DEDICATED with gratitude to the many individual authorities, protective agencies, civic and police experts, and departments which supplied information to help us help you best protect your home, yourself, your family, your business.

How To
Protect
Yourself
Today

How To Protect Yourself Today

Deputy Inspector Robert A. Hair
New York City Police Department
and Samm Sinclair Baker

STEIN AND DAY/Publishers/New York

The views expressed in this book are those of the
authors, and do not in any way represent the views
of the New York City Police Department.

CONTENTS

How To
Protect
Yourself
Today

1

WHAT YOU SHOULD KNOW ABOUT CRIME TODAY

IT IS vital to understand the significance to you personally of everyday police reports like these:

• "Houseworker admits to scores of burglaries in homes and apartments when left alone her first day on the job. . . ."
• "Moving van used to empty vacationing homeowners' houses and apartments while neighbors watch but don't report to police. . . ."
• "Unlocked front door admits thief who loots home while family eats barbecue dinner in backyard. . . ."

It adds up to this: the time to protect yourself, your family, your home and business is today. Tomorrow may be too late. The one safest step you can take is to act now to help prevent trouble *before* it happens. The old saying, "Prevention is better than cure," is truer and more urgent now than ever before.

You will profit by studying the basic protection facts you need to know, given here in simple, easy-to-use detail. This information is intended not to alarm you unduly but to spur you to take effective protection measures for your greater safety and peace of mind. As Emerson said, "Knowledge is the antidote to fear."

What you learn in this book can save you hundreds, thousands of dollars; it can even save your life and the lives of your loved ones. The extent of your gain will be limited only by how well you apply the recommended safeguards.

Your need for protection is greater now than at any other

time in history. You see the proof every day in newspapers and magazines, in TV and radio news reports. Note just a few of the many shocking crime statistics from authoritative sources:

• Crime in the U.S. is up 88 per cent in 7 years—rising nearly nine times as fast as the population. Crimes by types:

> Robberies up 86%
> Burglaries up 79%
> Larcenies of $50 or more up 103%
> Auto thefts up 100%
> Aggravated assaults up 66%
> Forcible rapes up 61%
> Murders up 41%

• Suburbs Draw City Burglars; Become Reverse Commuters and Loot Suburban Homes (*The New York Times,* page one).

• Mayor Opens Anticrime Drive. . . . 15,000 burglaries committed in the city each month, and the number is rising. . . . There is no community in this day and age that is free of a good deal of fear (*New York City Mayor's Criminal Justice Coordinating Council*).

• The total cost of crime in this country is variously estimated at 20 to 30 billion dollars annually. And this takes no account of the wrecked lives and human suffering (*Reader's Digest*).

• Over 44 million dollars worth of automobiles stolen in past six months in N.Y.C., an increase of over 25% for the same period last year (*Police Department Bulletin*).

• Crime Is Destroying America. It Must Be Stopped! One of the most menacing—and most unnecessary—problems in America today is the rampant lawlessness in every section of the nation, which is endangering our lives and our civilization (*Citizens Commission Against Crime*).

• Poll Finds Crime Top Fear At Home. . . . Crime topped the list when people were asked about problems facing their own community. Even other pressing local problems, such as crowded schools, transportation, and high taxes, take second place. The

(From *A Report by the President's Commission on Law Enforcement*)

report continues. . . . Official statistics indicate that crime is increasing almost everywhere in the United States, but it is growing fastest in the cities, next fastest in the suburbs, slowest in the rural areas. . . . One person in every three (33 per cent) in a recent survey admitted being afraid to go out alone at night in his neighborhood. Among women and persons living in the largest cities, the figure rises to about four out of every 10 (40 per cent) (*News story based on Gallup Poll*).

Don't wait to "lock the stable door after the horse is stolen." A French proverb puts it more pointedly: "When the horse has been stolen, the fool shuts the stable." Typically, a woman who was fearful of others entering her home talked about installing a burglar-alarm system . . . and talked some more about it . . . and talked even more about it . . . but did nothing about it.

Then criminals broke in and ransacked her house thoroughly. She complained, "They must have known I was going to install an alarm system next week!"

It's all too common for people to take precautions only after they've suffered losses. Don't let it happen to you; prevention is more pleasant and less costly than cure. Don't be upset if others laugh at you for being "a nut" about self-protection. You be safe; let the others be sorry.

Realize that even if you're not concerned about self-protection, you owe it to your family to safeguard them to the fullest possible extent. Most men are away at work during the day, and often evenings or when traveling on business. It's the wife and children who must bear the brunt of break-ins and other crimes at home.

"Opportunity Makes a Thief"

Never give a thief the opportunity. Never give any kind of criminal a chance. Take every possible and practical step beforehand. Thieves are constantly looking for the opportunity for a successful burglary. That applies at home, at business, on the street, with your car, and in respect to other possessions. Take

13

as your guideline the vow of a careful philosopher: "No one shall be a thief with me as his helper."

It is a mistake to think your possessions won't tempt a thief because you consider that their value is mostly sentimental; for one reason or another they might tempt a crook. Burglars can't be choosers—once they break in, they take whatever they consider of some value for their purposes. You'd be amazed at some of the weird things that are stolen. Police list such unlikely missing items as birth-control pills, pedigreed dogs, all sizes of objects from a dime-store ashtray to a grand piano, and even piles of old magazines.

One householder who was an avid tennis player reported two large buckets of worn practice tennis balls taken, along with his huge kitchen combination refrigerator-freezer. In a town in South Carolina, a flash came in that a building valued at $5,000 had disappeared; the investigating officers thought it was a gag, but discovered that it was true—a knocked-down pre-fab structure, 40 by 75 feet in size when erected, had actually been stolen. The point we are making is that it's not only jewelry, furs, and cash that get stolen. You can never tell what will tempt a thief.

Pay no attention to pessimists who may say that it doesn't pay to take protective measures since "nothing can prevent crime." All the facts prove that you *can* cut down chances of burglary or worse happening to you and your family and business. The professional burglar, who is willing to spend unlimited time, money, and effort, and take great risks in order to break into a structure, can probably find a way. But the burglar is looking for the "safe," easy entry with the least amount of danger. He tries to avoid the risks of a difficult, time-consuming, and perilous burglary. He seeks the unguarded, unlocked, or flimsily protected place where people are out for an hour, for the evening, for a day or longer—the longer the likely absence the safer the criminal probably feels.

A simple break-in is often available because of the occupant's carelessness. The burglar looks for an open window, an unlocked door, a darkened house with an unlit exterior. The tougher you make it for the burglar, the less chance there is that he'll enter your house, apartment, or place of business.

Sometimes, however, carelessness can accidentally cause the apprehension of a thief. A couple away for a month's cruise had a houseworker come in each Thursday to keep things tidy. The house being stuffy, the woman opened a window a few inches, forgot about it, and left it open when she finished her work. Then she locked the house and left. Fortunately in this instance, the owner had advised the local police that they would be away, and also mentioned the housekeeper coming in each Thursday. Officers in a patrol car checked the house routinely that evening. They spotted the open window, then proceeded to the end of the street, made a U-turn and came back. By sheer coincidence, as they returned to the house, they noted a burglar climbing through the open window and caught him. But people who count on this kind of coincidence are taking foolish risks.

Humorist Art Buchwald put it this way: "The people who are responsible for crime in this country are the victims. If they didn't allow themselves to be robbed, the problem of crime in this country would be solved . . . there is a current of opinion that our courts are being too soft on victims, and many of them are going unpunished for allowing a crime to be committed against them."

The best time to avoid becoming a victim of crime is before it happens.

Protection Is Needed Everywhere

You are definitely not safe from city burglars because you may live in the suburbs or even farther away from the urban area. Having autos, many burglars leave the city for a crime foray and drive twenty, fifty, and more miles to their target areas. They'll make a number of "hits" on homes, stores, and businesses, then head back to the city, arriving in time for dinner or breakfast, depending on whether they're working the day or night shift. Some burglars even commute to outlying areas by train or bus, but this is more risky. One disgruntled burglar was picked up by police at the railroad station after homeowners had reported a quick series of similar burglaries. The criminal was carrying a bulging suitcase and was waiting for a train which was already forty minutes late when police arrested him. He complained, "You can't depend on the damned train or bus schedules any more."

To make this book as helpful as possible, at the end of each of the following chapters you'll find a brief checklist of the principal points to remember. This is designed to summarize the advice and to serve as a useful one-minute "refresher course" any time you want to remind yourself of the key recommendations on any particular subject.

You'll also note that some recommendations are made more than once. That's because they apply to more than one area of crime, and we want you to have all of the relevant recommendations whenever you look up a particular subject.

Our purpose is to help prevent crime from affecting you by making it as easy as possible for you to *use* the information in this book constructively.

2

HOW TO GET NEEDED POLICE ACTION QUICKLY

WHEN YOU need police protection and action in a hurry, get to a telephone without delay. Tell the police clearly and con-cisely, how and why you need help instantly. In a crowded area, policemen or a police car may well be in sight, and you can summon their aid right on the spot.

When you report by phone, give the details briefly. First, pinpoint the location where help is needed so that the official on the other end of the line can dispatch officers to you at once, even while you're talking. Second, tell what is happening.

The speed of your report and the clarity and accuracy of the details you provide can make a life-or-death difference in an occurring or imminently threatening situation.

It must be repeated: when you need police help quickly, *be prepared to tell—in the first few seconds of your call—where it is happening and what is happening, in that order.* Then you can supply further information if needed, but the most important time is the first few seconds of your report.

Report All Crimes Quickly

Report even the smallest crime involving you, since it's a positive help in preventing further crimes. When police learn that small robberies are taking place in a neighborhood, they act quickly to tighten security measures there, often catching the thieves in the act. The criminals in such cases depend on citizens keeping mum so that authorities aren't placed on guard against

17

the increasing number of offenses—which may then build into a crime wave that might have been nipped in the bud.

A quick survey of unreported crimes turned up these typical instances.

• A man visiting from out of town pressed the buzzer in an apartment house vestibule, turned around, and found himself threatened by two men with knives; he gave up his wallet. Later he admitted, "I didn't report the robbery because it didn't involve much money and I figured the police couldn't do anything about it anyhow because the cash couldn't be traced."

• A woman returned home to find her television set and portable radio stolen. She told neighbors about it and one of them reported the burglary. The victim told the police she hadn't called them "because there was nothing they could do about it."

• A public official parked his car on the street, came back an hour later, and saw that a suit which he was going to leave at the dry cleaner was gone. Police authorities heard about this in a roundabout way, as one of a series of such thefts. When he was checked, the victim said, "I was too busy to call the police, and anyway what could they do about it?" The authorities stated that his report would have helped them take steps to help prevent more such crimes in the locality.

There is plenty the police can do about such crimes. The least they do is to order an alert on that type of theft in the areas where they occurred. Quite often one crime is followed by a series of similar thefts in the same neighborhood. What the police don't know hurts you when other victims don't report offenses against them. The failure of the public to call the police weakens the department's ability to deal with crime.

Each individual's failure to report his "one petty little robbery" contributes to an astounding, and crucial, total. A special survey by the National Opinion Research Corporation produced concrete evidence of the great number of unreported crimes in the United States. A sizable population sample, 10,000 people, were asked whether they had been victims of a crime, what was the nature of any such crime, whether they had reported it to the police, and if not, why not. Here's what they discovered in this federally financed study. During just one recent year there were in the United States *twice as many* robberies, aggravated assaults, burglaries, rapes, larcenies of fifty dollars and over than were reported in the crime statistics compiled by the nation's police departments and published by the Federal Bureau of Investigation—*twice as many*.

Report even "two-bit" crimes. In an instance involving a service station, a woman drove up and asked for two dollars worth of gas. She gave the attendant two folded one-dollar bills and drove away quickly. When he got back to the cash register, the attendant found that he had only one dollar bill. The woman had cut one dollar bill into two halves, and pasted each half to the same size pieces of blank paper so that when folded there seemed to be two one-dollar bills. Instead of shrugging off the dollar loss, the station owner phoned the police. An alert was sent to gas stations. The woman was picked up at another station nearby the next day trying to pull the same stunt. She admitted that she'd been picking up "lots of extra dollars" that way for months without being reported. She complained angrily that the station owner who reported her was a cheapskate.

When you are calling for help, don't be concerned about terms such as "burglary" or "robbery." Both represent a loss by any name. A *burglary* or *thievery* is usually the word for stealing from a home or apartment or building when the occupants aren't present. A *robbery* specifically covers taking property from the person of an individual, or when he is present, against his will, using force or intimidation. *Stealing* and *theft* refer to taking something from another, secretly or in his presence, with or without violence. In common usage, the terms are pretty much interchangeable. When a person comes back to his apartment and finds it's been broken into, he may start yelling, "I've been robbed!" without thinking whether or not he's using the correct phrase. One thing sure, it hurts when something of yours is taken, whatever you call the act.

To get the quickest help and most effective cooperation, it is vital that you cooperate with the police and other law enforcement agencies in every way possible. One way is to call the police whenever you see anything suspicious going on, whether around your home or on the street—anywhere. This doesn't mean that you become "involved," but you are doing your best to help prevent trouble before it happens. If yours is a false alarm, there's no harm done. If a crime is stopped, you've performed a service for others and for yourself, because you might have been the next victim.

The police authorities seek your cooperation. This printed statement is typical of steps recommended by police departments in cities, towns, and villages across the country:

THE CITIZEN'S PART IN CRIME PREVENTION . . . HOW YOU CAN COOPERATE: You can aid in the detection and suppression of crime and thus protect your property and welfare by being alert and telephoning the police whenever you observe suspicious persons or happenings or hear unusual noises, either at your home or in the neighborhood. Do not attempt a personal investigation, or turn on additional lights in the house, or make a lot of noise. That will only put the person in question on guard and prevent his capture if he is a criminal. . . . Don't delay! Don't look for an officer in the vicinity! Go to a telephone and quietly say, 'Police Department, Emergency,' or call [number]. . . . Your call will remain anonymous to the public. . . . If you witness an accident or crime, don't take it for granted that the police have been called. Telephone your police headquarters if no officers are about. If it was unreported, your action in telephoning may prevent or clear a crime, or even save a life.

Keep your eyes open and speak up. Police authorities stress that many cases are solved with the cooperation of area residents. You never know how much a tiny bit of information can help solve a case or prevent further crime. In one instance, a used-car salesman was arrested for robbery and the slaying of the victim. This came about because one person supplied part of a license plate number on a car speeding from the scene. Another citizen reported that he thought he had seen the criminal at a used-car lot. Putting the items together, detectives located he used-car lot, kept watch on it, and were able to arrest the suspect. Without those two bits of information supplied by helpful individuals, the criminal might have remained free to endanger others.

POLICE-ACTION CHECKLIST

☐ DO telephone the police instantly if there is trouble.

☐ DO give exact details of your location and what is happening immediately, speaking calmly.

☐ DO report even the smallest crime in which you are involved.

☐ DON'T fail to speak up about any crime you see.

☐ DO cooperate with the police if you're interested in controlling crime.

3

HOW TO GET URGENT HELP BY PHONE

AT HOME you should keep your local police telephone number (and fire department number) on the telephone instrument or next to it so you can phone directly without delay. A good idea is to take a small slip of paper and print on it the word "police" followed by your local police telephone number and below that the word "fire" followed by your local fire department number. (Of course, in some small communities the number is the same for both.) Then Scotch tape the number to the telephone instrument. If you have one or more extension phones, put these numbers on all the telephones because you can never tell which will be the nearest phone in an emergency. This can save you valuable seconds at a point when the slightest amount of time may be crucial to assuring your safety or apprehending a criminal.

If you haven't the police number available instantly, at home or elsewhere, don't take the time to look it up in the telephone directory. Dial "O" for "operator" directly. Control your emotions and your voice, or you may lose further precious seconds if the operator can't understand you. Say clearly and urgently, *"Police department, emergency."* You will be connected immediately.

National Emergency Number 911

Instead of dialing "operator," you'll get immediate action by dialing the national emergency number 911—if it is in effect in your community. There is a movement under way, already adopted locally by New York City, Huntington, Ind., and some other cities—more cities each year—to use 911 as an emergency number nationwide. Here's how it works: in a 911-adapted locality, if you have an emergency need to call the police for immediate protection or other help and don't know the local police number, you dial 911 and get attention at once. You don't waste time looking up the police number or going through the operator. The same applies in some places when you need emergency fire department or ambulance service—you dial 911 and tell quickly and exactly what you require in a hurry. Help speeds on its way.

Variations in the use of 911 occur according to the setup in each city. In New York City, for instance, at this writing the official instructions are stated as follows:

POLICE/AMBULANCE EMERGENCY: A citywide police phone number is available for emergency calls. It is 911. The Police Department requests that emergency callers be brief, explicit, and calm. All nonemergency calls should be placed through local administrative numbers.

FIRE: dial "O" for operator. Tell her you wish to report a fire. She will connected you with the Fire Department.

This emergency number does not apply everywhere in the nation at this writing. It is good only in localities where the telephone company is ready and willing to supply 911 as the emergency number, and where local governments adopt it. Eventually, if usage becomes countrywide, you'll be able to dial 911 wherever you are in the United States and get emergency service. That's a great advantage, of course, in speeding help needed urgently.

Dial "O" for "operator," as previously advised, where 911 is not the local emergency number, or if you're not sure about it. Tell the operator exactly what she needs to know, and she'll call the police, fire department, or ambulance service, whatever is required. Generally calls through the 911 emergency number bring help one or more minutes before the operator does. In spite of her efficiency and good will, the operator is a busy person with many duties. Once she gets your call, she in turn must dial a seven-digit number to convey your message to the proper department. But the only function of 911 is to speed emergency help. Saving even seconds on an emergency call can make the big difference between life and death in extreme cases of assault, fire, or illness.

You can dial 911 from coin telephones without using a coin, when this particular part of the 911 service is installed in your community. Look for the notice at the coin telephone which states that you can dial 911 without a coin; don't take it for granted, as this conversion is only beginning to take place. It is a great boon when you rush to a coin telephone to report an emergency, perhaps in a street or highway phone booth, and you haven't a coin and no one is around.

How to Give the Proper Description

When reporting a crime, emergency, or accident to the police, first give the bare essentials of (1) exactly *where* and (2) *what* is happening. Then be ready to supply further details if wanted by phone or by a police officer in person.

Study the typical listing here to aid in giving the proper description (this is the listing supplied to police officers by the New York Police Department). As general information, this can help you remember details which may be of great aid to the police when you are reporting as the victim or witness of a crime. It isn't probable that you can remember and fill in all these details, but the more specific your information is, the more likely that the criminal will be apprehended and the property recovered. Studying the list now will prepare you to give the most helpful description if you are ever involved in the future.

Description of Persons: give in sequence outlined below.

1. Name, include alias.
2. Address.
3. Sex.
4. Color.
5. Nationality.
6. Age.
7. Height.
8. Weight.
9. Build.
10. Clothes—jewelry.
11. How he (she) left scene: on foot, by auto; direction.
12. Peculiarities.
13. Posture.
14. Head—shape.
15. Hair.
16. Ears.
17. Face—shape.
18. Complexion.
19. Forehead.
20. Eyes—eyebrows.
21. Nose.
22. Mustache—beard.
23. Lips.
24. Mouth.
25. Teeth.
26. Chin.
27. Neck.
28. Shoulders.
29. Distinctive marks: scars, moles, etc.
30. Mannerisms.
31. Other characteristics.
32. Occupation.

Description of Property: include the following information where applicable.

1. Kind or type of article.
2. Shape.
3. Color.
4. Composition: leather, metal, wood, etc.
5. Brand or manufacturer's name.
6. Inscriptions— distinctive marks.
7. Serial numbers.
8. Contents.
9. Value.
10. Currency—denomination.
11. Bicycle: type, make, serial number, color, accessories.
12. Motorcycle:
    (a) Color, make.
    (b) Year, model.
    (c) Number of cylinders.
    (d) Saddle.
    (e) Position of speedometer.
    (f) Tire condition.
    (g) Accessories.
    (h) Distinctive marks.
    (i) License number.
    (j) Serial number.

Description of Motor Vehicle (escaping).

1. Color.
2. Make, year.
3. Body type: sedan, 2-door, etc.
4. Number of passengers.
5. Description of occupants.
6. Direction going.
7. License number, state, and year.
8. Body marks, bullet holes.
9. Size of car.
10. Radio antenna—location, description.
11. Tail light—description.
12. Wheels—whitewall, etc.
13. Distinctive features: tire racks, baggage racks, rear-view mirrors.
14. Damages: headlights, fenders, windows, etc.

PHONE-HELP CHECKLIST

☐ DO keep the local police department phone number on or by the telephone for instant use.

☐ DON'T look up the police number in the telephone directory—dial "O" for "operator" if you don't have the number.

☐ DO tell the operator, "Police Department, emergency," clearly—don't panic.

☐ DO dial emergency number 911 if it is functioning in your area.

☐ DO give the most detailed description possible.

4

HOW TO KEEP STRANGERS OUT OF YOUR HOME WHEN YOU'RE THERE

YOU MUST have a chain-guard on both back and front doors. A chain-guard is an indispensable protective device. It is a strong though short chain permanently attached to the wall or jam near the door, with the opposite end secured to the door itself. It is the latter end which can be released to open the door. With the chain-guard in place, the door can be opened enough to see who is there, but the door can't be opened wide enough for someone to squeeze in. It is a common mistake for homeowners to have a chain-guard on the front door, but not on the back door, even when tradesmen and others may call at the back door. Any door that lets somebody into the house should have a chain-guard.

A peephole viewer is a good added protection. A peephole viewer is an inexpensive, small, tube-shaped device that can be inserted in almost any door at eye level just by drilling the proper-sized hole in the door. The viewer enlarges what the person inside can see. This enables you to see who is outside your door before you even open the door on the chain-guard. (The peephole viewer is a hardware item, widely available.) The viewer usually comes with a slip-cover for the inside, so that no one can look inside; you simply raise or move the cover out of the way to look outside.

Don't admit a stranger at the door until you are absolutely certain it is safe. If you don't recognize the person, ask to see his credentials or identification card (meter inspectors, telephone company workers, electric company people all are required to carry identification cards). If you have doubts about the validity of the identification *for any reason whatsoever,* ask the person to wait a minute, close the door without removing the chain-guard (you don't want an intruder forcing the lock while you're away from the door for a minute), then telephone the company, giving the person's name, and ask if the caller is an authorized representative and is supposed to be paying you a visit. If the answer is "no," telephone the police immediately.

Watch out for one common trick. You may be handed a calling card with the individual's name, the company name, and a phone number. The phone number may be phoney. It is very easy to get phoney calling cards made up. Look up the company's number in your telephone directory. If it is different from the number on the calling card, call the police. If the number on the calling card is phoney, there may be an accomplice at the other end who will say that the serviceman or other visitor is "okay" when in fact he is not. Don't take chances: killers as well as robbers can get access to you through your own front or back door.

Never get careless and open the door without the chain-guard on. Be ready to slam the door shut and lock instantly if you see anyone looking at all menacing. Note this typical newspaper story: A semi-invalid sixty-eight-year-old woman with a heart ailment told the police that "her doorbell rang and she opened the door, thinking the caller was a relative. Instead, three men with handkerchiefs over their faces barged into the three-room apartment. One of the men, she said, 'told me this was a stickup and not to make any noise.' She started screaming, and the man began to beat her." Fortunately her police dog attacked the intruders and they fled. If she'd had a chain-guard on she probably could have slammed and locked the door, and her screaming and the dog's barking would have made the masked men run.

Be polite but firm in turning solicitors away—you'll be safer. Simply say, "We have a rule against door-to-door solicitation"— and stick to that rule. If there are reputable door-to-door firms and their representatives with whom you like to deal, make sure that the person is a bona fide representative by checking identification cards.

Take the license plate number of the car as it drives away if the person at your door made you suspicious. Report such calls to the police, providing the license number so that authorities can follow it up. That's the surest way to cut down on unsolicited calls at your door and at other homes.

Call the police if the person keeps hanging about or if his actions arouse suspicion.

Watch for this common routine with burglars: Rather than park a car and leave it suspiciously at the curb while they loot homes, a driver will drop off his partner, who will break into deserted homes, and then pick him up later with his loot at a designated time and place, often the same spot where they started. Police alerted by calls citing such a drop, where a man walks off in another direction, have caught many criminals by picking up first the car and driver, and then the partner.

Another ploy of burglars is to team up two men and a woman and drive to a selected street of homes. While one man slips into a house, the car is parked at the curb for a quick getaway, and the driver and woman stay in the darkened car— necking. Consider this a suspicious act and advise the police. (Genuine "lovers," please forgive us, but do find a safer place for your necking.)

The authorities not only welcome but solicit your calls, as in this typical leaflet distributed to homes and apartments by many police departments:

NOTIFY THE POLICE IMMEDIATELY IF:

Strangers ring your doorbell and ask vague and strange questions, or act suspicious in any way.

Persons without credentials ring your doorbell, seek employment, or attempt to gain admittance to your home to solicit and sell.

Strangers seek information about your family or neighbors, or their whereabouts.

Suspicious persons or cars are in your neighborhood

29

(many criminals have been caught sitting in their cars and looking over the neighborhood, as a result of a householder's phone call reporting the unusual occurrence).

Look any caller over carefully while talking to him through the opening with the chain-guard on. If it becomes advisable to report him to the police, your accurate description will help.

Investigate inexpensive intercom systems which are readily installed so that you can conduct a conversation from inside with someone outside your door, without opening the door. More complicated and more costly installations enable you to speak with someone outside the door from other rooms in your house or apartment.

Don't admit even a uniformed delivery man if you're at all suspicious. If he's on the level, explain your fears and ask him to leave the package outside the door for you to bring in after he leaves. You can sign a receipt with the chain-guard on, slipping the receipt through the opening. Fake uniforms are not uncommon disguises with criminals.

Never pay a solicitor at your door more than a small deposit, if anything, for merchandise that is to be delivered in the future. Too often merchandise that is paid for in advance never shows up, nor does the salesman who took your money; when you try to reach him, you find it's impossible.

Don't sign an order for merchandise at the door unless you're sure of exactly what you're signing and have read the order thoroughly, including the fine print. If there's too much fine print, or if the salesman tries to rush you, hand back the order sheet unsigned. If you sign, and the merchandise, such as a set of books, is delivered, read the order again. Chances are that there is a time limit of ten days or so in which to return the merchandise if you're not satisfied—even though you've probably been told that satisfaction is "unconditionally guaranteed." If you don't return the goods within the time limit, you may not be permitted to return it later under the laws of many states.

Never leave the door open while you go for your purse if

you've made a purchase. Close and lock the door. Otherwise you may find the "salesman" treading on your heels as you enter the house—then you may be in great danger. This is a common ruse to guard against when you're offered a bargain you can't resist and then the solicitor follows you in when you go for money. Many women have been robbed and attacked as a result.

Resist "incredible bargains" offered at your door. Chances are that the merchandise is stolen or defective. Shut the door firmly, double-lock the door, then phone the police if you are suspicious or fearful.

It's dangerous to trust a stranger at the door because he or she is very well dressed and looks "respectable." The most experienced crooks may be prosperously dressed, with smooth talk and polished manners designed to lower your defenses. Knowing that most people are nice and wish to treat others courteously, the criminal takes advantage of this with a suave, inoffensive approach. Keep that chain-guard on, remain firm, but turn the stranger away for the safety of yourself and others of your family who may be at home. If the stranger persists, and tries to push his way in, start yelling *loudly*. Convey the same cautions to your youngsters and to baby-sitters.

Don't admit strangers into your home unless you are absolutely sure that they're trustworthy. Be aware of the common approaches used to get into your house or apartment and then loot the premises or attack the occupant. For example, a man rings your bell and says that his car has broken down and he'd like to use the phone to call a garage; much as you want to help, it's safest to turn away such requests if you're a woman home alone or with children. Another common deception is for a well-dressed criminal, man or woman, to ask for "emergency" use of your bathroom. If a man asks to read your water meter, check your phone, or perform some similar errand, ask to see his identity card through the chain-guarded door.

A genuine representative of the water company or other service organization recognizes the good sense in this request for identification and obliges readily. If the man at the door starts protesting his honesty or gets unpleasant, become more suspicious at once, *and don't let him in.* Shut the door and phone the police.

If you let a stranger in, even for only a few minutes, that's enough time for him to tamper with the door lock so that he can get in easily when no one is at home, even if he doesn't rob you there and then.

It's safest to be suspicious of any "charity" solicitor who rings your bell and asks to come in and talk, unless he's a neighbor you recognize, of course. If you are at all in doubt, ask for an identity card, or turn the person away. Don't be satisfied if the person just flashes a card and puts it away; insist on taking it and reading it in order to be sure. The safest course is to tell the person, through the chain-guarded door, to write to you and then you'll decide whether to contribute or not. The same applies to telephone solicitations: ask the caller to write all details and information to you; don't just take down the address over the phone and then send money.

Don't admit "scholarship students," subscription agents, and so on who ring your doorbell. Such appeals should be made through the mail, at meetings, and through other means, but not by disturbing the privacy of your home, interrupting your day's work, using your time. A common approach still is for a young person to ring your bell and tell you he needs your cooperation to earn a scholarship for college, or he uses some other request aimed at arousing your public spirit. Keep your chain-guard on and simply say, "My husband doesn't allow me to admit strangers," or, "We have a rule in our home against *any* doorbell solicitations." Then close and lock the door.

Worthy charities have many other ways to collect funds. The stranger at the door must be regarded suspiciously, since many thousands of robberies and attacks annually, recorded by the police, start with the ring of a doorbell and the door being opened wide in response. Better be courteously suspicious than criminally attacked.

Be careful not to tell a stranger at the door that you can't talk to him because "I'm on my way out to go shopping" or "I have to rush to pick up my son at school," or any such information which informs him that you're leaving the house or apartment empty. Don't impart confidences such as, "We're going out to dinner tonight and I'm in a hurry to get ready." If the stranger is a thief, he's seeking just such information so that he can loot your home while you're out. In a typical case, a woman rushing out of her house locked her door and almost bumped into a man coming up the front path. He explained that he was a salesman. "I can't stop now," she said, "I'm late for a woman's club luncheon." Off she trotted. When she returned from the long luncheon, her house had been looted.

Scream or yell instantly and loudly if someone at the door tries to push his way in. Criminals fear noise which will attract attention. Your shouts can alert neighbors (especially in an apartment house) or passers-by who can summon help in a hurry. However, if you've let the thief in and the door is closed behind him, and he warns you to keep quiet while he takes valuables, it usually pays to be quiet. Try to remember details of what he looks like and exactly what he takes. Then call police as soon as he leaves. Your life and health are more valuable than any possessions you may lose.

Never buzz back a door opener in an apartment house unless you have been told who is buzzing, through the door phone system or some other means. If you press the buzzer to open the door indiscriminately, you are endangering not only yourself but also the other apartment dwellers. It's common for a burglar to press one or more buttons at random, then enter the building at the buzzer release. Once inside, he seeks out the empty apartments, picks their locks, and loots them. If a man rings your apartment bell and says, "Oh, I'm sorry, I thought this was the Browns' apartment," he may be checking to see whether *you're* out. If you see him go on to other apartments and ring the bell—and you don't know of anyone by the name of Brown (or whatever) on your floor—call the police and report the suspicious actions.

Warn any domestics or other workers in your home or apartment, including baby-sitters, not to talk to others about your comings and goings, your vacations, or other details about your personal life. Also caution all the members of your family against talking indiscriminately about such things. A long-experienced, smooth-talking burglar who was finally caught said he gained valuable tips from talking with maids, doormen, maintenance men, delivery boys, and others who had some knowledge about the people they worked for. Usually these people didn't know they were helping a criminal and would have been horrified at the thought. Nevertheless, by mentioning that "the people in Apartment C just left for Europe," or "the folks I work for will be away for the weekend (or for a week or a month) so I'm free then," can tip off a thief that he can try to enter without fear of anyone being home.

It's safer not to give information about your neighbors to any strangers at the door. They may be double-checking whether the neighbor is away for an extended time because the house looks unoccupied. The best answer is, "I really don't know." If you feel that the actions of the person inquiring are questionable, phone and discuss it with the police, who will check out the house and the neighborhood for any suspicious characters. Many thieves have been caught in the act of looting houses and apartments after such phone calls. Realize that such preventive calls save more time and trouble for the police in the long run than trying to track down burglars *after* a burglary is committed.

Don't let anyone remove anything from your home until you double-check that the person is authorized. For example, if you've called for radio or television repair, carpet or upholstery cleaning, or other services that may require taking the item to the shop from your home, be sure that the person is the authentic representative. There have been many instances when, for example, a TV repair man is called, the word leaks to a thief who comes to your home, looks the set over, says he has to take it back to the shop, and leaves with the set. An hour later, the genuine repairman shows up, but alas, your set is gone for good.

Make sure that the door lock is not in easy reach on an entry door with a window in it. If the glass is thin, the burglar can easily break it in a split-second while talking with you through the door. He quickly reaches in, unlocks the door, and forces his way in. There are locks available which make this reach-in opening difficult, particularly double-cylinder locks which must be opened with a key, not a simple knob. You can keep a key inside near the door but not on the door, so that the door can be opened only by you from the inside; the key would be out of reach of an arm thrust in from the outside.

CHECKLIST AGAINST STRANGERS

☐ DON'T admit a stranger at the door until you check his identity thoroughly and are completely reassured.

☐ DO keep the chain-guard on the door when talking to a stranger.

☐ DO install a one-way viewer so you can see who is at the door without opening it.

☐ DO keep out even uniformed messengers if you're unsure of them.

☐ DO call the police if a stranger hangs around or acts suspiciously.

☐ DON'T buy from solicitors or sign an order for merchandise without checking even the fine print.

☐ DO double-check the identity of "charity" solicitors before giving money.

☐ DO scream or yell if anyone tries to force his way in.

☐ DO warn domestics, baby-sitters, any others at home to observe these precautions against strangers.

5

HOW TO KEEP THIEVES OUT OF
YOUR HOME WHEN YOU'RE AWAY

SHAKESPEARE: *"Ho! let the door be lock'd."*

Effective home protection requires two-way action. First, it must include your personal measures to protect your home. Second, you must act in cooperation with the police, whose business it is to protect all people. If you don't take the proper, simple, basic precautions to help safeguard your home and the people in it, then no amount of police effort can keep you safe from criminal attacks. Without at least the elementary cooperation of every home and apartment dweller, the only solution would be to provide one or more policemen or guards for every separate dwelling and apartment—obviously an impossibility.

Police authorities repeatedly stress that the way to check and control criminal activity is twofold: (1) remove the desire for the individual to commit crimes; (2) remove the opportunity for criminal acts. You, an average citizen, cannot readily remove the desire from the potential lawbreaker, but you can take measures to remove the opportunity.

First, don't minimize the chances of your own home or apartment being burglarized. According to the police chiefs in a suburban county, home burglaries have reached "epidemic proportions . . . the No. 1 police headache, far exceeding auto thefts, assaults, rape and murders in volume. . . . One-third of the county jail's population are behind bars on burglary raps." Chief targets of the burglaries aside from cash are "TV sets, electric appliances, furs, radios, silverware, jewelry, and clothing."

Observe common sense care. Although some burglars are

smart and some incredibly stupid, careless people make their job easier. People leave their front doors unlocked while they go shopping or are busy out in back! They often leave garage doors open while they go shopping. Thieves can drive right into the garage, shut the door, and pile their takings directly into the car without fear of being seen by anyone.

Police records show that vans can drive up to the homes of people away on vacation without being reported. The neighbors may notice but don't call the police, even though they know the owners are away. They figure that the owners made the arrangements, or else they just don't want to get involved.

Just a little extra care pays off—you don't have to be a watchman twenty-four hours a day—just locking doors properly and other basic precautions can prevent your whole house being emptied.

"Public apathy is the biggest stumbling block to an effective burglary prevention program," a leading police magazine reported. "Most burglars are opportunists. . . . By installing adequate lights, locks, alarms, and other devices, the physical security of the property will deter the efforts of all but the most determined burglar [a statistical rarity]."

Don't be half-safe with halfway measures. *The Police Chief* publication cautions you: "A residence is not secure unless it is totally protected. . . . The strongest door will do no good if the burglar can quickly enter through unlocked windows. Each citizen should be sure his home is securely locked and lighted."

The amount of negligence by the public is very high and contributes greatly to increasing crimes of many varieties, particularly to breaking into homes. Many burglaries are due to unlocked doors and open or unlatched windows—invitations to the thief to "come in and help yourself." This is affirmed by a criminal who spent thirty-five years in what he called "government service"—that is, serving prison terms for assorted crimes. At age seventy he decided to go straight; he says, "Every city and suburban neighborhood is crowded with homes and apartments begging to be burglarized. Most people simply don't know how to protect their homes or apartments."

The first vital step in protection is to be aware of the

37

necessity—and then to do something about it. It's foolhardy to be like the smug householder who interrupted a burglar searching his home and said, "You're wasting your time, there's nothing anywhere. I've looked." Your home needs protection even if you own very few valuables. There have been cases of burglars leaving notes like this: "What kind of people are you? There's not a thing in the house worth stealing." Then they may wreck the place out of sheer indignation. Keep them out in the first place.

One police department recorded these statistics on how burglars get into a home, based on analyses of actual burglaries: 42 per cent force inadequate front door locks; 19 per cent break glass panels on back doors and reach in to unlock the door; 10 per cent force inadequate back door locks; 9 per cent break windows to enter; 7 per cent break front door glass and reach in to unlock the door; 6 per cent enter open doors and windows; 5 per cent break basement windows; 2 per cent enter with a key.

Insurance rates against burglaries are going up because, as one executive of a large insurance company said, "We're getting gun-shy" from accumulating losses through robberies. Said another insurance agent, "The insurance problem has been with us for some time, but it seems to be dawning on the public just recently." He pointed out that it's increasingly difficult for the apartment dweller, for instance, to get proper burglary insurance unless he lives in "a safe building, takes precautions, and doesn't make himself too obvious to crooks." As to the last point, if you own valuable jewelry, don't flaunt it around on the street or in public places; cover up lest you invite the burglary of your home.

Basic Measures for Protecting Your Home and Family

Rule One: Do everything possible to keep intruders out of your home. Don't ever take it for granted with crimes happening all over your community that your house or apartment will be an exception. (Be sure that every member of your family

reads this basic section carefully.) The records show that burglars will take just about "anything that isn't nailed down" and
will sometimes even rip out items that are nailed and bolted.
You name it—burglars will take it. It hurts especially somehow
when the burglar packs your own good suitcases and walks out
with them stuffed full of your possessions.

Your home may become a target either because of or in
spite of circumstances. It has been said that burglars primarily attack wealthy homes on large, well-shrubbed and therefore well-hidden properties; or that they prefer corner homes,
which offer more ways to escape unnoticed. Others claim that
burglars tend to avoid large, costly homes because there's too
much danger from sleep-in household help. Developments where
many homes are close together, or adjacent apartment houses,
would seem less vulnerable because so much activity goes on
with so many people living together, yet crime is high in such
locations as well. In short, protect yourself with your own measures rather than relying on theories or statistics to protect you.

Take steps to protect a house under construction, as well
as a completed home. Since there are no inhabitants, a house
in the process of being built or remodeled offers a safer target
for looting. In addition to stealing costly building materials,
criminals make away with refrigerators, freezers, washers and
dryers, and other valuable items that are installed before the
house is occupied. Such robberies can be defended against by
extra patrolling when the police are alerted, and by strong,
burglar-resistant locks and alarms installed early.

Always change your locks and keys when you move into a
new home or apartment. There's always a chance that keys kept
by the previous homeowner or apartment dweller will be lost
or handled carelessly so that a burglar can get them and use
them. Even in a brand-new house or apartment, where you're the
first tenant, it has happened that people concerned with building the place and supplying locks and keys have lost the original
keys. Others involved could duplicate or steal such keys before
you move in—then burglarize the place after you're settled. As
an example, when police raided a suspected loft, they found

not only a mass of loot but also hundreds of keys, neatly tagged with addresses of homes and apartment houses and numbers of individual apartments.

Never give duplicate keys to anyone you cannot trust one hundred per cent. Many burglaries have been traced to domestics and temporary workers whose keys had been copied, with or without their personal knowledge, then used to enter and burglarize the home.

Get back any keys given to dependable workers, including domestics, who have been in your employ for years and are totally trustworthy. In a typical case, a housekeeper retired from her job after more than twenty years, failed to return the key, dropped it in a bureau drawer, intending to return it "later." The key was found by a relative visiting the woman; he took it and used it to enter the house and steal a load of valuables.

Caution your youngsters who have door keys to keep them safe at all times. Many keys lost by careless youngsters, or taken when keys and other items are emptied from pockets for active play, have been used for burglaries.

Never leave house keys in the car when parking in a garage or lot where you must leave your car key. Keep car keys separate from the others, or use a key holder that enables you to remove and leave just the car key while you hold on to the others. Burglary gangs have been known to operate with a parking lot attendant as an accomplice. If you leave your house keys, he has them duplicated quickly for immediate use while you're out shopping or eating dinner, or the duplicate keys are used to enter your home weeks later when you're out.

Don't take lightly the loss of a house key. It may have been stolen, or picked up by a passing criminal who sees you lose the key. He may scoop it up, follow you back to your address, then enter later when he sees that your home is empty. The safest step is not just to make another copy of a key carried by another member of the family, but to have the tumblers on the lock (or locks) changed.

It's safest not to have an identification tag on your key

ring or key case. If you lose the keys, the tag is like a marker pointing thieves to your home.

Never hide keys where they can easily be found while you're out. Criminals make it a point to know the usual hiding places —in a mailbox, in the milk bottle box, under a door mat, on a hook nearby. No matter how ingenious you may think you are, the professional thief can usually search out the hiding place— that's his business.

Don't leave entry doors unlocked if you can possibly help it, whether you're at home or not. It may seem necessary at times when your youngsters are playing outdoors and keep going in and out, but try to limit this as much as possible. If the house must be open for them, leave only one door unlocked, preferably a door you have in sight much of the time, such as a kitchen door. Certainly there is no excuse when you're out and away from the house or apartment. An unlocked door is an open invitation to burglary, vandalism, or, even worse, attack on your person or other members of the family.

Always try the door to make sure it's firmly locked, tight, and secure when you leave the house. Spring locks can be opened quite easily and are not as safe as dead-bolt or double locks or other burglar-resistant locks you can get. Again, when you come home and close the door behind you, try the door to make sure it's firmly closed and locked against intruders.

Change any doors with pins on hinges exposed on the outside; this is true of many doors that open outward. A burglar can remove the pins from the outside hinges and swing the door open even if it's locked.

Close entry doors tight, never leaving a door ajar. This can be just too much temptation for a criminal passing by your house or going down the hall past your apartment who otherwise would probably never even have paused and tried to enter. Teach your youngsters, or anyone else living in your home, to close doors completely behind them whether coming in or going out.

Keep screen doors locked when the regular door is open for

fresh air or for any other reason. A screen door is a special temptation to a criminal, since dwellers are less likely to lock them than more solid doors.

Keep front and side entry doors locked at home if you're out in the back yard for work or play or a siesta. As previously noted, police records are filled with indignant reports of burglaries that took place while the family was resting or entertaining in the yard just a few feet away from the house.

Get extra protection on sliding doors and windows by wedging a strong stick, such as a broomstick cut to the needed length, in the bottom track, preventing anyone from sliding them open from the outside.

Double-lock your doors when inside or out if you have a "snap-type" lock. You get double or more protection by making entry more complicated and more difficult. The double-locking takes only a second or two but can make a big difference in protection.

Cooperate in keeping the apartment house street door locked. This will protect not only your own apartment premises but also others in the building. Burglars quickly learn which apartment houses are likely to have unlocked entrance doors, and they often commit burglaries repeatedly in that easy-access building.

Lock your apartment door behind you even if you're only going next door to borrow a cup of sugar or for a brief visit. A "few seconds" can easily stretch to quite a few minutes when you start to chat, and valuables can be emptied from the apartment in practically no time. Worse yet, if you're away only two minutes and a thief enters your apartment during that time, you may come upon him when you return.

Don't ever walk back into your house or apartment if you know you locked the door when you left but find it ajar or unlocked when you return. The safest move is to call the police from a neighbor's phone, and let them lead you into your home. The police not only welcome but invite such calls, even if it turns out to be a false alarm. Confronting a criminal in your home can result in violence and injury, even endangering your life.

Lock garage doors at all times, even if you're just "running out for some quick shopping." It need only take a few minutes for an experienced thief to empty the garage of lawn mower, garden tools, car tools, spare tires—whatever may be in there, even tools and a ladder to help him break into your house. Even if you are only in the back yard, and the garage faces the front out of your sight, keep the garage doors locked (not just closed). If the garage is attached to the house, unlocked doors make entry to the house that much easier for the intruder. A locked door creates an additional safety barrier, so get the locking habit and stick to it. Devices which open and close garage doors automatically are helpful in keeping them closed and locked.

Check every window to make sure it's locked when you go out. A burglar has patience; to gain entry he'll try every single window in hopes of finding one unlocked for easy entry. If you lock every window except one, that's the one the thief will use to enter; that's the only opening he needs.

Equip windows that open on or near fire escapes with special safety locks. Do the same with glass or other doors at entries or exits. These are all favorite places of entry for burglars, in apartments especially. Hinge-type bars are also acceptable within fire regulations.

Consider safety catches that allow a window to be raised only so far and no farther, so that there's no room for even the slimmest person to climb through. With such catches, readily available at locksmiths and most hardware and department stores, you can keep windows open for good ventilation, yet you get important extra protection against anyone climbing in. When installing any kind of window catches or locks, check the fire hazards involved, in case the window should provide an exit in the event of a fire. Make this a "must" whether you live in a house or an apartment.

Always check window locks to make sure they're not left

unlatched after a window-washer leaves. This is no reflection on the honesty of the window-washer; it's a double-check against carelessness in not closing the locks.

Don't rely on a chain-guard alone, as there are ways a professional burglar can slide out the chain and open the door *from the outside* if you leave the door ajar with the chain-guard on. It must be emphasized because so many people are careless—keep the chain on in any case whenever you open the door, in either a house or apartment. If the person outside is a stranger, or untrustworthy for any reason, don't unhook the chain. When installing a chain on the door, keep it tight enough that even the slimmest arm can't reach through the opening to unhook the chain or to grab you.

It's not safe to leave any note on or near the door stating that you've gone out and when you'll return. This is one of the signals that the professional thief, and even the amateur, looks for. You might as well leave a note directly to the burglar, inviting him to enter and help himself.

Don't leave a houseworker, or other temporary worker, in your home alone the first day on the job, not even while you go out for the briefest of errands. An honest houseworker will understand, since she (or he) would take the same precautions in her own home. There have been many cases of women hiring workers from want ads or agencies, and never checking the references. Agencies are supposed to check references, and most do, but it pays to double-check on your own—then you're sure.

Even references can be fraudulent, of course, so it's best not to leave the new houseworker alone until you're sure of her. In one instance, a woman arrested for burglarizing the home where she had been employed boasted that she had actually looted scores of homes on the first and only day she went to work there as a domestic. "Fools who trust anybody that much the first day," she said, "deserve to have their valuables stolen."

It's helpful to leave a second car in the driveway if you have two cars and are out in one. The standing car in the driveway or out front gives the house an occupied look, helping to ward off burglars who are seeking a house where no one is home.

You invite thieves if you leave a ladder lying around out-doors where a thief can see it and use it for a "second-story job." Police records show that this has happened thousands of times.

Cover basement windows from the inside with curtains, blinds, paint, or anything that keeps would-be intruders from looking in. If they can't see in, they can't see whether anyone is there or there's anything worth taking. If they can see some things they'd like to take—such as tools or sporting goods—and can also note that the place is empty, they may consider it an invitation to break in. Always keep basement windows locked.

CHECKLIST AGAINST THIEVES

☐ DO take double protection measures against thieves by (1) observing personal precautions and (2) using police facilities promptly.

☐ DO make locks on doors, windows, and every entry burglar-proof.

☐ DO use protection measures during the construction of a new home.

☐ DO change locks and keys when moving into a house or apartment.

☐ DO observe precautions against careless handling of keys.

☐ DO lock all entry doors and windows when at home or out.

☐ DON'T overlook the necessity for strong window locks and safety catches.

☐ DO keep basement windows locked and covered to prevent seeing in from outside.

6

A LIFESAVER: WHAT TO DO IF YOU MEET A BURGLAR FACE TO FACE

IF YOU awaken to find a burglar in your bedroom, *don't make a sound or movement*. The safest thing you can do is pretend to be fast asleep. If you jump up or out of bed or shout or scream, you may expose yourself and your family to grave danger. Often the first instinct of the burglar when suddenly alarmed is to react with violence.

Playing possum can well make the difference between life and death, for once violence erupts there is no telling where it will end. It can't be repeated too often: it is far better to lose your money and valuables than your life.

As soon as you're sure that the intruder is out of sight and sound, phone the police. Realize that you have a much better chance to aid a quick chase and capture if the burglar doesn't know you saw him. He leaves without realizing that the police will be after him in minutes; his getaway will be less hurried and his guard won't be up.

To aid in identification, later, peer through slitted lids while the burglar is in sight—but not if there's any chance he will catch you looking. Note and remember every possible detail of the intruder's appearance and movements. A good description can help the police catch him.

As advised elsewhere, if you enter your home and hear an intruder moving around, leave at once and call the police from the nearest phone, rather than face the thief yourself. If you enter your home and come upon the burglar face to face, don't make an outcry unless he threatens you with bodily harm. In the great majority of cases, if you are quiet, the intruder will be also. Yield your valuables and let him go—then call the police.

CHECKLIST WHEN ENCOUNTERING BURGLARS

- ☐ DON'T make a sound or movement if you awaken and see a burglar.
- ☐ DO try to see descriptive details through slightly open lids if possible.
- ☐ DO phone the police as soon as the burglar leaves.
- ☐ DON'T enter your home if you suspect a burglar is there; leave quietly at once and phone the police.
- ☐ Do keep quiet if you are faced by a burglar; yield your valuables, let him leave, then call the police immediately.

7

THE BEST WAYS TO BURGLAR-PROOF
YOUR LOCKS AND KEYS

IT PAYS many times over to check and install the most burglar-proof locks. Some pessimists will tell you that no lock will stop a burglar. While this may be true of the highly skilled professional burglar, even he is more likely to be discouraged by a well-locked door. He knows the necessity for working fast, and he'll usually pass up too tough a challenge. The amateur burglar or vandal is often stopped completely by a securely fastened door. The same extra protective value applies to window locks, storm windows, and also screen doors, since they must keep out intruders when solid doors are left open in warm weather.

Don't underestimate how easily professional burglars can get past an inadequate lock such as a common spring lock. In one instance, two well-dressed burglars entered a millionaire's city town house and took $3,000 in cash, an estimated $10,000 in family heirlooms and art objects, and a pen inscribed "Best Wishes . . . Lyndon Johnson." Fortunately, the police had been alerted that the two men were "casing" town houses in the neighborhood and had been following them for weeks. Officers arrested the burglars with the loot as they were about to put a loaded bag in a locker at the railroad terminal. The most significant point for you to remember is that the burglars opened the front door lock of the mansion by using only a thin celluloid strip!

Never leave the door unlocked unless it's absolutely necessary, even for a short period of time. The best lock in the world won't keep a burglar out unless it's used.

Install a strong chain door guard, as previously advised, setting it in with deep screws that can't be ripped out by a powerful push on the door from outside if someone tries to force his way in. Choose a heavy, not flimsy, make; some are available with locks to provide an extra door lock. Place the door part of the chain-guard so that it permits only a narrow opening, not wide enough for even a thin arm to push through and unhook the chain. You may prefer a type of chain door guard where the chain rolls back into a case, instead of dangling. The side of the chain case has a sliding bar which locks the chain in the recoiled position, providing an extra night latch as a further door lock.

It's unsafe to have spring-type locks. Almost any burglar can open them in seconds simply by inserting something stiff and thin. If you do have a spring-type lock, be sure to try the door again after closing it, to make sure the catch has caught and the door is locked, even if inadequately. Also, instead of the ordinary flat plate into which the spring-lock fits in the door frame, get a "safety strike plate" or a metal wedge, which makes it more difficult to push the lock back with a celluloid strip or a card or knife blade.

Replace snap-fastening locks, the type that you lock simply by pressing a button from the inside, opening with a key from the outside. This type of lock is also easily opened in seconds by a thief.

Consult a reliable local locksmith. Describe your premises, home or apartment, or have him look over your place. He'll tell you what types of locks can be installed to best protect doors, windows, and any other openings in your home, along with the costs. Keep in mind that saving a few dollars by installing an inferior lock can be very costly in the event of a burglary loss.

Check at least every six months to make sure that all locks on doors and windows are strong and tight. The looser a lock is, the easier it is to pick. Make sure also in checking that doors and windows fit snugly in their frames; the looser they are, the easier for a burglar to force them.

You can get good protection from strong pin tumbler cylinder locks on the entry doors. While you can get more protective locks for more money, sturdily constructed pin tumbler cylinder types serve well.

Consider a trigger-guard lock, which has an extra trigger-bolt added to the spring bolt that makes the lock much more difficult for a burglar to pick readily.

Add a dead-bolt lock above your present doorknob lock if you don't want to change your present lock. This may mean using two keys but is worthwhile for the extra protection. Place the strong, solid dead-bolt lock just above your doorknob. The dead-bolt lock takes up very little room and can become part of the plate of your present lock.

Investigate door locks with built-in alarms. If someone tries to use a key that doesn't fit the lock exactly, an alarm will go off and keep ringing until the correct key is inserted. By that time the burglar will have fled in most cases.

When you put an excellent burglar-resistant lock on your front door, don't leave flimsy locks on other doors and windows. All the burglar needs is to open one door or window. If you're concerned about carrying a mass of keys, you can have a locksmith fix the locks so that one key will unlock all the doors—but make sure that *all* the locks are good ones.

Never install locks with a few short screws flat on the door. The lock should be set firmly so that it can't be ripped out of the wood by a sharp, heavy push on the door, or the screws removed from outside the door. Observe the same caution in putting on a chain-guard or an extra bolt on the door. Locks, bolts, and guards are no stronger than the way they're attached; a few short screws won't hold the door locked even though the chain or bolt themselves are strong and heavy.

Don't skimp on padlocks for garage, basement, and other doors where they fit in well. Cheap padlocks are a poor investment, almost (not quite) as useless as no lock at all in keeping out the professional burglar. Padlocks, hinges, and auxiliary equipment should be heavy, strong, and installed deeply, not just screwed on with short, flimsy screws. Disc tumbler padlocks are cheaper but much easier for a burglar to open than the more complicated mechanisms of pin tumbler padlocks. Combination padlocks which open by turning a dial to a combination of numbers are good if you get a costlier, well-constructed type.

It's wise to get a strong, keyless combination door lock, such as goes on a combination lock safe. By having to turn the dial to a combination of numbers in order to open the door, you get an extra measure of security. You needn't be afraid of ever forgetting the key or be bothered carrying a load of jangling keys, but don't forget or lose the combination. And don't ever, as too many people do, write the combination on a card and keep it somewhere near the door—in a letter box, on a hook, or under the mat; burglars know and look in all such places.

Check locks on sliding glass doors as well as more conventional doors. Most such locks come right with the doors, installed at the factory, and put in place when the doors are put up (you can specify extra-secure locks before installation in some cases). You can add others, such as a strong wedge lock that enables you to leave the sliding door open enough to let in more air but not enough for anybody, even a child or a cat, to come through without your permission.

Investigate the big variety of window locks to fit your personal premises. Windows offer great temptations to burglars, since most frames are fitted with ordinary sash locks that a criminal soon learns to open easily. Get the lock that suits your purpose best: wedge-type so that you can open the window a few inches and lock it there; angled locks that are wedged into place when you secure the window and are much tougher to open than the usual sash locks; locks with keys which are difficult to open without a key.

Don't fit all the windows in the room with key locks which cannot be opened if the key isn't handy. In case of fire or other emergency, you may have to exit through a window in a hurry. Let one window in each room be your "emergency exit," without a key lock, and be sure every member of the family knows it; put on a strong lock that doesn't require a key to open it.

Check into modern double-safety pin tumbler locks, which

51

combine strong pin tumblers and magnets inside the cylinder. These are of course a big step ahead of the early Egyptian locks dating back to 2000 B.C., wooden locks using pin tumblers; other locks date back over 4,000 years and were remarkable devices for their period. In the modern double-safety locks, a special coded key releases the magnets in the cylinder and causes the lock mechanism to turn when you swivel the key. Another advantage is that the key can't be duplicated by an ordinary key shop, but must be processed by the manufacturer's factory or one of their authorized locksmiths.

There are many different models which fit the same apertures as standard locks so that the magnetic pin-tumbler type can be installed in a few minutes by an expert locksmith without new carpentry or other such work required. The locks are more costly than standard types but are more burglar-proof and worthwhile if you feel you can afford them.

Look for maximum security features on door locks. A modern lock which sells for about $40 advertises these features: "Steel clad ten-lever mechanism gives maximum protection against drilling, prevents picking and use of skeleton keys. Handle can be locked by key from inside or outside. Hook deadbolt resists forcing and gives positive engagement in staple. Bolt has reinforcing peg to resist cutting. Exclusive key combination to every lock unless specially ordered alike. Key registration prevents unauthorized persons obtaining duplicate keys. Cylinder cover shape resists gripping; concealed lugs and design of cylinder cover prevent rotation by force. Fixing screws are concealed when door is closed. Flanges on top and bottom of staple reinforce and anchor it to the door frame. Combines the security of a strong hookbolt mortise lock with the convenience of a self-locking rimlock, eliminates the need for two separate mechanisms." One thing sure, this lock won't be opened in seconds by a burglar with only a celluloid strip.

Replace skeleton-key-type locks—these are a cinch for the burglar to open with a master key or other devices he carries —or if there is such a lock on your door, at least add to it one of the other types of locks recommended.

When you need cabinet locks, locks for desk and other drawers, wardrobes, lockers, chests, trunks, or special-purpose locks for a showcase or cabinet with sliding doors, for a file cabinet, even for a telephone, it doesn't pay to buy the cheapest. You'll only be fooling yourself about the security value of the lock. Higher cost generally means better materials, more complex and more burglar-proof construction. Always examine a variety of locks for the purpose, in a range of prices, then choose according to your needs and means. As a general guide, the flimsier and simpler the lock and key, the less safety you're buying and installing.

Ask to see locks with round keys for greater home security, especially since such keys can't be duplicated at the ordinary key shop but must be made by a professional locksmith. The round key locks are also made better than average, and their more complicated mechanisms are more burglar-proof.

Look into "computer-type" locks, which provide excellent security. An average of twelve pinholes in the key are spaced and arranged by a computer. These keys can't be duplicated at a key shop; new keys must be obtained from the factory which originally made the key and lock. Such "maximum security" cylinder locks are sold and installed only by locksmiths specially authorized by the manufacturer. Cost including installation runs from about $50 to $100.

Also watch and wait when you have a key duplicated. If the man won't make it while you're watching, go somewhere else (unless it's a local dealer you know you can trust). It's too easy to run off an extra duplicate and turn it over to a burglar who will follow you to your address and use the key when the premises are vacant. Honest keymakers know this and will welcome this warning to the public; only dishonest individuals will resent the recommendation to "watch and wait" while your keys are being duplicated.

Never leave your keys in your jacket or coat pocket, or in any article of clothing that you hang up in a restaurant or other public place. That goes for clothing you leave in a checkroom as well. It's too easy for someone to have the keys

53

duplicated and returned to your pocket without your knowing the difference. You'll only realize what happened after your home is burglarized without any signs of forced entry.

Be careful with hotel or motel keys when traveling. It happens repeatedly that people dining in a restaurant, even the hotel or motel dining areas, leave keys in the pockets of coats hung on a rack. Pretending to get his own coat, a thief can lift the key from a coat pocket without being detected and then loot the room. At night he may even carry the motel room's television set to his car, parked conveniently near.

Consider carrying safety locks when traveling. For only a few dollars, you can get locks which weigh very little and take up minimal room in a suitcase, but give you an extra measure of protection. Stores have simple "travel locks" made especially to lock doors, windows, closets, drawers and cabinets in your hotel or motel room. While such locks may be opened by professional burglars, they definitely prevent many thefts by pilferers, prowlers, even temporary employees of the establishment.

Don't just get a duplicate set of keys made from those that belong to your wife or husband or roommate if you lose your own. As previously noted, you're better off changing the locks. The greater protection is well worth the extra cost.

It is also worth repeating that a name tag or other identification on your key ring or key case can lead a thief right to your home.

LOCKS AND KEYS CHECKLIST

☐ DO check all locks and replace with more burglar-proof types if advisable.

☐ DO replace any spring-type, snap-fastening, and skeleton-key locks with strong pin tumbler cylinder locks, and other improved types.

☐ DO install strong new guard locks.

☐ DO consider door locks with built-in alarms.

☐ DON'T use flimsy padlocks on garage, basement, and other doors; get disc tumbler and other strong new padlocks.

☐ DO check and install strong window locks.

☐ DO replace flimsy locks on sliding glass doors, cabinets, wardrobes.

☐ DO investigate locks with round keys for greater security.

☐ DON'T ever leave keys in the pocket of a coat hung in a public place.

☐ DO change important locks and keys if you lose a set of keys, or if they are stolen.

☐ DON'T have identification on keys.

8

HOW TO CHOOSE BETWEEN GOOD AND
BAD ALARM SYSTEMS AND DEVICES

A COMEDIAN says that the perfect gift for the family that has *everything* had better be—a burglar alarm. While nothing gives 100 per cent assurance against your house or apartment being broken into, burglar alarms have cut down the incidence of successful burglaries considerably, and increased the number of criminals caught.

A summer home, deserted between September 15 and June 15, was broken into time after time during the winter. Then the owner installed a burglar alarm system connected to the police station. Three different times the first year, as thieves broke in, the alarm system sounded at the station. Patrol cars reached the house so quickly that the burglars were caught. The following year there were no break-ins at all.

Prominently displayed decals on the outside of one attractive Long Island home stated: "This home is protected by an electronic device tied to the police station." In spite of the printed warnings, thirteen different burglars were caught by police during the owners' absence over a four-year period. One of the criminals was asked by police why he ignored the signs. He is reported to have replied, "I don't believe everything I read."

Perhaps the effectiveness of properly installed alarm systems is demonstrated by these remarks from the police chief of a suburban community: "This is a locality of homes, many quite luxurious, scattered over a considerable area. With hundreds of burglaries two years ago, we put extra patrolling into effect, along with other precautions, and urged homeowners to install alarm systems connected to a central board at the police station. Last year, home burglaries dropped a remarkable 72 per cent. A number of factors helped but we credit most of the drop to the widespread installation of good alarm systems."

Install alarms now if you're at all concerned about utmost protection and safety for your family and yourself. A good system is worth a great deal in peace of mind for those at home and for the husband when he's away. Said a traveling man, "I have a wonderful new feeling of assurance that I've made my family safer from the thief in the night." His wife said that it helped her to sleep when she awakened alongside his empty bed and was reassured by the glowing red button-light on the switch that the burglar alarm system was helping to guard her and the children. "That little red light," she said, "comforts me like a teddy bear in a sleeping child's arms."

On the other hand, delay in protecting your home can be costly. Disturbed by a burglary in the house next door, a woman wrote on her pad, "Look into burglar alarm systems." She saw the notation week after week, did nothing about it, then threw away the memo as her fears subsided and no further robberies were reported in the neighborhood. Three months later the family returned late from a weekend trip and found their home burglarized. She started looking into alarm systems the next day— a little late for that loss, but better than never to help safeguard their future.

Consider every kind of alarm system available to you, from simple inexpensive kits you can install yourself to more costly installations. Look under "Burglar Alarm Systems" in your classified telephone directory, and talk to suppliers in your area. Your police department can also give you the names of reliable burglar alarm companies that connect installations to the signal board in the police station. Choose what best suits your needs and your means, from a large number of possibilities.

Battery-operated alarms, some costing only a few dollars and others more complicated $100 or more, are effective to some degree in frightening off some inexperienced intruders. They're not considered reliable safeguards against skilled and experienced burglars. Devices are available which operate simply on penlight or flashlight batteries. You can attach them quickly, according to the fairly simple instructions that come with the units, to doors and windows. (Be sure to check instructions before you buy, to make certain that they can be attached to your own doors and windows.)

Once the alarm is set, opening the door or window will set off a buzzer alarm which may frighten away the intruder, as well as awaken people in the house so that they can phone police quickly or call for help in a hurry, scaring away an intruder. With this type of device, make sure that the noise it makes is loud enough to be heard in all parts of the house or bedroom, and preferably by neighbors or people passing by as well. Some alarms provide a little fire protection, too, as they are activated by fire as well as motion.

Some small buzzer alarms operating on batteries may also be carried as a "personal alarm" when you're out. The idea is that if you're accosted, you can press a button or pull a string on the device to frighten off your assailant and alert anyone near you to your danger. The device can be of value if you carry it in an overcoat pocket where you can reach it in a split second. However, if you have to open a handbag or briefcase, then reach in and activate the alarm, it's likely to be too late to do you any good.

If you carry a buzzer alarm device with you when you travel, you can attach it to a door or window in your motel or hotel room. It will give off a loud noise if the door or windows are forced, usually an effective protective signal in locations where other people are near.

If your property is on a lake or other shore, consider all the alarms described on these pages to help safeguard a boathouse, boat, boating equipment, and other valuable waterfront items. Some burglars specialize in raiding waterfront properties, often sneaking in and leaving by boat; special precautions must be taken against them, and good loud alarms provide one method that often is effective. The same is true for other types of vacation homes.

Professionally installed alarm systems offer excellent protection when properly planned and custom-fitted to your particular premises. Seek out particularly those companies that will connect your home directly to an alarm board at your nearest police station; as suggested, ask your local police officials for those names. Also look up in your telephone classified pages names of companies listed under "Burglar Alarm Systems." Call at least two or three alarm companies, have them give you a plan and estimate for your home, then choose the one that seems best for your needs. Be sure to get references and phone other homeowners in your area before signing a contract. Installation and maintenance cost depend on your requirements.

A variety of burglar alarm systems offers you wide choice. Most don't require any special power wiring, operating on standard wiring from the regular outlet. A basic system covers all entry doors to the house or apartment and a number of strategic doors to rooms inside, but not necessarily all doors. Windows may be attached to the alarm system also, but not necessarily. If the burglar gets into the house without activating the alarm, he is likely to set it off by opening one of the bedroom, study, or other doors connected to the system. When such a door or window is opened, a very loud alarm goes off on the huge bell located inside or outside the house, or both. The loud noise alerts you, neighbors, and passers-by, and the clanging alone is likely to make the burglar leave as fast as he can make his feet go. If you prefer, however, it can be a silent alarm, ringing only at a central station.

Most professional systems require lengthy, detailed, careful installation throughout the house or apartment. Be certain that no alarm system wires are outside the house where a burglar could cut them. Also make sure that the company you choose has fine craftsmen so that your walls aren't defaced by holes or wires showing. The only items that will show on your walls are two or three (or more if you have a very large place) plates the size and general appearance of ordinary light switch plates. The alarm plates usually have a slot for a key, and small red and white buttons.

Such a system operates very simply. When the system is off (during the day when you're at home, for instance), neither the red nor the white buttons are lit up. When you are ready to put the system on, at any hour of the day or night, you shut tight any doors and windows connected with the alarm system. This turns on the white light on the plates. If the white lights are not lit, you check all entries again to make sure they are closed tight; when operating properly the white light won't appear unless all wired entrances are closed completely.

When the white light appears, you insert a key (kept in a closed drawer or closet or other hidden place nearby) and turn it to the right; the red light goes on, the white light goes off. Now the alarm system is in active operation. If anyone—a burglar, one of the family, a dog, anyone or anything—opens a wired door or window, the gong sounds. Floodlights can go on also if wired into the system. In other words, as one house-holder put it, "All hell breaks loose!" That's true even if one of the family opens a wired door or window without thinking or realizing that the alarm system is on.

To turn the alarm system to "off," you simply turn the key to the right, and the red light goes off, the white light goes on. Then you open one of the wired doors or windows, the white light goes off, and the system is on "off"; the gong can sound only if the red light is on and a wired entry is opened. With the system off, the key is removed and put away in a concealed place. Operation of the system is almost as easy and uncompli-cated as turning a light switch on and off.

A big advantage of this kind of system is that you can also, in most localities, have it connected directly to the police station, where it is wired in to a special board. If a burglar or anyone else opens a wired door or window in your home when the system is on, a buzzer sounds and your light goes on at police headquarters. Police go into action; if there is a patrol car near you, officers can be at your house or apartment house in a very brief time. Many burglars have been scared off or caught by this police-connected home system. The connection is usually made through your phone system for which you pay a monthly fee to the phone company (charged on your phone bill), plus an installation fee.

Don't be upset if you set off the alarm system by mistake (one of the family going to the kitchen for an after-midnight snack, and opening a wired interior door, for example), as the police are very understanding about this. Simply phone the police immediately and report the mistake. (The police may come to your home anyway, because a thief could make the call as well as you.) Officials realize that such mistakes can happen, and would rather stop more burglaries and catch more criminals through such alarm systems than be concerned about false alarms.

If you cannot be connected to a police alarm system, for one reason or another, alarm services offer other variations. The system can be connected to a telephone gadget that rings police headquarters, or to a central service board at company headquarters. The operator there in turn immediately calls the police and sends company guards if available. Being tied in directly with the police station is generally faster and surer. In some cases, your system can be connected to both the police station and the alarm company headquarters, for an extra measure of safety.

Emergency buttons are also available for these alarm systems. These buttons are installed usually on the wall alongside your bed (in a higher position comparatively inaccessible to children), and at one or more entrance doors. Whether the system is off or on, pressing the emergency button sounds the bell alarm, or alerts police headquarters if your system is connected there. Thus, if you're at your front entrance door and someone is trying to push his way in past the door (you should have your chain-guard latched), you reach out and push the emergency button. Instantly the signal is activated, and police are at your doorway in a hurry. The intruder takes to his heels at once, but is often caught.

If you hear an intruder in your house or apartment when

you're in bed, you reach for the emergency button there, and the alarm bell and police go into protective operation instantly. For this reason the emergency buttons are an important feature to consider with any alarm system; you may never use them, but even one occasion could save your life from an attacker. The button signal is also useful in getting quick help in case of a heart attack or other emergency where you need aid instantly.

Alarm installations are generally operated on your electric system but include a battery connection, so that if your electricity goes off in a blackout or for any other reason, the burglar alarm system still works. The mechanisms for most systems are inclosed in one or more boxes about a foot square which are placed in an out-of-the-way spot on a pantry or laundry wall or in a closet. They are constructed to be tamper-proof in case a burglar gains access and wishes to disconnect the system.

Your alarm system should be custom-planned and fitted to your special needs. It can be wired to a safe or vault; it can be combined with a fire alarm system. For whatever is desired, there is an installation charge and an annual service charge, usually paid monthly or as arranged. Costs vary, usually involving over $100 and perhaps considerably more—especially if the system is connected in some way to the police station.

After your system is installed and operating properly, have it checked again *one week later* and at least once every six months to make sure it's functioning to protect you. In one instance, a homeowner had a good system installed and connected with the police station. The family felt greatly reassured about their protection; the little red alarm light glowed comfortingly each night when the alarm key was activated. After nine months, the red light began to flicker at times, so the service crew of the alarm system company was called.

A company mechanic arrived the next day, asked the lady of the house to phone police to ignore alarm signals from the house, as he would be testing. The mechanic fixed the flickering light, which required only a slight adjustment. He then tested all parts of the signal, opening and closing each wired door with the system on, checking everything out thoroughly. "It's working perfectly," he said to the lady. "Please phone the police that we're finished testing." She called and was told by a puzzled policeman, "Your alarm here hasn't been signaling at all, but the signal for an address around the corner from you has been going like mad. We checked out that house and there's no trouble there. Better send the company man down here. . . ."

It turned out that the company had made the installations in both houses at the same time—and put the name and address card of the other house on *both* signals at the police station. If a burglar had tried to break into the house being checked, the signal would have sent the police to the other house "around the corner."

(If you're curious, the company—with face very red—refunded service fees and telephone charges for the nine months that the system had, in effect, not been properly connected.)

This kind of system, combined with strong locks and other basic measures recommended here, is probably the best protection you can buy for your home or apartment. It must be repeated that nothing can be guaranteed to stop 100 per cent the highly skilled professional criminal who wants to get into your house. The better *your* planning, however, the more time and planning are required on his part. Unless your home contains fabulous, costly treasures which would produce easy exchange and big money, remember that the burglar is seeking a pushover entrance, not a difficult, alarm-rigged entry.

You're far safer with a good alarm system. The overwhelming majority of people who have professional alarm systems installed, as described, feel that their homes are far more burglar-proof— and according to the records, they are. When you go shopping, out for an evening, or away for a lengthy trip or vacation, or when you close a summer or country house for months, your mind is far more at ease. A year after installation, a typical homeowner wrote, "It has been almost a year since our protection burglar-alarm system was installed. We haven't had a single break-in incident since, after having a number of burglaries before, along with vandalism which was costly and upsetting when we would return to a ravaged home."

Consider the "extras" if you look into a burglar alarm system of the type described. Special external signals work purposefully to warn off the burglar who is thinking of breaking into the house. The glowing red light tells the burglar that the alarm system is guarding the house. Small, neat decal signs on the wall by each entry door (usually one sign placed on each side of the house) state that "THESE PREMISES ARE PROTECTED FROM BURGLARY." The criminal usually passes by such a house or apartment—again he figures that it's tough enough to make a dishonest living without taking on more difficult challenges.

Probably the prime reason burglars respect an alarm system is that they know the police can arrive with astonishing speed when the signal flashes at the police station. One burglar who broke into an apartment with an alarm system managed to work his way past the front door but tripped the alarm when he entered an inner bedroom, in spite of being extremely careful. As he headed for the front exit he heard sirens and realized that he couldn't beat the police from the building. Quickly he stripped off his shirt, trousers, socks, and shoes, and pulled on a pair of the owner's pajamas. Just then the doorbell buzzed. He opened the door, acting as though he lived there, and apologized to the police that he had tripped his own alarm by mistake. Right after the police left, so did he. Caught soon after, he revealed his quick-thinking but futile trick. Burglars rightly hate alarms of any kind.

It's vital to understand that a burglar alarm system doesn't take care of all the protection you need in your home. It's the combination of all basic recommended steps that will serve you best.

Check your insurance agent to learn whether you're entitled to a discount on your burglary insurance premiums once you install a good burglar alarm system, as is the case with some policies for business establishments.

In addition to these standard systems, there are radarlike burglar alarms which come in various types. They consist of ultrasonic and microwave detectors. When set in operation, any motion caused in a room by an intruder, or anybody or anything else, will activate the system. You can arrange to have the intrusion result in a call to a number which is all set to reach the police with a prerecorded message: for example. "A burglary is taking place on the premises of George Brown, 150 Home Street, Apartment 2F." Or the system will sound a loud alarm bell or turn on floodlights, or both, according to how you have it set up. This type of alarm is adaptable for use in homes and apartments, as well as in stores and other business establishments.

There is a popular single unit you can install yourself simply by plugging it into an ordinary electric outlet. It is about a foot long and a few inches deep and high, and costs about $100. This unit has no outside connection, does not transmit any message to the police or anyone else. Each unit simply covers an area of about 15 to 20 feet, protecting one room in the house or apartment. In some cases one unit can be so positioned as to protect several small rooms, but generally one unit is necessary per room. Depending on the number of units used or necessary, protecting a home or apartment runs from a few hundred dollars into thousands. Or you may rent a system of this type for an installation fee of $100 or more, and a service fee of a few dollars per month.

Professional installation rather than do-it-yourself is recommended, although mail-order ads tell you to simply set the device in a room and "it plugs right into an ordinary 115-volt outlet." Unless you have professional know-how, your own installation may result in much less protection, as well as cause many false alarms.

These devices, as noted, are activated by motion in the room intercepting the invisible "rays" or waves beamed out in circles to cover the area. The waves keep circling and bouncing harmlessly off walls, ceiling, floor, furniture, and other still objects in the room, with nothing happening to the alarm system as long as the waves leave and return to the device without interruption. If any object, such as the person of a burglar, breaks the normal

65

paths of the waves, the frequency is altered and the alarm system is activated. If it is attached to a bell, when the gong goes off, hopefully the burglar will, too.

An added advantage here is that the device can usually be turned on from outside the room or apartment or house when you leave. Then you turn it off similarly when you return, before entering, so that your own body entering the waves will not cause a false alarm to sound. The unit can also be equipped with a "panic button" on the wall by the front door which you can press if an intruder tries to force his way in: a very desirable accessory.

If you haven't a burglar alarm system, you can install a panic button separately at bedside. Various types operate on house current or battery. Pushing the panic button sounds a gong or siren or puts on floodlights outside to alert neighbors and passers-by—whatever you arrange to scare off a burglar and get help for yourself.

If this kind of protection fits your needs, investigate electronic call button systems. With one unit about the size of a small transistor radio, the pressure of your finger activates an electronic signal which is received immediately at a central point. There the unit dials the local emergency number and plays a pre-recorded tape giving whatever message you have designated, including your name and address. Help is sent at once.

The call button unit has no wires, and since it's only about the size of a pack of cigarettes, you can carry it in your pocket, or keep it on a bedside table, in a desk drawer, and so on. Use it in your home, apartment, office, store—wherever you feel you need protection most. You don't alert a criminal who has entered your bedroom, for example, because pressing the call button makes no sound when it signals for help. Most such systems involve an original cost running to hundreds of dollars, plus a small phone installation fee, and an extra fee added to your monthly phone bill, as it operates via the telephone company.

There are also electric or battery-operated pads which fit under rugs, carpets, or doormats. They lie very flat and are quite invisible, creating little or no bulge. When they are turned on, stepping on the alarm-mat will sound a loud bell or buzzer, frightening away an intruder and alerting you and others. Some pads activate loud barking sounds, very lifelike, for all the world like a large, angry dog, designed to frighten away an intruder before he bothers to look around to see the dog. In cases where burglars with plenty of time to operate cut a hole in a door to crawl through, bypassing alarm system wiring around the door, an invisible alarm pad under the rug just inside the door can trip them up by signaling the intrusion. In an instance where burglars used an electric handsaw to cut through the door, the indignant homeowner said, "What gripes me most is that the crooks plugged their electric saw into an outlet on my porch, and used my own current to rob me!"

Keep abreast of other types of burglar alarm devices and systems which are being developed as the number of burglaries increases and people recognize the need for protecting their homes and themselves. Before you buy any of the items or systems described here, ask the opinion of your local police authorities about its efficiency for your purposes.

If you live in an apartment house, discuss security measures with other tenants to make sure you're all getting maximum protection. For example, instead of old buzzer systems which enable a burglar to ring one person's buzzer and then use the opened lobby door to reach another apartment, there are new and safer direct-dial apartment intercommunication systems. Each tenant's name is listed but *not the apartment number*. A visitor presses the button, communicates with your apartment through an intercom system, and identifies himself before you tell him the apartment number and press a button to release the lobby door.

"Better dwell in the midst of alarms" than in an unsafe place, living with fear. By relieving your fears to a considerable extent, a good burglar alarm system will help you live a happier (and perhaps longer) as well as a safer life.

BURGLAR ALARM CHECKLIST

☐ DO realize that burglar alarms cut down immensely the incidence of break-in.

☐ DO order a professional alarm system, preferably connected to the police station, if at all practicable for you.

☐ DON'T skip battery-operated alarms if you can't go for more costly systems.

☐ DO look into radar-type alarms, electronic call buttons, panic buttons, under-carpet and door pad alarms, and others.

☐ DO take other recommended precautions in addition to burglar alarms and devices.

9

SPECIAL PRECAUTIONS FOR APARTMENT DWELLERS TODAY

LEARN all about the security measures in your apartment house, in addition to following the preceding recommendations for utmost security. Learn the building layout, spotting where intruders are likely to enter and how you can safeguard yourself, and suggest desirable extra safety measures to the building manager. For example, one helpful device is an internal television system which enables someone in the lobby to check what goes on at all entrances and exits, in the elevator, in halls, and in other places where crimes most commonly take place. Burglar-resistant locks are available which use pushbuttons instead of keys; each tenant has a combination of different numbers which he pushes to unlock his door.

Make a note of where you can get help quickly if needed—from neighbors, the building superintendent, and workers, from an alarm button in the apartment or building. Having this knowledge *before* you are faced with a safety crisis can save valuable minutes to relieve your fears, help stop a crime, or help catch a thief.

Install strong, extra locks on your entry doors to which only you and your family have the keys. The regular apartment locks may be opened by a master key in many cases, and if the key falls into the wrong hands you're in trouble.

Don't bypass your immediate neighbors and other building tenants. Get to know them, even if only slightly, for mutual cooperation and protection. Looking at tenants helps you to recognize them on sight; this can be very helpful as an aid in identifying strangers and suspicious-looking characters quickly.

It's safer not to ride the self-service elevator with anyone who looks at all suspicious to you; it's safer to step out before the elevator starts, and take the next trip. If you're going up or down, be sure the indicator registers the right direction (if you're on the 10th floor going down, for example, and someone pushes the button to "up," this may indicate trouble). Note where the "alarm" button is in the elevator, and try to be near enough to push it instantly if necessary.

Beware of being lowered by the elevator to the basement, where many crimes occur. It's safest when the elevator doors open to reach in, press the basement button, then wait for the elevator to come *up* from the basement so you know it's not on the way *down* to the basement. Look into the elevator to check that no one is lurking in it, then step in and press the button to your floor.

Never go to the laundry room in the building at night, or at hours when the laundry is likely to be empty, without taking a companion. Arrange with one of the other tenants you know to do your laundry together, for mutual protection. The laundry room is a favorite spot for criminals to attack a woman (or even a man) alone, where an outcry or other noise probably won't be overheard.

You can't rely on the chain-guard to keep out burglars if you leave the front or back doors ajar for ventilation, as some people do when their apartments get hot or stuffy. This is a dangerous practice, as a husky intruder can break the chain by force or slip it off from the outside with a device.

Report any suspicious-looking characters to the building superintendent or the police. This helps prevent crimes *before* they happen. If the person accosted by the police is there for a good reason, he'll have no problem explaining his presence and will realize that he's being questioned for the protection of all in the building.

Take extra precautions if you're a woman living alone. Ask your neighbors, building manager, superintendent, and attendants to keep an extra check on your apartment for anything or anyone with a suspicious look.

Your mailbox and apartment registry listing should use your initial rather than your first name; for example, "B. Brown" rather than "Beatrice Brown." Such an initial listing is safer in the telephone directory also, as criminals often seek out the woman living alone as less of a risk for them.

Before you agree to a roommate, check every detail of her references, background, and habits thoroughly. If you detect anything suspicious, don't make an arrangement, as many thefts and other crimes have occurred from the "inside."

When you are going out on a date, or for an evening appointment, it's safer to let someone know, perhaps a neighbor, friend, work associate. Tell them whom you'll be with and, if you know, where you'll be going. If you're missing or robbed, this information is essential to help you most quickly.

Inform the authorities if your apartment manager fails to institute proper precautions or rectify unsafe conditions such as inadequate lighting. The proper authorities can help make desirable corrections and additions for tenant safety, without revealing your identity.

APARTMENT CHECKLIST

☐ DO check all security measures in the apartment house, in addition to installing your personal safeguards.

☐ DO learn how to get help quickly from apartment house employees and neighbors.

☐ DO install the strongest, most burglar-proof locks possible on doors and windows.

☐ DO take the precautions recommended in riding self-service elevators.

☐ DON'T go to the laundry room alone at night.

☐ DO report suspicious-looking characters to the building superintendent or police.

☐ DO observe the specific added safeguards listed if you are a woman living alone.

10

SPECIAL PRECAUTIONS FOR SUBURBANITES AND IMPORTANT EXTRA GUIDES FOR ALL

LEAVE a light on, or several lights, when you go out for the evening. The lighted windows should be visible from the street. If yours is a two-story house, leave a light upstairs as well as downstairs, facing the street. Use a special timing device, if you have one (described later), to turn lights on and off in different rooms at intervals as though someone were moving from room to room naturally.

Close the blinds, draw curtains, or pull down shades when you go out at night, along with leaving lights on. Otherwise, a thief can look through the window for some length of time. If he sees that the room is unoccupied, with no movement at all over a long stretch, he may take a chance on entering. However, if shades or blinds are drawn so he can't see into the room past the lighted window, he's likely to look for a more inviting place. In closing blinds, tilt slats upward so anyone looking in can see only the ceiling. Pull window shades all the way down—don't leave a crack at the bottom for anyone to look through and see that the room is empty.

Double-check before you leave for the evening that all doors and windows are locked. Burglars brag at how easily they "walk right in" because a side, basement, or other door has been left unlocked. Often when you "know" the doors are locked, you have forgotten that you opened one for a delivery man, or a dayworker left without locking the door behind her, or the kids unlocked it for dashing in and out. It only takes a minute to double-check and can save you hundreds, even thousands, of dollars.

Lock up tight especially when you're off to a wedding, a funeral, or any event—a dance, lecture, concert—which is public knowledge. Professional burglars watch for such happenings, find out who might be going, and loot the empty homes or apartments. In the case of one neighborhood association dance at a country club, a number of homes in the area were looted while the occupants were attending the affair.

Never keep large sums of money, jewelry, negotiable bonds, and such at home. They're all much safer in a bank vault for ready access whenever you need them.

General Hints for All Kinds of Homes

Prepare a list of your valuables, jewelry, cameras, typewriters, portable TV and radio sets, particularly noting the serial numbers. Keep separate lists of the numbers on automobiles, bicycles, fans, washers, and so on. Do the same with credit cards, travelers checks, and other negotiable papers. Keep a record of any savings bonds, other securities, preferably in a bank vault where the bonds themselves should be kept. Note detailed descriptions of jewelry, costly vases or other valuables, with sketches or snapshots to help identify them. If your home is looted, these listings help police to recover what was stolen from you.

A well-equipped police department can often perform "miracles" in recovering stolen merchandise, such as identifying cameras in the laboratory by checking the photographic negatives made from them. When the police cover pawn shops and secondhand stores looking for stolen merchandise, clear photos or drawings of your jewelry and other valuables, along with detailed descriptions, can make the difference between recovery and loss of your possessions.

Take action if you see suspicious characters lurking around your house, or outside or inside your apartment house, near the entrance, in the lobby, in the halls. If someone seems to be hiding near the dark entrance, turn around and call the police from the nearest phone booth; don't try to enter the building until a police car arrives. If you suspect anyone hanging around the lobby, elevators, stairways, or halls, call the police as soon as you enter your apartment and lock the door behind you. By phoning instead of shrugging off your suspicions, you will be helping yourself and family, neighbors, and the police. Criminals depend on citizens' inaction to give them plenty of rope with which to hang you.

Observe proper precautions upon returning home and finding that burglars have been there. If you see signs of a break-in before you enter, such as a lock broken or the door open, don't enter; call police from the nearest phone and wait for them before entering the house. Otherwise you might surprise the burglars in the midst of the robbery, and violence to you and yours could result.

If you enter the house and find that thieves have been there and gone, phone the police immediately, preferably from a neighbor's phone rather than your own. Walk around and take an inventory of what seems to be missing, but *don't touch or move anything* until the police arrive and give you permission. Otherwise you might destroy indicative clues, even fingerprints. In many cases, burglars leave familiar traces of how they worked, what they took, the way they left the rooms, and so on; these can help the police to track them down and recover your property (this is known as their M.O., "modus operandi," meaning the way a particular criminal or gang usually works).

If you fail to report the intrusion, you're making it more likely that your home will be robbed again. Even if only a few minor items have been taken, call the police. The least help they can give you is to advise how your premises can be made more burglar-proof. Also, they'll be more watchful of your place from then on.

If you do walk in on a burglar, try not to panic lest you incite him to violence. Try to keep as cool as possible. There have been cases of particularly well-controlled individuals who have come upon an intruder after entering the house or apartment and said, "Oh, I'm sorry, I must be in the wrong place," then walked out before the burglar could get over his surprise. Admittedly, few people can act that quickly and cleverly, but at least try not to panic.

Arrange cooperation with your neighbors in a house or apartment house. Make a pact that you'll report any suspicious characters around his place, and that he'll do the same for you. This is one of the most effective ways to help check the activities of criminals.

In one such case, a woman saw men carrying items from her neighbor's house into a truck in the driveway—in broad daylight. She phoned her neighbor to ask whether she could be helpful. When no one answered the phone, she became suspicious and immediately called the police (unlike other cases cited where neighbors did nothing). The truckmen, hearing the phone, became upset. They bustled out of the house carrying a large color television set, put it in the truck, closed and bolted the truck doors, backed out, and headed down the street. An approaching police car, answering the neighbor's call, blocked the truck at the corner. The merchandise was returned to the house; the burglars were returned to the prison from which they had been released a few weeks before.

Never leave jewelry, money, or other valuables exposed in your house, particularly in the hall or downstairs rooms. A delivery man or other caller who would not be tempted otherwise might return for the obvious valuables as soon as you leave your house or apartment. Also, a purse or wallet left on a hall table offers the temptation for someone to grab it and run.

Don't leave important papers, a purse, or any small valuable within reach of an open window. A passing thief can reach in, grab whatever is there, and vanish without even being noticed.

Never keep sizable sums of cash around your house or apartment, no matter how safe a hiding place you may think you have. Police know that there are no safe hiding places from burglars—the professionals search thoroughly and seem to "smell" money wherever it is tucked or locked away.

Notify the proper authorities if street lights are out in front of your house or nearby. Do this as soon as you notice it, as crime thrives in the dark.

Leave on lights outside your house from dark until bedtime; make this a habit whether you're at home or have gone out. It's even better to leave the lights on all night, keeping the outside flooded with light, as the cost of the electricity is still cheap protection. Lights at each entry door are desirable. Criminals hate light; they tend to stay away from lighted places where they can be spotted by neighbors, by people walking along the street, or by a passing patrol car whose officers are on the lookout for any suspicious persons and movements around a home or apartment house and will usually stop to investigate. By putting light on the subject who is thinking of burglarizing your house, you're protecting your home with another vital deterrent. Never forget that the criminal wants better than an even break when he picks a target for looting.

Keep a radio on when you go out of your house or apartment if there have been burglaries in your area recently. The combination of lighted, shade-drawn rooms and sound from a radio helps discourage burglars and sends them on to seek some other target—which, hopefully, is similarly protected.

Never leave valuables such as clothing, rugs, costly blankets, furs, and so on, out on a line or porch railing or fire escape for airing while you go out, not even if it's only a brief errand. Too often the items are gone when you return.

Protective Light-Control Devices

It's safer not to leave lights on 24 hours a day when you're traveling or vacationing. This may alert a burglar to the fact that the family is away—how many people normally leave lights on in the daytime? But a house left continually dark also invites criminals. The safe step is to get a special timed light switch. These devices range from simple ones for under $5.00 to more complicated setups costing about $100 or more.

The least expensive switches work on light-sensitive cells

which turn on the light when the room grows dark at twilight, and turn the light off again as the light of day moves in at sunrise. A disadvantage here is that a criminal checking the neighborhood night after night will spot your house as being lighted all night long, again a break in the normal family pattern and a signal that the house is deserted.

More complicated and more costly types of light-and-time controls enable you to vary the lighting in rooms in a number of ways. You can regulate one or more lights in the house or apartment so that lights go on about 7 P.M. and off about midnight, or whatever is your normal time of turning out lights as you go to sleep. You can fix the device so that a light is on in one room for a couple of hours, as many as you wish according to your setting; then that light goes out and another light comes on in another room, and so on. By this method, you create the effect of people staying in one room to chat, then going to another to watch television, leaving that to go to the bedroom, approximating your usual living habits. This adds an extra measure of protection.

More sophisticated timed switches provide extra settings, too, for turning a radio on for a few hours or longer, or even the television set and other appliances. You can use these devices for other on-off uses, too—in cooking, for instance, turning an electric stove or coffee maker on and off automatically as you wish.

Extra Care and Cooperation Vital

Help protect your neighbors as you would want them to help protect you and your family. This recommendation cannot be overstressed. Every police authority will assure you that cooperation among individuals, neighbors, and families is essential to the prevention and deterrence of crime.

Check your burglary insurance every year or two. Changes in your personal as well as in general conditions may necessitate changes in your insurance policies for maximum protection and for compensation of loss by burglary or vandalism. Be warned by the popular cartoon showing a man intruding in a dark bedroom, shining his light on a terrified, just awakened couple in bed; he carries a briefcase marked "Safety Insurance Co.," and says, "You're probably thinking, 'A burglar—and I have no insurance!'"

Valuables are not safe because you lock them up in a small tin box. One of the first items the burglar will note to carry away is that small tin box. Don't keep lists and descriptions of valuables in the box (they're safer in a drawer), as they'll be gone along with the "safety" box. If you do use a strong, well-locked safety box, preferably kept within a safe, make sure that it's bolted down securely so it can't be carried away.

Be careful not to brag about your possessions or about family collections that may have considerable value—small antiques, stamps, coins, other valuables. Talking about such items to strangers, or to friends in a crowded place like a bus where you can be overheard, often results in tragic losses. Too often there are reports in the newspapers of a home being raided with little taken other than something like "a stamp collection worth thousands of dollars."

When someone in the family dies, it is a good practice *not* to list the address of the deceased in the obituary. According to a front-page article in the January 5, 1970 edition of *The Wall Street Journal,* "Obituaries and paid death notices are among the best read parts of a paper, and the readers include burglars who like to pay their respects by visiting the home of the dead person during the funeral."

Lock up liquor and other valuables rather than leave them around out in the open as temptation for easy pickings by anyone in the house or an intruder from outside. A variety of locks including attractive combination locks can be used on cabinets, closets, other closed places. A workman who had been in a house for several weeks returned when the family went on vacation and tried to break in. Fortunately for the owner, an alarm system brought the police, and the would-be thief was caught.

He complained, "When I was working there they left all this valuable stuff around loose as though they wanted somebody to take it."

Keep one or more powerful flashlights and candles in your home in case of a fuse box or general power failure. Put them on so that you show light in the house or apartment. Since burglars operate best in darkness, many take advantages of power failures.

Look over the neighborhood carefully from a protection viewpoint before you buy a house, or rent or buy an apartment. Consider safety hazards for your family and yourself. Is the street well lighted? or so dark at night that the dimness invites criminal activity? Is it a neighborhood where suspicious-looking persons are seen generally on the streets? Is the street well patrolled by police or hired guards? or is the area empty and dangerous in the later hours? The accent here is on checking *before* you make a commitment and move in.

Check the crawl space, if any, under your house, and eliminate the opportunities for places where a criminal could hide in waiting in the darkness.

Keep breezeways from garage to house well lighted at night and not covered with heavy foliage to afford a criminal a hiding place.

Make sure that any skylights and other roof openings are well locked, with strong grills if necessary to keep out intruders.

Check basement windows to be certain that they are secure against easy entrance, with strong protective grills if necessary.

Be careful when entertaining that your guests don't leave pocketbooks and wraps in a bedroom or other room that could readily be entered by an intruder from the outside. Make sure before your guests arrive that the windows in the room are securely locked. Burglars seek just such opportunities as a party or gathering to slip in and gather up purses, costly furs, other valuables that are scattered about.

Don't take off rings, wristwatches, jewelry and leave them on window sills (as on a kitchen sill by the sink) when washing up or for any other reason. People passing by or looking in might see them and decide to steal them. Strangers such as persons making deliveries might spot the valuables and grab them there and then while your back is turned or come back to steal them later.

Call the police promptly if you see anyone suspicious lurking about your house or apartment, or an automobile parked out front where it shouldn't be for a long period. Usually criminals look a home over carefully from the outside *before they choose it as a target.* A patrol car in the area can check suspicious cars and persons readily. Many crimes have been prevented by such cooperation. You're protecting yourself while protecting your neighbor—in many cases a burglar looting an apartment, surprised in the act, and trying to escape pursuing police, will break into a nearby apartment to avoid detection and will endanger any occupants there.

Ask the cab driver to wait and not leave until he sees that you've entered your house safely at night. Use a wave of your hand at the door as a prearranged signal. You'll be safe from attack by intruders hiding in the shrubbery or in the darkness around a corner of the house.

It's better not to trust itinerant workmen who ring your doorbell and offer to resurface your driveway, trim your trees, repair your roof, or do other jobs—all usually at "bargain prices." A typical offer is to repair your driveway "for $50— would usually cost you over $100, but I'm from the next town, just did a job near here, and have a load of material I'd rather use on your driveway than drive back to the shop. . . ." Instead of saving money, you'll probably be throwing out $50 on messy work that must be done over next year. No matter how convincing his "guarantees" may be, your chances of getting your money back if dissatisfied are less than slight.

Homeowners who have hired "a passing gardener" who offers to do "one more job for practically nothing before I head for home" have not only lost the $25 or so they paid to "save a sick tree"—but have also lost the tree, which might have been healthy before it was hacked up. Many who have paid a bargain price to a passing workman for "quick roof repair" have unhappily tried to dodge the rain dripping through on them in the next heavy storm.

For your own protection, call in dependable local companies, get their estimates, look at a few of the jobs they've done in the area, and check with those homeowners for a recommendation; then make your selection. The local firm wants your good will to help get future jobs; therefore it can't use fly-by-night tactics. Furthermore, local authorities can help you get recompense if not satisfied, whereas they have no jurisdiction over companies in other areas.

SUBURBAN AND GENERAL CHECKLIST

☐ DO leave some lights on when you go out for the evening, and use timing devices if you'll be away for a day or longer.

☐ DO close blinds, curtains, and shades when out at night.

☐ DO check that all doors and windows are locked when leaving.

☐ DON'T keep large sums of money and valuables at home.

☐ DO keep a list of valuables, jewelry, and other such possessions.

☐ DON'T enter your home if it has been broken into—phone the police and wait for them.

☐ DO notify the authorities if nearby street lights are out, or lights in your apartment vestibule and lobby

☐ DO leave on outside lights and a radio when you go out.

☐ DON'T leave valuable items outdoors, in yards or on porches.

☐ DO arrange cooperation with your neighbors for mutual protection.

☐ DO examine the neighborhood from a safety viewpoint before deciding to live there.

☐ DO check crawl spaces, breezeways, and other spots in and around the house from a protection viewpoint.

☐ DO examine strangers carefully for later description if needed.

☐ DON'T do business with itinerant workmen.

11

THE PROS AND CONS OF KEEPING A GUN IN YOUR HOME

SOME PERSONS insist that the only way they can feel they and their families are protected properly is to keep a gun handy in the house or apartment. This is particularly true of certain individuals who live in lonely and remote dwellings or in areas which have suffered from many burglaries. They claim that without a firearm they feel defenseless, and that "a gun is the only thing that will scare a thief away and keep him away."

Some men who have served in the armed forces during a war claim that they have been as well trained as a policeman and that they can handle a dangerous situation if they have a rifle in the house. They argue that only inexperienced people should *not* be allowed to have a gun for protection.

Others feel that a gun should not be used to thwart a robbery, but that in these turbulent times a rifle is necessary to protect your family and scare off rioters (by showing the rifle and, if necessary, by firing it in the air). In some communities, the police forces are not large enough to handle a riot of any size. Many people claim that the only precaution possible is owning a rifle.

Law enforcement authorities, however, are in practically total agreement on warning the average citizen *not* to keep a firearm in his house or apartment. Violence begets violence. In the case of a burglary, if you make a move to use a revolver or other firearm, the intruder is likely to react with some form of violence, such as shooting you first. Better submit to being burglarized than take a chance on being maimed or killed.

The lawbreaker is a professional at violence—you are not, even if you had a good war record—so the odds are with him and against you. Avoid owning and using any firearms for burglary protection.

There are many dangers in keeping a gun in the house: children injuring themselves . . . wives being shot when cleaning a shelf and knocking a loaded revolver down, or when emptying a drawer containing a gun . . . a firearm being used in another crime after having been stolen from a home by a burglar.

Guns have been fired accidentally, injuring or killing a person in the next room or apartment. Youngsters have found live ammunition and maimed themselves and friends while trying to explode a bullet with a hammer or a rock, like "fireworks." In one case, a child pushed a bullet into a toy pistol and exploded it.

The man who feels he needs a gun as protection from intruders admits there is a dilemma. If the gun is not loaded, or the gun and ammunition are in a locked box for the safety of the family, it may not be available quickly enough for an emergency if an intruder breaks in.

The real dilemma concerns a possible riot in a town where law enforcement authorities are not strong enough to handle it. One can sympathize with the man who says, "I have a responsibility to protect my loved ones. What do I do when a riot develops in an adjacent area and a frenzied mob starts ransacking the homes around us? The three policemen in our village can't handle it. I've got to have a rifle."

According to authorities, the best protective action anyone can take to keep you and your family from being injured or killed during a riot is to leave the scene. Your life and the lives of your loved ones are more important than your property. This advice may not satisfy some people who live in riot-torn areas— or in areas where riots seem imminent. It is the safest course of action, but it is depressingly frustrating to contemplate and does not deal with the long-range problem. If you live in a town that seems marked for trouble and you are not content to take a passive stand, discuss the problems with your neighbors, work on ways to eliminate possible causes of riots, study plans of cooling inflammatory conditions, and develop precautionary steps in case all else fails. These steps may involve a family-evacuation plan and a temporary civilian guard led by the police. The situations may differ from community to community, so the best that can be said here is to seek and follow the advice of your elected officials and lawful authorities.

FIREARMS CHECKLIST

☐ DON'T keep a gun in your house or apartment except under very special circumstances.

☐ DO realize that the criminal is a professional in violence, and the odds are on his side in using firearms.

☐ DO understand the great danger of accidents if there are firearms kept in the home.

12

HOW A DOG CAN HELP
PROTECT YOU

BY ALL means have a dog if you love a pet and want to get whatever measure of protection he can provide. But don't count on a dog to replace strong locks, burglar alarm systems, and other protective measures recommended here. The main value of a dog is in his bark rather than his bite. Any dog trained to be so vicious as to attack, maim, and even kill intruders is probably unsafe to have around the house with children, guests, even yourself.

By barking loud and fiercely when he hears an intruder, your dog can be a living burglar alarm system at times. However, you must realize that his value is limited here, too. If an intruder carries delicious meat or other goodies, most dogs are more likely to lick than bite the hand that feeds them. Any dog may be put out of action by a burglar who uses chloroform, of course, unless the dog attacks too quickly for him.

The dog does act as a deterrent to some burglars because the intruder can't know whether the dog will attack or just bark. Some people insist that posting a "Beware-of-the-Dog" sign also acts as a deterrent—whether they indeed have a dog or not. But again you should not count on a dog or a sign so much that you forget other precautions.

Your dog can be an extra measure of protection when you're working around the house outdoors, or taking a walk alone on the street, or shopping. A sizable, loud-barking dog is a deterrent to criminals, at your side or in your parked car while you're in the supermarket.

Your dog is safer indoors or behind a fence than roaming the streets. Use a leash when you take him for a walk. It's the law in many areas, and it is good sense. Dognapping is becoming more commonplace, particularly in cities and suburbs where there is a sizable dog population. It is estimated that the number of dognappings in New York City, for example, runs into the thousands annually. Some dogs are stolen in order to return them for the rewards. Most of them are taken by well-organized criminals who sell the dogs to laboratories for an average price of $40 each. If operators steal and sell fifty dogs a week, they collect about $2,000. That's a lot of dog biscuits, and not at all funny for the dog owners.

Take this further protective measure—have your pet marked with your social security number. A qualified veterinarian will tattoo the number on the relatively hairless part of the stomach just inside the hind leg; the process is quick and painless. The number may then be registered with a special agency, or the dog's owner may be traced through government authorities. Laboratories tend to refuse to buy dogs so marked, as this is more dangerous for them; they risk being connected with buying stolen merchandise rather than being able to claim that these are deserted dogs. Also, it's harder if not almost impossible for a dog thief to resell a valuable purebred animal when he's marked indelibly with identifying numbers. Thus, a lost dog so marked is more likely to be returned to you for a reward.

Rewards can really be remunerative to thieves if the dog owners involved are affluent. An advertising executive spent hundreds of dollars in newspaper display advertisements to recover his mongrel, which had cost him only a few dollars to buy originally. Of course, not all people who return lost dogs are thieves or even reward-seekers.

Report a lost dog to the authorities quickly if you want to help cut down on dognapping for rewards or for sale to laboratories. If all dog owners did this, and the same person kept popping up to return the dog and collect the reward, this kind of racket could be checked.

Burglars have been known to use well-trained dogs for illegal purposes. Some seek to evade suspicion by walking a dog around a neighborhood by day or night, and sizing up houses that might be vulnerable for looting. While the dog pauses at a tree or at the curb, his master notes locations of doors, windows, and shrubbery around a house, to facilitate his break-in when the owners are absent. One such operator said proudly, "Nobody suspects a man and his dog, figuring that a dog owner can't be all bad. I've even taken my dog along when I break into a home or apartment, as I've trained him to warn me with a low growl or tug on my jacket if someone is coming in." In such cases, a dog can be a burglar's best friend.

DOG PROTECTION CHECKLIST

☐ DO have a loud-barking dog to help protect your family and home.

☐ DO take along a loud-barking dog on the street and when shopping.

☐ DON'T rely on a dog for full protection. Learn his limitations.

☐ DO guard against dognapping of a valuable pet.

☐ DO have your dog marked with your social security number for identification.

13

SPECIAL TELEPHONE PRECAUTIONS, HOW TO HANDLE CRANK OR OBSCENE CALLS

NEVER give any information to strangers on the phone. Don't ever reveal your name or address in response to any such pretext as, "I'm trying to check somebody. . . ." Or a caller may say, "I'd like to speak with your husband—when will he be home? What time should I call him back tonight?" That's one way a potential assailant tries to find out when you'll be out or alone, so that it's safer for him to break in. A caller may ask when you're going on vacation, pretending to provide some pre-vacation service. Don't be taken in by any excuse. If you're doubtful, ask for a number you can call back and a name and address to go with it. Then check the telephone book listings before phoning; chances are that the caller will become evasive or just hang up.

Don't just overlook a batch of "wrong number" phone calls, or nobody answering your "hello" when the phone rings several times in a row. Report these to the business office of the phone company (see number in your telephone directory). They can take steps to check out your phone carefully. Understand that burglars often operate this way: they size up your house or apartment as a likely prospect for looting, and get your name from a lawn sign (a good reason for displaying only your house number but *not* your name on a sign outdoors), mailbox, or apartment listing. Then they phone to see whether anyone is at home. If there is no answer, they may break in, assuming the premises are deserted. Usually they will keeping trying until there is no answer, so take precautions against this common criminal procedure.

If someone phones more than once making obscene suggestions or disturbing you in any way, call your telephone business office; steps will be taken immediately, including police help if necessary, to track down the caller. One woman who was upset by nuisance calls said that they stopped quickly when she bought a shrill whistle, cupped her hands around the mouthpiece, and blew loud and long, blasting the caller's eardrums.

Refuse to talk to anyone annoying you on the telephone. Don't try to reason with the other party or to "talk sense" to him —just hang up immediately. Do the same if the phone rings and no one answers at the other end but you hear someone breathing —hang up right away. If the calls continue, say that you are going to inform the telephone company and the police. Then do it—call the business office at the phone company, and if the caller is threatening in any way, report it to the police without delay. New electronic devices are helping to track down unwanted callers. Don't be embarrassed or hesitant about reporting crank calls; you'll get willing aid in restoring your peace of mind.

Tell your children, household help, baby-sitters, or anyone at home to be sure to inform you if there are mysterious or crank phone calls, so you can take action as advised here.

Leave the phone connected if possible during any extended absence on your part. If a potential intruder calls to check and is told that your telephone is "temporarily disconnected," that's a revealing tip that the occupants are away.

TELEPHONE CHECKLIST

☐ DON'T give any information to strangers on the phone.
☐ DO report repeated "wrong number" or "silent" calls to the telephone company.

☐ DON'T ignore "crank" or "obscene" calls; quickly inform the phone company and the police.

☐ DO leave the phone connected while you're away, since "disconnected" informs a potential intruder that your home is deserted.

14

HOW TO PROTECT YOUR CHILD
AT HOME AND AWAY FROM HOME

At Home

A WISE man said, "Where crime is taught from early years, it becomes a part of nature." Just as truly, where awareness of the value of protection is taught from the start of understanding, it becomes a valuable part of your child's equipment for a good life.

Have your youngsters themselves read the next few chapters particularly, and hopefully the whole book, as soon as they are old enough. What they learn can help safeguard them and they will benefit more from the protective measures you urge on them. Clearly, everything you do, for instance, to protect your home from easy entry by burglars and other intruders, helps protect your children.

Keep reminding children as necessary to observe your home protection rules for the good of themselves and the whole family. Windows and doors must not be carelessly left unlocked. Strangers must not be admitted to the house. Go over with them at intervals, as you find essential (you know your own child best), the precautions which apply from other chapters.

Don't close the door of your child's room completely when he's sleeping. Thus, unusual noises can alert you.

Leave your home well lighted at night, outside and inside, if you have to leave the children home alone.

Teach your children to call the police if they hear intruders when they are home alone. Leave other emergency numbers for them as well—a neighbor, or a phone where you can be reached.

Away from Home

Drum into children's minds these basic precautions:

• Never talk to strangers who stop in an auto; don't go near the car.

• Never go anywhere with a stranger on the street, in an auto, on a bus—not anywhere.

• Never hitch a ride with someone you don't know.

• Report at home or at school any strangers who try to get you to go with them.

• Try to remember and write down the license number of the auto driven by any stranger who tries to get you to come into the car.

• Don't accept candy or other gifts from a stranger or anyone else who makes you suspicious or uneasy.

• Yell or scream as loud as you can if you need help.

• Ask a policeman at once for any kind of help you need, and tell him if a stranger has approached you and tried to take you for a walk or ride. Tell the policeman about suspicious-looking persons so he can check on them. The policeman's work is to help guard you and keep you safe.

• Keep in mind always that the policeman wants to be your friend. His job is to help you stay safe. If anybody else tells you otherwise, don't believe him.

• Don't walk or play alone in places or buildings where there is nobody else around.

• Don't take shortcuts that are deserted or that go through dangerous areas such as a thick woods. The shortest way isn't the safest if it's a lonely area.

• If delayed from getting home from school right away, let someone know at home that you'll be late or where you'll be.

Always call home if you have to stay at school for a meeting, a rehearsal, or anything else; the school office will let you use the phone in such cases.

• Tell someone at home if you expect to be late getting home from school, or from anywhere else.

Know when your child is expected home from school, allowing for regular closing hours and travel time. If the child is much later than usual, check first with his or her friends. Then call the authorities if the delay is prolonged.

Warn your children to take a well-lighted route if they are returning home from a friend's house or anywhere else after dusk. It's much safer if they're not on the streets alone at all after dark, or even with just one or two playmates. If they must come home after dark, you should pick them up if at all possible; if not, arrange transportation or companionship for them.

Never drop your children off at a friend's house, a boy scout get-together, a church meeting, or anyplace else without waiting and checking to make sure they get in all right and that all is well. In one tragic case, parents dropped off their little girl for an evening church meeting and drove right off to a movie. The child found the church locked; it turned out that the meeting was actually scheduled for the following night. On the long, lonely walk home, the little girl was attacked and killed.

Make sure that your child has enough money for bus fare, or to phone you or a friend if he needs assistance.

Find the happy medium, as a wise and careful parent, between overwarning your child so that he is in danger of becoming "a scaredy cat," and instilling in him the sound, sensible precautions listed here.

Furnish your children with some identification, even just a little card bearing your name, address, and phone number, so that a policeman or someone can reach you in case of an accident or any trouble. Tell them to seek out a policeman or other official or someone they know, not a stranger who might remember the address and come there to break in at a later date.

Warn your youngsters to wait for buses in well-lighted places.

If the bus stop is dark for any reason, they should move on to a lighted spot. The same applies if they're waiting on the street to be picked up in a car by you or a friend.

Urge your children to be with a friend when out on the street or elsewhere; two or more are safer than being alone.

Try to keep your youngsters off the streets at night as much as possible. Have your teenagers read these statements from others like them who know: "My brother was jumped and beaten by a couple of hoods." . . . "I was walking my dog at night and a car stopped alongside and they tried to get me to go for a ride." . . . "Anybody could attack you anywhere, even in a good town." . . . "I used to feel pretty safe in my own neighborhood, but now there are too many people, including kids, out for kicks."

Instruct your children not to play in junk piles, or mess around with trash waiting on the roadside to be picked up by garbage trucks. Aside from obvious dangers, some discarded items almost qualify as lethal weapons. For example, an old TV set or picture tube can become a menacing "bomb." If children throw rocks at the tube or hit it with a club and puncture it, the big tube will first implode (bursting inward) and then shoot out heavy, spearlike glass splinters to a range of 20 feet. Warn your youngsters against this and similar little-known hazards. It's safer in every way to stay away from trash piles, which may also be frequented by vagrants.

See that your youngsters keep good company and stay away from others who are "out for kicks." It's true that "a man may thrive on crime, but not for long." Inevitably, when mixed up with companions who lean to lawbreaking, there's big trouble ahead, trouble from which no one may be able to save the youngster. That's not just "adult talk"; it's authoritative fact straight from the experts' mouths. An executive of a noted government research center states definitely, "Many youths get into trouble not as a result of so-called criminal tendencies but because of a desire to obtain status with friends."

Keep instilling in your youngster that the police and other authorities are there to help. Trouble is likely to develop as soon

95

as a teenager, or a child at any age, starts labeling police and other authorities as the enemy.

Try to make sure your children inform you before they go anywhere with anyone, particularly for as long as an hour or more. If they're going on a trip, check to be certain that they have adequate supervision.

Don't take it for granted that all is well if your youngster says that he or she is sleeping over at a friend's house. Always call and verify that this is so, using some pretext, to be sure that he actually is there, safe, and well.

Visit your child's school; meet the teachers and officials of the school to check on safety precautions there, as well as on other matters that concern you. This is one way to learn about undesirable behavior or companionship on your child's part so that you can help prevent trouble before it happens and breaks into serious and perhaps irreparable dimensions.

Never hire a baby-sitter without adequate knowledge or references as to reliability. A case in point is that of a 12-year-old baby-sitter who took off with a two-month-old baby in her charge. Fortunately she was soon caught; the girl explained that she "wanted the baby to be her own."

Follow these further precautions:

• Always leave telephone numbers which the baby-sitter can call in an emergency—the number where you'll be, if possible . . . the numbers of nearby relatives, friends, or neighbors . . . the child's physician . . . police and fire departments.

• It's a good idea to instruct the baby-sitter to phone you at a specific hour (such as 10 P.M.) if you're at a number where you're easily reached; that way you know that the sitter is alert and attentive to your instructions.

• Phone in if you can after you've been away an hour or two in order to double-check that all is well.

• Caution the baby-sitter *every single time* that she (or he) is not to admit strangers under any circumstances.

Don't let your daughter (or your son) baby-sit unless you check up on the reliability of the people who hire her—beforehand. Make sure that when she is driven home, the driver waits until she's safely in the house and has closed and locked the door behind her. If her employer brings her home at an hour you consider is too late, don't let her sit for that family again.

Report to police or other authorities any suspicious-looking persons you see around schools, playgrounds, buses, on the street. Also report any ominous incidents or possibilities that your children tell you about. Such reports have helped to prevent innumerable crimes against youngsters as well as adults.

Take advantage of special training courses for your youngsters. Check your community authorities and schools to learn what is available. Many police departments teach safety in a Preschool Child Traffic Training Program. Here, often through demonstrations with dolls and toy autos, children learn how to be safe, careful pedestrians, and how to conduct themselves through traffic to and from school, and at all times. A father said that his tiny daughter was teaching *him*; she warned him when he was impatient at the wheel, "Daddy, you don't go on the yellow light—it's not your turn."

CHILD-PROTECTION CHECKLIST

☐ DO teach your children how to take the steps advised to protect themselves.

☐ DO inform your children of the basic home-protection rules and the importance of observing them.

☐ DO keep the door of your child's room open at night.

☐ DO instruct children how to call the police if needed.

☐ DO teach your children not to talk to strangers or accept rides or gifts, as well as these other basic precautions:

☐ DO ask a policeman for help at once if needed.

☐ DON'T walk or play alone in lonely, deserted places including streets, woods, empty lots, shortcuts, buildings, junk piles.

☐ DO tell someone at home if delayed at school or away for any reason.

☐ DO keep children at home after dark as much as possible.

☐ DO have your child carry some identification always.

☐ DO check the company your children keep and encourage them to have companionship wherever they go.

☐ DON'T hire a baby-sitter without checking reliability thoroughly.

☐ DO observe the basic baby-sitter rules, never letting up.

15

ON-THE-STREET PRECAUTIONS TO INSTILL IN YOUR CHILDREN

IN ADDITION to the protection given in preceding chapters, make sure that your children learn the following basic safety guides when on the street or traveling in a car:

• Never cross the street against traffic; always wait for your green light, no matter what other children with you do.

• Don't cross a street in the middle of the block. Always use the crosswalk—those few extra steps can save your life.

• Never dart out between cars into traffic to chase a ball or for any other reason. Better lose a ball than your leg or your life.

• Look to both left and right, even on a one-way street, before crossing. Accidents have happened on one-way streets from cars backing up or going down the wrong way by mistake.

• Never cross at corners without watching to make sure that no cars are turning in your direction.

• You can't trust drivers to stop even when the light turns red. Wait for the cars to stop, then cross. Many accidents have been caused by drivers trying to beat the red light across, then hitting a pedestrian who watches the light but not the cars. It doesn't help much to say that you were right and the driver was wrong—if you are badly injured.

• It's unsafe to play on the streets where autos travel. Even if no cars are in immediate sight, they can zoom in. This is a prime cause of injuries to youngsters.

• Always fasten your seat belt as soon as you get into any

car. If there is no seat belt handy, sit well back. Don't ever stand up in an auto while it's in motion. The same is true in buses and other vehicles: wait until it stops, then get up to get out or to change seats.

• Never take dangerous risks such as racing across a street, leaning out of a window, or anything dangerous and therefore foolish. An accident that takes only seconds to happen can cripple someone for a lifetime.

• Don't ride a bicycle on unsafe streets where there is a lot of traffic, where the paving is broken up, or where it may be deserted. Observe the safety rules provided when the bicycle is purchased.

• Get a good, strong safety padlock for the bicycle. A flimsy, cheap lock is almost as useless as no lock at all.

• Keep a record at home of the bicycle serial number. That's a big help in recovering a lost or stolen bicycle, often the only way to identify the bicycle so that you get it back.

CHILD-ON-STREET CHECKLIST

☐ DO wait for a green light on the corner before crossing the street.

☐ DO look to right and left first before crossing, even on a one-way street. Check the traffic as well as the light.

☐ DON'T cross a street against traffic, or in the middle of the block.

☐ DON'T trust cars to stop quickly when a light turns red— wait until they are stopped before crossing the street.

☐ DON'T play on streets where autos travel.

☐ DO observe bicycle-protection tips, never riding on unsafe, heavily-traveled streets.

☐ DO get a strong safety padlock for the bicycle, and keep a record of the bicycle serial number.

16

FOR EMERGENCIES: WHAT TO DO IF YOUR SON OR DAUGHTER IS MISSING

IF YOU are convinced that your child is missing, the first and foremost advice is this: don't lose your head, don't panic, because if you do you will lose precious time and effectiveness in locating your youngster. At this stage, every minute can count to help assure the safety and recovery of your child. The necessary fact to reassure you, and to help yourself and others in your family keep relatively calm, is that *most missing children are found unharmed*—it is the exceptions that usually hit the headlines. This is proved conclusively by police records.

Your first action step, without question, should be this: *notify the police immediately.* Police authorities will put all of their available manpower, resources, and know-how to work instantly, as time can be of the essence in locating a missing person of any age. The professionals know this best of all.

Police are able to mobilize quickly vast amounts of personnel and equipment. As a result, detailed search of large areas is conducted systematically and most efficiently with minimum waste of time and activity. If needed, police authorities can utilize all types of search apparatus—radio-equipped patrol cars, jeeps, horses, helicopters, boats, special maps of the area, and public address systems.

The police also have access to communication media for public announcements when necessary, and use of teletype systems to other jurisdictions and states if needed. This is particularly important where runaway teenagers are involved.

With all these facilities and widely coordinated manpower available, the importance of *immediacy* in notifying the police cannot be overemphasized. No civilian do-it-yourself search operation could quickly gather such resources or hope to achieve the results that experienced police can. So don't waste any time or have second thoughts about notifying the police at once.

Another reason for calling the police immediately is that they may have already located your lost child and be attempting to identify and reach you, the parents. Both parents and child will thus be reassured at once, avoiding much needless suffering.

In order to help the police act most quickly and effectively, be prepared to give an accurate, detailed description of the missing child: clothing worn . . . where last seen . . . and, if at all possible, the destination or direction in which the child was proceeding.

If you have reason to believe that foul play or kidnapping has taken place, be sure to so inform the police. Give all your reasons for believing that this is the case.

If you think your child has run away from home (not uncommon with teenagers), tell the police so frankly, and give your reasons. False pride can impede an investigation dangerously. Be completely open and straightforward; you and the authorities have the same common goal, to find the youngster most swiftly and safely. Quick action here often brings the youngster back before he gets into serious trouble.

It is extremely important in any case of a missing person that the police be given instantly any new information or developments that you may learn about or that may come to mind after your original report. Do it immediately.

If the missing child turns up or is found by others than the police, notify the officials at once. This enables them to call off the search and return their men, equipment, and attention to other duties or other urgent demands.

Additional Important Steps

After you have notified the police of your missing child, tell your neighbors, friends, relatives, and the youngster's playmates. Seek any information they may have of your child's possible whereabouts. Give them a detailed description of the child, the clothing he was wearing, and his probable destination or the direction in which he was proceeding.

It is helpful to keep a list handy of your children's usual playmates, their addresses and telephone numbers, and the places where they are most likely to congregate. This is a great aid, and may be a lifesaver, if your child is missing and you need to check at playmates' homes.

Neighbors and friends may volunteer to assist in the search for the child, supplementing police efforts. In a rural area particularly, perhaps with insufficient police manpower and equipment, private resources will have to be relied upon more. The local police authorities will probably enlist the aid of private radio operators, boat operators, airplane pilots, car owners, and others—anyone or anything that might be helpful in the search.

The activity should be started in the area where the child was last seen. Particular attention should be given to rooftops, attics, basements, crawl spaces, vacant buildings, excavations, construction sites, recreation areas, caves, ponds, streams, wooded areas, abandoned articles such as refrigerators, ranges, and boxes with snap-shut doors.

In short, search all possible places, especially those which might appear attractive to a child.

Method of Search

Organize the search, working under police supervision, so that there is no duplication of effort. The searchers should be divided into teams with specific areas to cover, on a block-to-block basis in urban and suburban areas. In wooded, desolate areas, assistance should be sought from Forest Rangers and natives of the vicinity who are familiar with the territory.

It is vital to remember that a civilian search should always *supplement,* not replace, a police operation. Unless impossible for some reason, such civilian search volunteers should be under the direction of the police. Otherwise whole areas or hiding places might be skipped and valuable time lost.

Above all, don't hesitate to call the police right away if your child is missing an unusual length of time, and you've checked without success the places where he normally would be. Police would rather track down alarms, including false alarms, than have a child in danger. The same is true of school authorities and any others who might be involved in your child's welfare and safety.

MISSING-CHILD CHECKLIST

☐ DON'T panic if your child is missing; keep your wits about you.

☐ DO notify the police at once.

☐ DO think about and provide accurate descriptions of your child and where seen last.

☐ DO inform neighbors, friends, playmates, relatives, to enlist their help.

☐ DO search the area where the child was last seen, including all places that might attract a child.

☐ DO notify the police immediately if the child shows up or is found by others.

17

HOW TO KEEP YOUR YOUNGSTERS OUT OF TROUBLE

IT IS your responsibility to get this basic guideline across to your youngsters: *one sure way to help avoid trouble is not to be there when trouble happens.* Of course a dangerous situation may erupt suddenly, without warning, but this is the exception. When it does, your youngster should be instructed to get away from there in a hurry. Most of the time one can feel trouble developing and leave the scene beforehand.

Whether the dangerous situation explodes unexpectedly or comes about slowly or through premeditation, it usually can and should be avoided by not getting involved, primarily by getting out of there, whatever the conditions may be.

Pass on to your youngsters this warning from a specialist in juvenile delinquency: "Youthful behavior, even though it may be the result of thoughtlessness, can mean tragic results of something that started as 'just a ride around town' (with troublemakers). If the spur-of-the-moment mischief of a youngster who has never been in trouble before results in being convicted of a crime, he will suffer society's consequences the remainder of his life."

It is never too early to teach respect for the law. Criminality can begin with the youngest and smallest. In a country jail in Missouri it was found necessary to place the bars of a cell closer together after a youngster weighing only seventy pounds squeezed through the bars and slipped out.

Don't minimize the danger to and from wayward youngsters. A typical fact: "Juvenile crime is growing at a much faster rate

105

than the overall crime rate . . . [in a recent year] more than one-half of all arrests for burglary, larceny, and car theft were in the 11–17 age group." In Florida a seven-year-old boy was caught burglarizing a home. He admitted that he had broken into the home three times before, as well as into another home. In all, he had taken radios, walkie-talkies, and a ring—total value $200. Police said they "would try to work out something with the youngster's father," since the boy was under the minimum age even for Juvenile Court jurisdiction, which starts at eight years of age.

Never take a dare that might involve lawbreaking. This is a forceful point to make to youngsters. Here's sound official advice: "It takes more courage to turn down the dare than to accept it—and your friends know this. In the long run they will respect you for having the courage and foresight to turn down a dare involving a breach of the law. Remember, it is better to be a live 'chicken' than a dead duck."

Advise your children of the difference between a "childish prank" and a crime. Sometimes there seems to be just a shade of difference, but it can result in real trouble from which you want to protect your youngsters. For example, stealing apples from someone else's tree may seem like a "childish prank," but it's not far removed from crime: stealing apples from a grocer's basket will lead to arrest and prosecution. Chalking a line on a store window on Hallowe'en is "mischief," but smashing the plate glass window is a crime; the difference in degree must be stressed as a safeguard.

Two teenagers in Utah "had fun" cutting off the valve stems on the tires of thirty-three automobiles. They were caught and could have been jailed by a stern judge. In this case the boys found out how long it takes and how much backbreaking work it is to inflate 132 auto tires with a hand pump—that was their sentence.

It's easy to pass off the blame on "society" or on "someone else" if your youngster gets into trouble with the authorities. Fair or not, society's fault or otherwise, your child is your responsibility, first, last, and always. You and your child suffer most if he gets into trouble; it doesn't help much then to blame the world.

A parent was being interviewed on a television show about his son's troubles, which had made headlines. Suddenly the father shouted at the studio audience, "You're the ones who are to blame, the trouble is not with my son but with society, the atom bomb, racism. . . ." Whether or not he was right, it was his son who was in jail for a criminal act. One point here is obvious, that the youngster had not had instilled in him a knowledge of and respect for the law and for moral and ethical standards.

A leading official stated emphatically that society has let down the nation's youth primarily in "its failure to teach them the meaning of discipline, restraint, self-respect, and respect for law and order and the rights of others." Whether or not you agree with this viewpoint, it certainly merits consideration in respect to protecting your youngsters from the dangers of involvement in violence, not necessarily of their own doing.

Help your youngsters to join good, supervised Teen Clubs, Boys' Clubs, Explorers' Clubs, and other organizations which have been found to be effective for the members and the community. One such club whose activities were aided by individual policemen showed their appreciation by creating the slogan: "Respect the police—they are human too." When such a relationship is established, there's a far better chance not only for law and order in the community but also for justice for all. A teenage girl involved with such a program wrote to a police officer: "I learned that you are an ordinary man like any other, and that you don't like to arrest anybody unless you have to."

Stress that it's the stupid youngsters who usually commit crimes. A teenager who had been in and out of a reformatory was captured and thrust back in again in a town in England. He was caught in the act of stealing twelve pairs of shoes put outside of room doors in a hotel corridor for shining, a custom there. The young criminal found out that the shoes belonged to officers attending a police federation conference.

Seek the advice of police and other authorities if you think your youngster is getting involved with undesirables. The police are professionals; they want to help, and they usually can.

Safeguard your youngsters by seeing that they stay away from riots, fights, fires, wherever there is obvious danger. The best way to keep from getting injured in riots and other violent situations is to get away in a hurry and stay away. Your children should be instructed to head for home at the first sniff of violence erupting.

Emphasize the dangers of physical injury in mingling with lawbreakers. Police trying to control fights among teenagers come upon dangerous, unique home-made weapons which can maim and kill. There is always a chance of a flare-up among criminal elements at any time. Stress to youngsters the importance of staying away from those who are against the law. Warn them to keep out of fights and to get away quickly if there is an outburst. Leaving the scene is by far the better part of valor.

Most parents know that youngsters are much more prone to taking unreasonably risky chances. Somehow, the older people get, the more cautious they are about endangering their own lives. When it comes to automobiles, the highest risk period is up to age twenty-five, which is why you pay a heavy insurance premium if you have a teenage or early twenties driver in your family.

But parents ask, *"How* can I get this warning across to my children?" The best procedure, of course, is to be as specific as possible. One father in upstate New York knew that his two teenage sons, who had qualified for their drivers' licenses, drank beer on occasion in their friends' homes. He knew he couldn't stop them from drinking beer; if he tried to, knowing teenagers, he thought they'd just drink more. And so he concentrated his conversation with them on drinking safely. He asked them what it felt like after a few beers. The boys, at first embarrassed, finally said something like, "You know, dad, you get a bit woozy-happy, you talk too much, maybe a little unsteady on the feet, depending on how much you've had."

The father said, "Okay. Now suppose you needed an operation, would you want the surgeon to operate on you after *he'd* had a few beers?"

Both boys responded immediately and negatively. "His hands might not be as steady as they should be."

"Maybe he wouldn't see too well, not double, that takes a lot of drinking, but you know, just a bit out of focus like."

This gave the father the opening he was looking for. "Well, boys, you know the incidence of something going wrong on the operating table is much lower than something going wrong on the road. More people are injured or killed by accidents involving some drinking—even just a few beers—than are ever lost on the operating table. Besides, I've never heard of a surgeon who drank before an operation—he'd lose his license. Well, drivers lose their licenses for drunk driving, but they just don't seem to make the same connection between the responsibility of, say, a surgeon, and a driver of four thousand pounds of steel down a country road while under the influence."

The psychology this father used worked because he didn't try to stop the boys from drinking beer or from driving, but from *mixing the two* and taking the kinds of chances teenagers are most likely to take. His story was a good one because on Saturday nights, when they took the car out, he'd say something like "Remember the surgeon who had a few beers!" The kids would laugh, but they'd remember, and that's what counts.

If you suspect a teenage driver uses marijuana, it might be useful at an opportune moment to use an approach tried by a state trooper with his own son. He suspected that a large number of the youngsters in the local high school used marijuana from time to time. He had cautioned his own son. But because, in his job as state trooper, he was on the road a good deal of each day, he was most aware of how even something that supposedly isn't addictive can make a good driver careless and lead to accidents. What he said to his son went something like this: "I know that the kids around here say that the pot they smoke is a lot less harmful than the alcohol used by their parents. Maybe yes, maybe no. But what the kids say is that marijuana gives them a high, makes them feel real good, not weighted down with worries. Well if you're driving a car, I *want* you to worry. If you want to stay alive, you have to drive defensively, which is what they teach you in school driver-education courses. How can you be defensive, and on the constant alert, if you're the slightest bit detached or high? Pot may make you care less, but it also makes you careless, and if you're driving, that's dangerous."

Later, that state trooper admitted that talking to his own teenage son was embarrassing, especially beforehand when he was a bit nervous about it. But he knew the necessity of having the talk, and doing it in a pleasant way so that his son would listen and know that his father was trying to help and not "be a policeman." In less than a week, that lesson may have saved another boy's life.

As it was reported, the trooper's son saw another boy, a school friend, getting ready to drive home while fairly high on pot. He tactfully asked to drive the car because he "needed the practice," and the other boy agreed. The trooper's son stopped the car in front of the boy's house and backtracked on foot to his own less than a block away. Before he reached home he heard a terrible crashing noise and ran back to his friend's house. The friend, still high, was no longer euphoric. In driving the car just into his own garage, he misjudged his distance from the wall and possibly his speed, because the right side of the car was badly scraped and dented. The damage came to several hundred dollars and they had to report it in order to collect on the $100-deductible collision insurance. Not only did it cost $100 but the insurance rates were upped next time around for the boy's father. The important thing is the boy might have had a far worse accident on the road if the trooper's son hadn't spotted the condition he was in and offered his help.

Point out emphatically that drinking, drugs, and driving form a dangerous combination that causes many auto accidents and deaths among youngsters (as well as adults). Those driving under the influence of narcotics or alcohol are a menace not only to themselves but to all others in the car and on the road.

Encourage your teenagers to take a safe-driving course at

school. Not only can they often get a license at an earlier age, but they learn basic protective rules, safety regulations, and the value of obeying them to save life and limb—along with a lower insurance rate from some companies.

Action Against the Crime of Shoplifting

Shoplifting by youngsters has shown a frightening increase in the past few years and has assumed epidemic proportions among teenagers in some communities. The FBI reports a shocking increase in recent years of close to 80 per cent in arrests for shoplifting. It is estimated that about 50 per cent of the shoplifters are juveniles.

Chances are that your youngsters will never be involved with shoplifting, which is true of the great majority of young people with watchful, attentive parents. However, the best way to keep this tragic act and its consequences from happening in your family is to take simple, basic protective measures.

Emphasize to youngsters in a discussion of the subject that shoplifting is not a lark but a crime which can blight an entire lifetime. The following statement tells it "like it is"; this is a brief excerpt from a Precinct Community Council bulletin, worth noting carefully by every adult and youngster:

> Rarely is this crime committed out of economic need. The reasons given by apprehended youth are: "For kicks"; "Impulse"; "Keeping up with the crowd." In other words, to them it is more a sport than a crime. This is a serious misconception on the part of the youth involved. The law makes no provisions for a "sport." Shoplifting is a *criminal act,* and as such, it is prosecuted to the full extent of the law. The enormity of the problem has induced previously reluctant merchants to assist the police and the courts in the apprehension and prosecution of the perpetrators.
>
> Some youngsters display indifference in respect to getting arrested. Too often the attitude is, "Suppose I do

get arrested? So what?" They fail to realize that a record of arrest follows one for the rest of his life—wherever he may go, whatever he may do. He will be called upon to explain the arrest whenever seeking employment, admission to a college, applying for a Civil Service job, entering military service, attempting to practice a profession, or applying for a special license. And this list is by no means complete. An arrest record could make it very difficult to obtain a desirable job or attain other goals. An arrest record could ruin a youngster's future.

The danger of being caught, sentenced, and jailed is increasing. There are now close to a quarter-million formal arrests annually for shoplifting. Losses to stores are estimated at over $9 billion a year—yes, *billion*. As stores install more electronic and other devices and take other measures to catch the criminal, the percentage of shoplifters caught and prosecuted is on the rise. Modern developments, including private radio systems, closed-circuit television, and two-way mirrors, are increasing in use in stores.

Shoplifting is not a minor matter. No youngster or adult should make any mistake about it: *a shoplifter is a criminal.* That's true whether he steals a 10 cent candy or a $10,000 mink coat. The difference is only in degree; the act is a criminal act no matter how little or how much is stolen.

Officially, shoplifting is petty larceny or grand larceny: in short—stealing and thievery. Anyone can be arrested if he wrongfully takes for his own use money or property that belongs to another, regardless of its value—even a penny or a pencil. If it's possible to find the owner of the money or property, then it's illegal to keep the items. It should be stressed to youngsters especially, who may not realize it, that you can be arrested and punished for an illegal act even if you say, "I didn't know it was a crime!"

Don't ignore the subject with your youngsters. Instilling enlightenment on the crime of shoplifting doesn't involve any slightest indication of accusation when handled matter of factly. When parents look the other way, youngsters often get the idea that they don't care.

Note carefully and pass on these plain facts and recommendations to help protect your youngsters and their friends from becoming involved in shoplifting.

1. Most shoplifting begins by going along with the wrong crowd; it often starts with a theft amounting to only a few pennies, then mounts into increasing dollars; inevitably it leads to arrest and disgrace. It's vital never to commit the *first* act. Shoplifting that starts with a penny value can be a lifelong expense.

2. If a youngster is along with the crowd which commits shoplifting acts, he can become involved and branded as a criminal even though he hasn't stolen anything himself but was "just along for the ride." It has been pointed out that "whoever meditates a crime has all the guiltiness of the deed." If your companions start talking about going into stores to try shoplifting, or any crime, leave them; go away from there at once. It's better to be called unpleasant names than to have your name blotted on a criminal record. It's a mighty smart "chicken" who runs away from even the chance of becoming implicated in a criminal act.

3. Tell youngsters to stay away from others whom they may not even know who go into stores carrying oversize pocketbooks, shopping bags, large plastic envelopes. They may be innocent or they may be using these common "drop" containers for goods pilfered from the counters and shelves. The safest step is to stay away from them.

4. A common tip-off that a youngster is shoplifting is when he comes home with more items of assorted kinds than he had the money to buy. This should be investigated thoroughly and stopped without delay. Statements such as "Mary gave me this new scarf because she has one just like it" should not be accepted carelessly.

5. When a youngster mentions being in one or more stores with a group of others, look into it carefully. Make sure that he

stops going with those companions if there is anything at all suspicious. Such aimless "shopping" expeditions too often lead to or cover up shoplifting.

6. The parent's attitude has a strong influence on the children. If the father or mother, hearing talk about "petty" shoplifting at the table, just laugh it off, youngsters tend to feel that there's nothing really wrong with this kind of thievery.

Don't overlook your responsibility as parents to prevent and stop youngsters from shoplifting. Records show that children aged eleven have been caught at the crime. A sociologist states: "If the young shoplifter can believe he has a great deal to lose by continuing to steal, he stops." According to one investigation, fourteen-year-olds are "the largest single group of youthful shoplifting offenders."

Shoplifting can start at any age, even younger than teens. An official law publication reports: "About teenage shoplifting offenders, it is generally conceded that they become involved to derive 'kicks,' or because it's the 'fad' or the 'in' thing to do, or because it is considered a 'status symbol' among their peers. They seldom look upon shoplifting as stealing." That's one of the main points to remember in taking effective protective steps with your children. They think it's not stealing because "the store is so big, they'll never miss it."

Girls are not exempt—they as well as boys are among shoplifters who have been caught. All classes of society are represented, not just the poor but children of the very rich. Fewer than one out of a hundred youthful offenders was found to be in need. Many were carrying enough money on them to have bought the article stolen. Items taken from the store are frequently found in street trash baskets nearby.

Punishment for shoplifting is becoming more severe. It used to be necessary to catch the individual after he had actually left the store's premises with the stolen items, but arrests can now be made if the articles are hidden on the person. In some states, such "petty theft" by adults is punishable by up to six months in jail, or $500 fine, or both. In other states, sentences can be as high as four years in jail, no matter how little the stolen merchandise is worth. In every state, shoplifting can mean a jail sentence.

Don't wait to take action with your youngsters against the slightest possibility of their becoming involved, even remotely, in shoplifting. This can lead to crimes of ever greater gravity. When a parent is called by authorities and told, "We are holding your child on a charge of shoplifting," it may already be too late.

CHILD-TROUBLE CHECKLIST

☐ DO instruct your children to stay out of trouble-prone places, and to leave a scene instantly if trouble is imminent or develops.

☐ DON'T minimize the dangers of a child's keeping bad company.

☐ DO warn your children never to take dares that might involve lawbreaking.

☐ DO help your children join good, supervised clubs and other groups.

☐ DO stress that it's the "stupid youngsters" who commit crimes.

☐ DO consult authorities if you think your child is involved with undesirables.

☐ DON'T ignore the possibility of children engaging in shoplifting crimes which can blight an entire lifetime.

☐ DO absorb the facts and recommendations about shoplifting and discuss them with your youngsters.

18

HOW TO KEEP YOUR DAUGHTER FROM BEING ASSAULTED

THE DANGERS to your children from child molesters is a difficult subject. Targets are girls usually, but increasingly, attacks on boys are involved, too. There are a great many more attacks than are generally known, since authorities estimate that as many as 95 per cent of cases are *not reported* for fear of embarrassment or further injury to the child, physical or psychological. Nevertheless, there are over 100,000 sex arrests yearly, the FBI reports, with many of the offenses directed at children.

"Don't have anything to do with strangers" is the basic warning to instill in your children. What to do is stressed earlier in this book but bears brief repetition here; see that your child understands and stays away from strangers accordingly:

- Don't stop to talk with strangers . . . don't accept auto rides . . . don't take gifts of candy or money or anything from strangers . . . don't play with older strangers . . . don't go to the movies with a stranger, or to an amusement park, or anywhere . . . don't let a stranger touch or fondle you . . . *get away from him or her* as fast as you can go.
- Start screaming if a stranger is annoying you.
- Tell a policeman, your parents, your teacher, a friend, anyone you know, if a stranger is annoying you or stopping you, and remember so you can describe exactly where and when it happened, and what he or she looked like.

• Never get into a stranger's car for a ride or a lift if he stops to ask directions. Stay far enough away from the driver so he can't grab you.

• Take down the license number of the car if a stranger bothers you, and tell your parents as soon as possible. Write the number on paper, or on the sidewalk, or in the dirt.

• Tell your parents, a teacher, a policeman, right away if you see a stranger hanging around a playground or any place where children gather normally, or if you see him partially undressed or acting peculiarly, as in a car parked on the street. Tell them about any older person who makes dirty remarks to children.

• Never play in deserted buildings or streets or alleys, or any other lonely area.

• Don't loiter in or around, or play near, public toilets.

• Take friends with you when you go to a playground, to the store, to school, the movies, other places outdoors.

• Stop and tell a policeman about anything suspicious that happened or that you saw. The policeman's work is to help and protect you.

• Don't wander away from the crowd or from friends at a picnic or other outing; always stay within sight and calling distance.

• Never hitchhike.

Warn children against the well-dressed stranger and the "nice guy," as well as others. Sex offenders come from all classes, all incomes. Too often the weeping youngster attacked by a child molester cries, "But, Mommy, he looked like such a nice man. . . ."

As you know from reading and hearing news reports, some of the most horrible sex crimes have been committed by rapists who make an exceptionally favorable impression. They do this by putting on a special act of being charming, by radiating good will, by using a most gentlemanly approach. Impress your

117

youngsters that the nicer a molester may appear, the more dangerous and ruthless he may be.

Preventing Assault of the Older Child

Fathers and mothers are sometimes worried that their daughter who is no longer really a child might be raped by a stranger, or even a schoolmate, or by a gang of boys. What advice can be given?

Instilling precautions about staying away from poorly lit, deserted areas and places where rape has occurred before is most important. But even when all the best precautions are taken, a girl can still be attacked. And you can't assume that only those girls who "want to be raped" will be. "Wanting to be raped" may seem a contradiction in terms, but many people believe that only those who look for trouble find it. There may be cases where this assumption is correct—especially if the girl is victimized frequently—but it is an uninformed generalization.

And a girl need not be ravishingly beautiful to be the target of rape. A rapist, even if sane, is not in control of his reason or emotions. He is trying to force his will on somebody. Even an unattractive girl may be the victim of a rape. Just remember how many elderly women are rape victims.

One extreme solution comes from a twenty-three-year-old, very pretty social worker who found that she was frequently in danger of rape—and that her best defense was to wear several pairs of panties. Although multiple panties isn't a practical solution for everyday use, there is a simple lesson to be learned from it. It is easier to rape a girl who doesn't wear undergarments than one who does.

The most important rule: *if you are attacked, make noise.* Yell as loudly as you can. Your screaming may unnerve the potential assailant as well as attract help. For girls who sometimes have to walk in isolated or dark areas, a pocket siren device can be of help, because the sound carries farther than a voice.

118

A girl has many protective weapons in her purse, if she wants to think of them as such: fingernail files, ball-point pens, even the corner of a hand mirror. The problem with any of these devices is that the victim may not have a chance to get to them. In a respectable area of Seattle where elderly women were being molested, ladies of all ages began wearing large hat pins—and made certain that the fact was well publicized. A heel jabbed down onto a man's instep or a knee raised sharply into his groin can be quite painful. At least the momentary anguish will give the girl a chance to run away. And escape, of course, is the most important goal.

Rape is a dangerous and revolting experience, and it can have severe psychological consequences in the case of younger girls, but the greatest danger is that a significant number of rapists subsequently kill their victims. That is why the frequently heard school joke is so inappropriate: "Confucius say if rape is inevitable, relax and enjoy it." Surely a potential victim should not sacrifice her life to defend her virtue, but equally she should recognize that her life is sometimes at stake if a rapist is attacking her, and learning ways to escape is the wisest course.

CHILD-ASSAULT CHECKLIST

☐ DO teach your youngsters not to have anything to do with strangers, not to accept rides or gifts, and never to hitchhike.

☐ DO report to the police if a stranger annoys your child, and instruct your youngsters to do the same immediately, also telling about anything suspicious or frightening and about any stranger hanging about play areas.

☐ DON'T let your child play alone in lonely areas, or go places alone particularly at night.

☐ DO warn your youngsters against wandering away alone at picnics and other outings or gatherings.

☐ DO caution children against even well-dressed, well-mannered, "nice" strangers, a possible guise for sex offenders.

☐ DO teach teenage girls that if all precautions fail screaming and making noise is the most important thing that they can do.

19

HOW TO GUARD YOUR CHILDREN AGAINST OTHER VIOLENCE

THE SAFEST and most sensible course is to realize that your youngsters can become involved in acts of violence or crimes against society such as looting and vandalism if you don't take proper precautions. You must start at a very early age to shape and lead your child toward helping to build and safeguard society rather than reacting *against* it. This is dramatized by a cartoon showing a boy about twelve wearing an eye-mask and carrying a gun; he is walking out of the house at night while his listless mother remarks to the yawning father, "I think maybe we'd better have a heart-to-heart talk with Junior about what he intends to do when he grows up." This is an exaggerated picture, of course, but is not far off the mark as a warning to parents who fail to have heart-to-heart and head-to-head talks with their children.

Reread the recommendations on shoplifting again. The same cautions and actions apply in respect to other possible criminal involvement by youngsters—choosing good companions, not taking "dares," understanding the lifelong damage due to an arrest, and so on. Apply these suggestions with your youngsters early.

Choose other toys than guns for your youngsters. Discourage others from giving them similar toys and gadgets of violence. Many toymakers themselves have stopped making guns and weapons because they have become convinced that these items are incitements to violent thoughts and actions. One of the nation's largest toy distributors, and a leader of a citizens' movement called "Toy Disarmament," marked his entire stock of toy guns for a bonfire. He stated: "Everybody talks about disarming the world, but we believe a practical step is to start at home." His group's aim is to stop the manufacture of such "violence items." Part of the drive is a campaign in which children turn in their toy guns and are given buttons printed, "I turned mine in."

Don't permit your children to watch TV shows of violence. All too true is a cartoon showing a young child glued to the TV screen and begging his beckoning parent, "Please, Pop, let me watch just one more killing!" While it's hard to pin down the exact effects, many psychologists are convinced that watching lots of TV violence disturbs the youngsters and can incite them to commit or be injured by violent acts. If you're doubtful about the deeply harmful effects of TV shows of violence on your child, remember this: No child was ever injured by a TV show he *didn't* watch. The two best ways to stop the emphasis on violence in TV shows are these: (1) tune out the show—as listening audience drops, the show will be dropped; (2) write the *presidents* of the station, network, and sponsoring companies, protesting against the show, stating that you've prohibited your youngsters from watching it any more and that you won't buy products advertised on such programs.

Instruct your children that, when they come upon violent acts in schools, on the street, anywhere, to leave the scene. Teach them how to protest against what they consider injustices in the school system and elsewhere by legitimate constructive action, avoiding violence completely. Most important, train them to *get away from there* if violence of any kind erupts; they won't be injured if they're far away from the commotion.

Instill respect for law and order in your youngsters. They will benefit by cooperation with police and other authorities. Help them understand that guardians of the law are working to protect them. It is natural for the young to rebel, but teach them to rebel not against protective authority but against injustice.

BASIC CHILD-PROTECTION CHECKLIST

☐ DON'T ignore the recurring possibility of children engaging in shoplifting or other lawbreaking disguised as "childish pranks."

☐ DO choose toys other than guns for youngsters.

☐ DON'T let your child watch TV shows of violence.

☐ DO instruct your children to leave scenes of violence immediately.

☐ DO try to channel a youngster's natural inclination to rebel in constructive ways, letting him fight injustice rather than the laws that protect him.

20

HOW TO INSTILL IN YOUR CHILD
A SENSIBLE
ATTITUDE ABOUT DRUGS

YOU MUST get across to your youngsters that it's not only not smart to experiment with or to use drugs, but that it's downright stupid. Don't just bypass the terrible menace of drugs with the self-assurance that your own children can't become involved or badly affected. A high U.S. official warned: "Many parents seemingly do not concern themselves about organized crime and drug traffic because they feel that the consequences of this type of crime will never reach them." The figures on drug usage by youngsters are staggering; the percentages of increases are even more horrifying, to parents especially. According to the vice-chairman of a State Narcotics Commission, the use of drugs among school-age youngsters assumes epidemic proportions. He reports: "Surveys show that 20 to 30 per cent of all students (primarily in their teens) have experimented, mostly with marijuana but also with pills. One-quarter of these say that they take drugs on a regular basis."

The drug that is most widely used is marijuana—"pot," "tea," "grass"; cigarettes rolled from the leaf are dubbed "reefers," "sticks," "joints." The number of arrests for its usage, according to the national Bureau of Narcotics, as much as doubles each year, with about 40 per cent of the users under twenty-one.

Other drugs are often used by youngsters: LSD to get "out of this world"; amphetamines (called "pep pills," "bennies," "wakeups") "to get going"; glue-sniffing "to get a charge"; barbiturates ("goofballs") "to slow down"; Dexadrine "to pep up"; methamphetamine or "speed"; and even cocaine ("coke," "snow"), heroin ("horse"), morphine ("M, white stuff"), and other menacing drugs referred to as "hard stuff." The use of any can lead to tragic results; for example, barbiturates are the second most commonly used agent for suicide, by a sometimes "unintentional" overdose. Sniffing glue and fumes as from an aerosol can of cocktail-glass chiller, in search of cheap thrills, has caused death or long-lasting suffering, including brain-cell damage.

Know and understand what causes drug usage among juveniles, since knowledge gives you the power to help keep it from happening in your family. A concerned psychologist, after emphasizing that "there is no single cause," sums up the primary reasons for you:

1. Emotional deprivation such as is engendered in broken homes and lack of interest on the part of parents.

2. Overindulgence, at the other end of the spectrum, with a lack of disciplinary training.

3. Difficulty for the child in identifying with a parental figure and forming a proper ideal, such as might be found in a broken home or one in which parent(s) are away too much or have a bad relationship.

4. A distrust-of-authorities displacement, generated by an unhappy interaction with the primary authority figures, the parents.

Reason number two, parental permissiveness resulting in self-indulgence of children, is often stressed by psychiatrists as a cause of drug abuse among juveniles. A psychoanalyst at the Psychiatric Clinic for Children states: "A lot of parents believe that you have to let kids do what they want to or they'll get depressed or neurotic. They're also afraid their kids won't love them if they put restrictions on them." As a result, many youngsters have no guidelines on how they should behave—a terrible responsibility foisted by well-meaning parents on children who haven't the experience and judgment to make sound decisions. Too many of these youngsters turn to drugs.

"The common factor," an authoritative publication states, "is the attempt to escape from either physical or emotional problems." There is general agreement that for parents to maintain "a working relationship" with their children is one of the strongest checks against drug use and abuse.

Absorb the reasons youngsters give for trying drugs. They usually boil down to "experimenting with something everybody's talking about" . . . "keeping up with the gang" . . . "getting out of the dumps" . . . "needing to feel peppier" . . . "getting rid of feelings of disappointment, insecurity, inferiority" . . . "getting some new kicks out of life." The real reasons are almost always much deeper, as previously noted.

Don't think that drug usage is limited to certain classes and types of youngsters. The facts are clear: juveniles of all classes, rich and poor, all colors, religions, and backgrounds, from high to low in mental capabilities, have been found using drugs. While usage has been greater in large cities, it has now spread to and is increasing in rural areas, villages, towns, and smaller cities throughout the country. Police know this and use every possible legal means to help prevent the spread of drug usage before it gets out of hand. On occasion, police use dogs with "a nose for marijuana," not for attack, but to track down caches of the drug. A German shepherd in one demonstration took less than one minute to weave his way through twenty people crowded in a room, nuzzle open a closed locker, and claw through a plastic sheet covering a suit jacket in which a package of marijuana was hidden.

Acts of violence may arise from the need to obtain drugs. This is proved by an analysis of a good many case studies. One basic way to keep your youngsters away from crime is to keep them away from drug users and usage.

Study these common symptoms which are often related to drug usage, and watch for them in your youngsters:

- Eyes and nose watering excessively without a cold.
- Loss of appetite.
- Nicotine-like stains on fingers.

• Symptoms like those of intoxication, without the smell of alcohol.

• Sores appearing on arms and legs.

• Lethargy, lack of initiative.

• Sudden bursts of anger for no good reason.

• Appearing unresponsive, remote, dulled—a change in character.

• Becoming nervous, tense, high-strung, without apparent cause.

• Acting with exaggerated emotion, as seldom before, with sudden changes to loud laughter or uncontrollable crying, or showing extreme fear with no real foundation.

• A sudden drop in interest in school and grades.

• Becoming excessively talkative, with the words pouring like a torrent.

• Convulsions, hallucinations, shocks, even seemingly mild and harmless ones.

• Appearance becoming sloppy, eyes looking "funny."

• Muscle-twitching, vomiting, diarrhea, sleeplessness.

• Finding illicit material in child's room or drawers.

DRUG-PRECAUTIONS CHECKLIST

☐ DO instill in your child the downright stupidity of using drugs, and give the sound reasons why.

☐ DO understand the main reasons why youngsters may use drugs, including parental permissiveness, and take steps accordingly.

☐ DO realize that drug use exists among all classes and types.

☐ DO guard against the acts of violence which may be due to the need to obtain drugs.

☐ DON'T overlook the common symptoms of possible drug use, as listed.

21

FOR EMERGENCIES:
WHAT TO DO IF YOU FIND THAT
YOUR CHILD IS USING DRUGS

TAKE CONSTRUCTIVE action at once if you think or know that your youngster is taking some kind of drugs. Don't refuse to face the shocking possibility. Don't try to shrug off the symptoms or put the blame on other factors. Here's what you should do:

• Don't try to handle the problem alone; seek professional help without delay. Consult your doctor, your clergyman, or police officials, whichever is more appealing to you, but do ask those who know. They will tell you whom to see for immediate professional assistance to stop your child's use of any harmful drugs.

• Get detailed literature on the subject from your local police department, library, health department, school office, other local sources.

• In addition to getting professional help, establish calm, quiet discussions with your youngster about the problem. Angry denunciation and demands, without taking positive steps to help, can make matters worse.

• Reread the recommendations given previously to help keep your child from shoplifting and other criminal acts. All those specific suggestions apply here to drug-taking and any other antisocial actions. Undesirable excesses of any kind, such as excessive drinking, often lead to experimentation with drugs.

• Cooperate in organizing school activities against drugs,

with conferences, lectures by professionals. The principal of a midwest high school which undertook such parent programs reported: "Once the parents were made aware, our problems subsided."

• Don't ever say, "It can't happen to my children. If we ignore the whole problem it will go away." Learn all you can about drugs so you can speak to your youngsters from knowledge, so your children can never say, as many do, "We know a lot more about drugs than our parents do."

• Emphasize to your youngster: if people say it hasn't been proved that smoking pot and using some other drugs is harmful, that neither have they been proved *not* harmful, and that one fact cannot be evaded: *they are against the law.* There are severe legal penalties for possessing, using, or selling marijuana (and many other drugs). It becomes a criminal act which, too often, leads to worse crimes that can ensnare you and mark you negatively for a lifetime.

DRUG-EMERGENCY CHECKLIST

☐ DON'T delay action if you find that your child is using drugs, as use is likely to increase unless stopped.

☐ DO get professional help quickly from your doctor, clergyman, school, and police authorities.

☐ DO discuss the situation calmly with your youngster, avoiding explosive anger.

☐ DO emphasize to your youngsters the harmful and law-breaking aspects of using drugs.

22

A LIFESAVER:
HOW TO PROTECT YOURSELF ON THE
STREET UNDER TODAY'S CONDITIONS

UNDER today's conditions there is constant need to be wary when you or any of your family are out on the streets, particularly after dark. Three to four times as many street crimes occur at night during the darkest hours as by daylight. There is four times as much crime on the street at 11 P.M. as there is at 6 A.M. Thus, chances are about four times higher at night that you might be mugged or robbed if you're not watchful. Referring to street crime, President Richard M. Nixon warned of dangers due to an "88 per cent increase in muggings, robberies, rapes, and assaults over the past seven years."

Jokes abound about robbery on the street. In one case a woman asks a criminal who is taking her purse, "Would you mind giving me a receipt? I have to account for every penny to my husband." A man tells a robber taking his wallet, "I don't care about the wallet, but could I have the money back? It was left to me by my grandfather."

In spite of the joking, a survey shows that over 30 per cent of Americans admit that they are afraid to go out alone at night now, even in their own neighborhoods. The figure increases to 40 per cent among women and people living in large cities.

Practically anything can happen on the streets at night, all over the world. In Brazil, police hunted a gang of thieves who terrorized the women in a suburban area. Their "thing" was stopping women alone on a street in the dark, cutting off all their hair, and selling the stolen hair to wigmakers.

It is not easy to prevent crime on the streets. The forces of law are trying increasingly. A New Jersey engineer invented eyeglasses with a rear-view gimmick. An inconspicuous tube in one of the temple pieces points backward and deflects into a prism at the front. Thus the wearer can see whether anyone is following him. The inventor says that the rear-view eyeglasses enable people to get away fast if there is menace from someone coming up from behind. He mentions that under today's crime conditions there is bad advice in the famous saying attributed to former baseball pitcher Satchel Paige: "Don't look back. Something might be gaining on you." Now it has taken on new meaning.

While rear-view eyeglasses aren't generally available yet and would be of only limited value at best, there are many simple, effective measures you can undertake to help protect yourself and members of your family against becoming victims of crime in the streets.

Study and pass on to others close to you the basic precautions given in the pages that follow. These recommendations can save your life and the lives of your family if kept in mind always, becoming part of your instinctive thinking and action.

Avoid walking on poorly lit or dark streets. Take a well-lighted route to where you are going. Don't take any shortcuts across vacant lots, down dark alleys, or anyplace where you're likely to be caught alone.

It's safer to walk the street with company. The more people you are with, the less chance of robbery or attack. "Safety in numbers" is more than a catch phrase.

Carry a small flashlight in your pocket or purse when you go out at night. It comes in handy to light up a murky area on a dark street, to help find your keys quickly in your purse as you approach your door, or for other protective purposes.

Stay out of parks at night, even small "pocket parks." These are favorite haunts of muggers, rapists, and other criminals. Remember the too-common headlines: "Couple Mugged in Park" . . . "Woman Assaulted and Killed in Park" . . . "Man Robbed, Injured in Park."

Walk in the middle of the road if you must walk down a deserted street, perhaps past vacant lots. You are less likely to be accosted out in open space than against a fence or building. Also, you can more clearly see someone approaching, and you have more room for dashing away. Avoid walking close to bushes alongside a pavement, or next to other growth which might conceal a waiting attacker. Keep to the middle of the sidewalk. Beware of passing close to dark hallways and dark entrances to alleys, as well as vacant lots. Don't walk along too close to parked cars from which someone could reach out or jump out and pull you in.

Be especially watchful when walking past darkened homes and buildings, deserted office buildings, factories, or warehouse areas after working hours. Also avoid such lonely places as closed schools, playgrounds, parks.

Let people know where you're going and when you're due to arrive there so that they can look for you if you're overdue. If you're approaching the building on a dark, lonely street at night, you can phone ahead to have someone waiting for you at the building entrance.

Wait for buses and taxis or a friend's car only at well-lighted places, never in the dark.

Never carry more money than necessary. Instead of a lot of cash, carry blank bank checks, travelers checks—anything but a lot of bills which invite thieves and make the risks greater. And, of course, don't wear costly jewelry on the streets, or carry negotiable securities or other valuables.

Avoid flashing money around in a public place—you may be watched and then robbed on the street soon afterward. When you pay out money in restaurants, stores, filling stations, or wherever, try to keep your wallet concealed as you remove the needed bills.

Notify police promptly if you see suspicious-looking persons loitering on the streets you normally have to walk at night. Report especially anyone hanging around on the street near your home. If you're in danger, stop at a phone booth if possible and summon the police.

Never carry a purse loosely (close to your body is best) lest it be snatched easily out of your hand by a sneak thief who grabs and runs, even on a crowded street. Some thieves wait in a parked car, jump out, grab your purse, and speed away almost before you know what has happened. If you're carrying a shoulder bag, hold onto it, at the lock preferably. You're safer keeping your money in a pocket wallet on your person, if possible, and not carrying a purse on the streets at night. Rather than keeping a lot of money in your purse or wallet, hide it somewhere on your person if it's practical.

Don't put down your purse on a bench if you're waiting at a bus stop, for example. That makes it too easy for a passer-by to snatch it and dash away in a split second. Hold the purse with a firm grip in your lap—make it a habit.

Try to know what's in your purse, taking inventory before you go out if possible. In case of theft, a listing and description of items helps police catch the thief and recover your stolen property—or helps you collect on your insurance.

Carry clear identification with your name, address, and who should be notified in case something happens to you on the street and you're rendered unconscious.

Arrange for an escort to meet you at a bus stop or subway exit if the rest of your route home is on dark or lonely streets.

Call the proper community authorities if the street lights go out in your area, leaving the street dark and therefore more dangerous.

Be very careful "window shopping" on the street alone at night. Even if the window is well lit, a person standing alone is a likely target for a purse-snatcher or a quick frisking for a wallet.

Use a police call box if one is handy to bring help quickly if you're terrified, or if you're robbed, mugged, or attacked on the street. In some communities, the telephone company has arranged the phone boxes so that anyone can call the emergency security number without need to insert a coin; keep those phone locations in mind. If you don't report to the police, your silence aids the criminal, protecting him, inciting him to further crimes.

There is always some chance of recovering stolen possessions.

Never accept a ride from strangers in a car, even if a polite, well-dressed gentleman or a seeming lady pulls up to the bus stop and says he's heading in the same direction as the bus route and will drop you. Whether you're a woman or man in that situation, you'd be taking a big chance on being robbed or attacked as the car heads quickly for a lonely spot.

Don't wait to see what happens if a passing car pulls up quickly alongside you and stops suddenly. Turn and run as fast as possible in the opposite direction from which the car was coming, and scream or yell for help as loudly as you can if you are chased. The car will have to swing around in a U-turn to go after you—more likely it will head away in a hurry.

Be alert. Don't "nightdream" as you walk along a street at night. Keep alert to detect and get away from anyone loitering in front of or following behind you, and for any suspicious actions.

Make wide turns in rounding a sharp right-angle corner or passing a corner on a lonely street at night. You're safer on the outside or middle of the sidewalk from a thief or mugger flattened against a building and waiting to spring.

Don't approach a parked car if you're beckoned, even though someone is asking for instructions and you don't want to be impolite. It's better to be ungracious than unconscious. If you do stop to answer, stay far enough away from the car so that no one inside can reach out to grab you and pull you in. It's common for a criminal couple to operate from a car this way: the auto pulls up alongside a woman on the sidewalk, and the man driving calls out to the pedestrian, asking for directions. As she comes near the car to answer, a woman accomplice in the back seat of the car jumps out, snatches the victim's handbag, and leaps back into the car through the open door. They drive away, having accomplished the theft in seconds.

Bypass any strange noises that might be made to cause you to stop and investigate. It's safer to keep going about your business on the street at night; however, notify the police as quickly as possible. Nor should you stop on the street if you're approached by a stranger at night for "a light for my cigarette," for address instructions, or for any other reason. Close up, he can grab your purse, wallet, jewelry, briefcase, and be gone with your valuables in less than a minute. Be suspicious; keep moving. Even if the individual is a very attractive woman or man, an accomplice may be handy to mug and rob you while your attention is engaged in conversation.

Try to see as far down every block as possible before you walk it late at night when most people are indoors. If you see anyone or anything suspicious, take another route, or wait for other pedestrians to come along. Then follow fairly close to them.

Ring the doorbell of a lighted house you're near if you fear that you're about to be robbed or attacked by someone lurking or approaching. To allay the homeowner's suspicion, your first words should be, "Please call the police"—then explain.

If you think you're being followed, step off the street into a lighted building, or stop and talk with someone, perhaps pretending to ask directions, to throw off anyone following. If you see a policeman, stop and talk to him; don't hesitate—he'd rather prevent a crime than have to investigate it later.

When you get off a bus or other public transportation at night, or leave a public place such as a restaurant, notice whether anyone else follows you. If you slow up, speed up, or cross the street and still see the person following you, scream or shout.

A woman is more likely to invite attack on the street if she is wearing tight, "sexy" clothes. If you are heading for a party in a décolleté costume or an extra-brief skirt, it's best to ride up to the entrance rather than walk. Your intentions are undoubtedly perfectly innocent—but your appearance is nevertheless inviting. In a northwestern city, even nuns wearing habits had to be provided with protective escorts when leaving work late at night from a hospital to walk one block away to the convent.

Never go walking blithely down lonely streets if you've had a few, or more, intoxicating drinks. Even though you're not "drunk," alcohol tends to reduce normal caution and protective reactions. Remember, people who have had one too many are easy victims of street crime. Better have someone drive you home if you can't sleep it off where you are.

You can't rely on a dog for 100 per cent protection on a dark, lonely street, although you are safer walking with a loud-barking dog than alone.

Plan your route ahead of time whenever possible if you have to walk any distance to your destination. Choose the best-lighted, busiest streets rather than a dark, lonely thoroughfare. If the only way you can figure to get there is dangerous for walking, don't go unless you can ride by bus, taxi, your own or a friend's car. Keeping your fingers crossed while walking a lonely route at night is no protection at all.

How Best to Defend Yourself

Restrain yourself from fighting back if you're in a holdup where the thief grabs your purse or takes your wallet and valuables. Your life is worth more than any material possessions. A tragic example to keep in mind is that of a forty-six-year-old widow who was attacked on the street when returning home late at night from her job as nurse's aide at a hospital and apparently resisted the holdup man. Hearing her screams, people ran out from an apartment house and found the woman lying on the sidewalk, bloodied from stab wounds. Just before she died, the woman whispered, "They pushed me and tried to grab my purse. . . . " Better lose your purse than your life.

The plain fact is that the criminal, already outside the law, is prepared to attack, using violence if he must to gain his ends. The law-abiding citizen, in practically all cases, hasn't planned to ward off an attack, since crime is not his "business." The arsenal of the robber, even when it looks innocent to you, may be lethal. For example, you might not be alarmed, as you should be, if you saw a thief pull a harmless-looking comb out of his pocket. Actually its use could make the difference between life and death for you. Law enforcement officers who are familiar with the criminal's weapons know that a comb may conceal a three- to four-inch needle-sharp spike imbedded in its top length. Pressing a small button at one end releases the stiletto-like spike, which springs out instantly, locks into position, becomes a murderous weapon. Fighting back, unless absolutely necessary, against a criminal so armed can cost you your life.

Scream or yell if you learn that the criminal's aim is a physical attack endangering your life. Police records prove that if you scream and run away, your chances of escaping safely are better. If you stay and try to fight back when your attacker has a gun or other lethal weapon, the odds of winning are overwhelmingly against you.

Try to talk an assailant out of a crime, speaking calmly and reasonably (no, it's not easy to do). Sometimes it works, if you haven't been able to scream and run away. Women have saved themselves from sexual assault by convincing the criminal that they had a venereal disease, or were pregnant, or afflicted with a horrible contagion. Men have pleaded poverty and illness. The danger is usually increased if you start cursing your assailant.

It's better not to try to disarm a criminal in the first few seconds if you decide, foolishly, to fight back. In the first few seconds of a holdup, your attacker has the height of his attention focused on you, is most alert and least likely to be caught off guard; all that reduces your chances of winning. If you must counterattack, wait for a letdown on his part, for a moment of carelessness, then make your move.

It's unsafe to rely too confidently on "safety devices" which you carry on your person, although such items have proved helpful at times in warding off street crimes. You can get widely advertised, pocketsize alarm signals for a few dollars, which are, in effect, noisemakers to frighten off an attacker. You can carry a shrill whistle to scare off a criminal and to bring help. If carrying such devices makes you feel safer, do so by all means, but understand their drawbacks and limitations.

A typical ad in a newspaper urges: "You Don't Need a Gun to Save Your Life If You Carry a Shrieker in Your Purse or Pocket. Now you can walk down darkened streets, ride the subways, or work the night shift without worry—if you carry the

Shrieker to terrify molesters and muggers. One touch of the ingenious pocket-sized Shrieker (only 3½″ long) does just that: it wails an ear-splitting alarm that summons help from blocks away. . . ." The danger here is that the advertising, and carrying the item, may lull you into ignoring other essential protection measures.

A small alarm gadget that is activated by pressing a button, pulling a string, blowing, or some other means may be just about useless when kept in a woman's handbag. It's quicker to scream or yell and to start running away (unless menaced with a gun). If you're too frightened to scream or yell when in danger, then the pocket alarm can be very helpful—provided your reflexes are fast enough to use it in time.

Never fight "fair" if you're in a struggle to save your life. Use whatever weapon you can. Hat pins once provided a natural defense weapon for a woman, but who wears a hat pin (or a hat) these days? A ball-point pen is more common; it can be used as a defense tool if driven into the face, eye, ear, or neck; it may at least leave a mark which can't easily be wiped off, and has proved helpful to police in identifying attackers.

If you *must* fight back to stay alive, then realize that you are not involved in a gentleman's or lady's sporting event. You have to win, no matter what. You must kick to the most vulnerable spots, especially the groin, shins, kneecaps. Gouge at face, eyes, nose, mouth, using your fingers and nails. Bite, scratch, bash, batter; hit at the head, bridge of the nose, or the windpipe with a heavy purse, a book, a rolled-up newspaper or magazine, any other heavy object you may be carrying; in addition, use your hands, arms, and elbows. Butt with your head. Jab with an umbrella if available, slam with a briefcase. Stamp on feet, shins, instep with your heels. Fight in every possible way with the fury of a tiger defending her young. Don't rely on the manly, upstanding one-two punch with which the hero of a TV drama often knocks out the villain in a split-second.

Learning judo or karate will not automatically make you the winner either. A quick course in such mysterious self-defense techniques is no defense against a gun, knife, or other instant-action weapon. By all means take up judo or karate if you enjoy it as exercise and sport, but realize that a very small percentage of people ever become fully qualified as experts, and definitely not after a quickie course of a few sessions. The owner of a karate academy frankly states the situation this way: "Women come to my classes because they think judo will protect them. They stay for a few weeks, then quit when they realize I haven't a magic wand. Even a few lessons, though, makes them feel better."

You may be better able to cope in a life-and-death struggle with a criminal if you know karate or judo or have had some boxing or wrestling training. However, in a holdup, don't rely on such defense or attack techniques; give up your valuables and save your life.

Again, it can't be repeated too often: don't fight back; do give up your possessions—unless you are positive that you must use force as a matter of life or death.

You should not carry tear-gas devices if they're illegal in your state. Such pocket-size tear-gas units, offered in stores and in mail-order ads, have reportedly caused blindness, loss of nerve function, or other tragic damage, often by accident when touched off in error or ignorance. Regardless of arguments that the criminal deserves what he gets if seriously hurt by tear-gas or another defensive item, if it's illegal in your state don't use it.

One ad for a neatly designed tear-gas device promises, "Highly potent tear gas spray (in 4½" pocket size aerosol cartridge, $5) renders attackers helpless on contact, yet leaves no lasting effect. . . ." First, it's not necessarily true that use of the gadget "renders attackers helpless on contact. . . ." If the item doesn't work, you're probably in even bigger trouble as the criminal counterattacks. Second, it has not been proved that tear-gas "leaves no lasting effects," as the ad man promises.

Take heed of this landmark case: A woman who claimed that a man was bothering her, in fact scaring the wits out of her, pulled out a tear-gas pen and squirted the spray into the man's face. This happened in a city that prohibits use of such devices. The woman was arrested and charged with assault, unlawful possession of the item, and weapons-law violation. She could have been sentenced to jail for up to two-and-a-half years. She fought the charges over a period of eight trying months, piled up high legal expenses, and lost her job.

ON-THE-STREET CHECKLIST

☐ DO use well-lighted thoroughfares, not dim, dark steets, alleys, shortcuts.

☐ DO try to have companions on the streets, the more the safer.

☐ DON'T go in parks at night, nor in vacant lots or lonely places.

☐ DON'T walk too close to parked cars, dark hallways, or entrances.

☐ DO advise someone where you're going, and when you'll arrive.

☐ DO wait for buses, taxis, cars in well-lighted spots.

☐ DON'T flash around or carry a lot of money, jewelry, or other valuables.

☐ DO notify police at once of suspicious-looking persons or actions.

☐ DON'T carry your purse loosely or put it down out of touch.

☐ DON'T accept a ride from strangers or stop to talk with them.

☐ DON'T stop to investigate strange noises.

☐ DO hurry to a safe place or into a lighted house or building if you're being followed.

☐ DO take along a loud-barking dog on the street if possible.

☐ DON'T fight back physically in a holdup if you can help it; better yield your valuables than life or limb.

☐ DON'T rely too confidently on "safety devices," nor use any that are against the law in your locality.

☐ DON'T fight fair if you're necessarily struggling to save your life; use every possible tactic and weapon, as recommended.

23

FOR EMERGENCIES:
HOW TO PROTECT YOURSELF
IN CASE OF A RIOT

THE BEST protective action anyone can take to keep from being injured and even killed in a street riot is summed up in four words: *stay away*—if you see or hear about a riot in your area; *go away*—as swiftly as you possibly can if you're caught in or near a riot. If you see the potentials of a riot in signs of rising anger and violence in a crowd, notify the police at once, then leave the area.

Wherever your sympathies may lie, understand that rioting is an unlawful act, and no matter how innocent you may be, if you're in the middle of it you're liable to arrest—not to mention personal injury.

Take cover as far inside as possible. Once you're indoors, in your own home or somebody else's apartment, office, or anywhere, get to the interior rooms or to the wall and corners farthest away from the windows and doors. There is a tendency to go to the windows or open the door a crack to look out and see what's going on. That's very dangerous. Innocent persons have been killed by stray bullets or maimed by rocks, bottles, or other objects thrown during a riot. Usually such results are accidental, but in some cases, where rioters are attacking anything and anybody, the sight of someone at a window or half-open door is just another welcome target.

If you feel for some reason that you absolutely must look out the window, at least stand to one side as you peer out, back from the glass, showing as little of yourself as possible. Never silhouette yourself in the center of the window frame where you'll form an inviting, easily reached target for attack with rocks, bottles, bullets.

Head for shelter in the nearest building if you are caught outside in a riot. Climb to the top floors and seek the deepest interior shelter—if you can't get out of the area completely. Above all, get off the street and away from the spots where the action is.

RIOT-PROTECTION CHECKLIST

☐ DO lock up tight and stay indoors if a riot occurs in your area.

☐ DO take cover or get out of the area at once if caught outdoors during a riot.

☐ DON'T venture into a riot area; stay away.

☐ DO go away from the spot instantly if there are the slightest signs that a riot may occur.

☐ DO take refuge in the nearest building if caught in a riot, and climb fast to the top floors and deepest interiors.

☐ DO stay in interior rooms in a riot, always away from windows and doors, which should be locked up tight and barricaded if necessary.

24

WHAT TO DO ABOUT CRIME ON YOUR STREET

CONSIDER extra protective measures in addition to all the personal precautions recommended if a number of crimes are taking place on your street, particularly in the city, so that you find it unsafe at night. Get together in a meeting with other people living on the street to discuss and decide what can be done. Check with your local police precinct for an official representative to attend your meeting and advise you as to just what measures would be most effective in your situation.

Look into the volunteer situation. In some cities the police accept qualified citizen volunteers for training as auxiliary police. These volunteers wear uniforms and serve without pay because their intent is to help protect their families, neighbors, and friends. Being professionally trained, they have proved to be an effective deterrent in many instances.

Investigate the possibilities of hiring one or more protective custodians, men who patrol the street during the night hours with the approval and help of police authorities. The cost per person can be small if split up among many families on the block.

The president of one such block organization stated: "We've had a guard almost every night for the last two months. We've stopped quite a bit of crime. There's been only one mugging, and at least a 40 per cent drop in thefts. I'm not saying that we're free of crime, but the things that happen on the streets—the holdups—are almost down to zero."

He explained further: "There are enough police floating in the neighborhood to make arrests, and they do a good job. But our program of hiring a street guard is not for arrests; it's more for crime prevention."

Think about and discuss another means of mutual protection: neighbors on some streets provide pairs of watchers from among themselves to patrol the block at night. Just the presence of a pair of men on the street acts as a deterrent to criminals. Other measures are described by a tenant: "We try to get some tenants with dogs to patrol outside during the evening. A group of tenants has agreed to work on an emergency basis. If somebody in the building is going to be out at night, she can call one of the tenants who owns a dog, and that person will come downstairs and wait outside the building on guard until she comes in."

None of these measures is guaranteed to work perfectly. All of them help to some degree. The safest course is to stay indoors at night, but that is quite impossible for most people. While you can't protect yourself 100 per cent against any mishap in life, you will be safer by taking every possible precaution advised, and cooperating with other citizens.

How to Report a Street Crime

If you observe a crime on the street, or are a victim of a holdup or other crime and the criminal has left the scene, call the police at once and try to provide details on the phone:

1. Give the exact location of the crime.

2. Tell briefly what has happened.

3. Give your name and the location and phone number from which you're calling.

4. If an automobile was involved in the crime or getaway, give the license plate number if you can, a brief description of the type and color of the car, and how many people were in it. A search for the car can then be started at once while police are on the way to the scene of the crime.

The police will undoubtedly instruct you to wait at the scene, and will probably arrive in a radio car just about as soon as you've completed the call or very shortly after.

Be as observant as you can during a crime so that you can

report to the police in most helpful detail the appearance of the assailant: age, sex, color, height, weight, plus other identifying characteristics such as peculiarities of speech, a scar, twitch, or limp.

Act quickly to call the police. If you're a victim or witness, don't take it for granted that others on the scene have phoned the authorities; do it yourself. Your identity will be withheld if you prefer.

STREET-CRIME-CONTROL CHECKLIST

☐ DO cooperate with the police and neighbors to check street crimes in your area, under supervision of the police.

☐ DO consider joining with other qualified citizen volunteers under police auspices, as arranged in some cities.

☐ DO investigate hiring protective custodians if special protection is needed on your street.

☐ DO consider forming patrols by pairs of neighbors with dogs.

☐ DON'T fail to report a street crime speedily, as victim or witness, and know how to give clear, accurate descriptions.

25

HOW TO STAY SAFE FROM ATTACK
IN YOUR CAR

ALWAYS keep in mind that you are not safe from attack just because you're inside your car. The statistics of thefts and assaults on the occupants of cars prove that you must stay alert and careful at all times against trouble from outside when you're parked, or even riding.

Don't put your pocketbook or a valuable package on the seat alongside you when you're driving alone. When you stop for a light or other reason, a thief can reach in the window or open the door, snatch your purse, and disappear. It's safer to keep your purse out of sight, in a spot such as on the floor behind your seat.

Keep your doors locked at all times while driving, stopped, or parked (as well as when you leave the car, of course). This prevents a criminal from opening the door and jumping in when you're waiting for a red light or are parked.

Look into the car carefully, both front and back interior, before opening the door and entering. This is a "must" in case an intruder is hiding inside, usually in back, waiting to rob or attack you while the car is in operation or when you arrive at your destination.

Have your car key in hand, if possible, when approaching your parked car. It's safer to insert the key and drive off, rather than to sit inside the stopped car fumbling in purse or pocket for your key, especially in a large parking lot without others nearby.

Avoid parking in a secluded location by night, and even by

day, where an assailant could accost you unnoticed by others.

It's not safe to park in a dark "lover's lane" location. These are favorite haunts of criminals for robbery and attack. If you insist on stopping in such a dangerous spot, or on a dark street to say a long goodnight, be sure all the doors are locked and the windows not open wide enough for anyone to force his way in. Keep the key in the ignition for a quick getaway. With all these precautions, you're still a sitting duck for an armed assault.

Never forget that it is dangerous to keep the motor running for heat or for any other reason when you're parked. Many deaths have been caused by carbon monoxide filling the car, and a long nap or a long goodnight turns into the long sleep.

Lean on your horn and keep sounding it with intermittent blasts if someone is trying to force his way into your car, or if you're in other trouble. The repeated blasting of the horn (not a long, steady sound as though the horn is stuck), helps to drive the assailant away and to bring help faster.

Lock yourself in the car until help comes if your auto breaks down at night, first pulling or pushing the car to the side of the road. Open your hood and leave it up to show that you're having trouble. Display a white handkerchief or other white marker from the driver's window or driver's door handle, preferably held up on a stick such as a jack handle, or from the radio antenna, or preferably from both door and antenna. That's a signal for help recognized by many. Talking through your closed window, ask anyone who stops to call the police for help.

Never let your gas gauge go down to near zero. If you're being chased by an assailant and you run out of gas, you're in deep trouble. If you run out of gasoline in a lonely spot on a dark road, or even in daylight, you're inviting danger from passing criminals.

Don't drive to an isolated spot such as your own driveway at night if you're being followed by an assailant, particularly if no one is at home. Instead, keep driving and stop only at a well-lighted place with plenty of other people around. Or pull up alongside a policeman or police car. Keep blasting your horn intermittently meanwhile to attract attention and scare off the car following you. If it's daylight, blink your car lights on and off as another signal to attract the attention of others to the fact that something is wrong.

Consider a new "dummy" item if you're a woman who often drives alone at night. Some stores offer an inflatable vinyl balloon that blows up to a man-size figure and head. Set on the seat alongside, it looks like a man sitting beside the woman driver. Use it if it makes you feel safer, but don't count on it to replace the other protective measures recommended.

Try to travel on well-lighted streets as much as possible rather than very dark roads or alleys. It's better to go a longer way on a lighted, well-traveled street than to take a shortcut via dark streets and alleys.

Stay out of "dangerous" neighborhoods where crime abounds if you can possibly do so. As stated before, a prime rule for avoiding trouble is to stay away from trouble areas.

Keep toward the center on a dark, lonely street or road rather than close to the side where someone may jump out of bushes or a dark hallway.

Avoid stopping to fix a flat in a dark, lonely spot on the road or street. Keep driving slowly until you're in the light or reach a service station. It's better to ruin a tire by riding on it than to be robbed and attacked.

Never stop in a traffic lane to fix a flat, as you're inviting death from oncoming cars. Drive on slowly until you can pull over to a safe spot.

Don't ever pick up a stranger, no matter how innocent-appearing, woman or man. Make it an ironbound rule: no hitch-hikers; a young, pretty girl is often a decoy for a hidden accomplice. If you stop, they may both hop in, and you're in serious trouble. Don't take a stranger for a demonstration ride if you're selling your car—it's safer to have someone else along. The same is true when you're buying a used car from a private party.

If nothing else, these figures should shock you into passing up all hitchhikers. In a recent survey along a stretch of road in Arizona, 96 out of 100 hitchhikers had some previous or current difficulties with the law: 84 of those thumbing rides had criminal records; 12 others were either juvenile runaways or AWOL servicemen; only four of the 100 questioned appeared free of lawlessness except, of course, violating anti-hitchhiking regulations.

Don't drive right up to your house, garage, or apartment indoor or outdoor parking place without slowing up and putting your bright lights on to make sure no one is lurking around, waiting for you to park your car and get out in order to rob or attack you.

Leave a light on in your garage when you go out at night for extra safety. If the light is out when you return and you're positive you left it on, don't enter the garage. Call the police and wait for the police car. There is a good chance that the bulb hasn't burned out but that an assailant may be waiting in the dark garage.

CHECKLIST AGAINST CAR ATTACKS

☐ DON'T leave your pocketbook or valuables on the seat beside you if driving alone.

☐ DO keep all car doors locked when driving.

☐ DON'T park in a secluded spot at night, or in a "lover's lane."

☐ DO try to travel on well-lighted streets rather than on dark, lonely lanes and alleys.

☐ DO stay out of dangerous, crime-ridden areas.

☐ DON'T ever pick up strangers or hitchhikers.

26

HOW TO KEEP YOUR CAR FROM BEING STOLEN

A THIEF steals a car every 57 seconds. Note carefully the following facts from the National Automobile Theft Bureau, FBI Uniform Crime Report.

• The box score in just one year (increasing each year) reveals these shocking facts: 815,000 cars stolen, for an economic loss of more than $250 million. In other words, nearly one out of every 100 registered cars in the nation has been stolen by car thieves. About 200 cars a day are stolen in New York City alone.

• The prime targets are late-model cars, sporty models, high-powered models (but car thieves aren't that choosy; they'll steal anything they can get in a pinch).

• It may seem unbelievable but it's true: 80 per cent of stolen cars are left unlocked by the operators when they leave the car. And 50 per cent of the cars stolen, where thieves have found the doors unlocked, also have the key left in the ignition.

• Two-thirds of all thefts occur at night, one-third in the daytime. That still means that over a quarter-million cars each year are stolen in daylight, primarily because of unexcusable carelessness on the part of their drivers.

• A significant fact about stolen autos is that 90 per cent of the people arrested for car theft are under age 25. This is usually the first serious offense committed by young people, who may go on from there to a life of criminal activity if not checked.

If your car is stolen, partly because of your carelessness in leaving it unlocked and perhaps even leaving your key in the car, you have not only invited and aided the theft, but you are endangering others. FBI figures prove it:

• A stolen car, driven by a thief, is 200 times as likely to be in an accident as when the owner is driving it. This newspaper story is typical: "In White Plains, N.Y., a 16-year-old boy stole a car from a shopping center and hit and killed a 60-year-old woman as he sped away."

• Almost one out of every ten cars stolen is used in committing other crimes. Time after time, when the license number of a getaway car used in a crime is reported by a witness, a quick check shows that the car was reported stolen just a few hours before (having the license number has still been useful in many cases in catching the criminals before they change the plates or abandon the car).

• About 50 per cent of the getaway cars used in bank robberies, and tracked down, are found to have been stolen.

• In one year, more than 150,000 stolen cars were involved in accidents, with a tragic toll of more than 20,000 injured, many crippled for life, and 600 persons killed in the smashups.

Not all car thieves are professionals; one reason so many cars are stolen is that many more amateurs will take a car than will try such crimes as breaking into a house or store. Here's a breakdown of car thefts by type of thief:

• 46 per cent of auto thieves are "joyriders," generally under age 25, who steal a car "for fun or kicks" and usually abandon it after they've had their fling. During the joyride, however, many of these cars are involved in smashups.

• 35 per cent are "transportation thieves" who take the car for their own specific purposes: 27 per cent to "get someplace"; 8 per cent for use in committing a crime. In these cases also, the stolen cars are usually abandoned after being used for an illicit purpose.

• 15 per cent are professional car thieves who steal for

the purpose of selling the cars; these cars are not abandoned. Cars taken for resale total about 125,000 per year.

• The highest percentage of car thieves apprehended are amateurs; they get caught because they act nervous and are unfamiliar with the stolen vehicles and with methods of trying to escape detection.

Note these further facts about auto thefts; knowing them may prove helpful in protecting your own car from being stolen and in aiding officials to apprehend car thieves:

• *Places of theft:* 29 per cent of cars are taken from congested residential areas; 28 per cent from parking lots; the balance from transportation terminals, from other places such as shopping centers where large numbers of cars are parked, and from higher income residential sections.

• *Methods of entering:* in over 75 per cent of thefts, car thieves get into the cars through unlocked doors; other methods are use of master or duplicate keys . . . breaking windows . . . using a wire hanger to pull up button of door lock through partially opened windows . . . forcing windows through use of common levers such as beer can openers, bent screw drivers, or other instruments. The last method usually results in such telltale signs as windows cracked, chipped, or broken and the window frame areas scratched, chipped, or dented.

• *Ways of starting car:* most stolen cars, a whopping 43 per cent, are started by using a key left in the ignition or supposedly concealed somewhere in the auto (under a mat, attached to the sun visor, in unlocked dashboard compartment). Other methods are use of a master or duplicate key . . . a special jiggler-type key . . . a jumper wire or hot wire under the hood . . . starting through other electrical equipment in the car such as dash lights . . . inserting foil or steel wool in back of the switch to bridge contacts and close circuits . . . pulling out ignition wires and twisting them together . . . unplugging the ignition switch from the regular auto switch and using the thief's own switch to replace it, along with his key for that switch.

When some of the preceding techniques are used, there are

definite observable signs like: the motor is running in a darkened car with no lights or other electrical equipment such as windshield wipers in use . . . motor running but no key in the ignition . . . wire or switch hanging from under the dashboard. Law officers are constantly on the lookout for such telltale signs, as well as for indications of the driver's unfamiliarity with the car, such as bucking, jerking, stopping short, stalling. They have recovered many stolen vehicles in this way. In one case, a police officer noted a driver acting nervous and saw a loose wire hanging below the dashboard—but there was a key in the ignition. Nevertheless the officer ordered the car to pull over. When he examined the car, he found that the thief had wedged the back half of a key into the slot to look like the ignition key at a passing glance, then had started the car by pulling out and twisting the ignition wires.

• *Ways of disguising plates:* professional thieves usually have a set of replacement plates which they attach shortly after stealing the car . . . or they wire other plates over the auto's plates in a few seconds for a fast getaway . . . or they change the letters and numbers on the plates by use of colored tape so that in a few seconds an E becomes an F, a 4 becomes a 1, and so on. With more time, stolen cars may be given a complete new paint job, change of accessories, replacement or addition of seat covers, so that even the owner wouldn't recognize his own car a few hours after it was stolen.

Never leave your car doors unlocked, not even if you are only dashing into the supermarket "for a few seconds, to get a carton of milk." Certainly it's a nuisance to lock the car, then go to the trouble of fumbling for your keys again to unlock it—especially when you're only going to be gone for what you consider an instant in time. But that's long enough for a thief to hop in and drive your car away, perhaps trying so hard for a quick getaway that he smashes into your best friend's car and cripples her as he's trying to speed out of the supermarket parking lot. This kind of thing has happened all too often.

You can't consider any place safe for an unlocked car. In a

typical instance, a homeowner in a quiet suburb made a habit of leaving his car unlocked, with the key in the ignition, in his garage. He explained later that he had once mislaid his key in a bureau drawer, couldn't find it the next morning when he was late and in a desperate hurry to get to the office. After that he took to leaving his key in the dashboard "so I would know where it was, without bothering to think about it." He also left his overhead garage doors open overnight because "I used to wrench my back opening and closing those heavy doors."

One night, about 1 A.M., he heard shouting, then a motor starting with a roar. He dashed to his bedroom window in time to see his own car zooming out of his driveway to streak away up the street with a screeching of tires. Dashing out, he found his neighbor talking excitedly with officers from a police car which had just arrived. They had been summoned by a phone call from the neighbor's wife. He said that he had awakened, heard noises, and surprised a burglar in his downstairs study. The intruder had scrambled out, jumped into his neighbor's car (which he had apparently checked beforehand, noting the key in the ignition), and made a quick getaway.

The indignant neighbor said that the thief wouldn't have gotten away if the unlocked, ready-to-go car hadn't been available. No amount of apology was able to soothe the justifiably angry man. The car was discovered an hour later, smashed up against a tree a few miles away, with no traces of the driver. The crestfallen car owner mumbled, "I didn't think it could happen that my car would be stolen from my own garage."

The theft of your car can happen *anywhere,* even when you've only walked a few steps away after you park it. That is particularly so if you not only fail to lock the car doors but also leave your key in the car.

Never leave your motor running, even if you're only running into a store to grab a newspaper, or to mail a letter at a corner mailbox. You're subject to a traffic violation in most states. Many cars with motors left running have been driven off in less than half a minute by watchful thieves.

Always check windows when you're locking up your car to

make sure that they are also locked tight if they have latches, or closed snugly at top and on all sides. The least opening will admit a strong blade-tool on which pressure can be applied to break the lock, enabling the thief to open the window, reach in, and unlock the door. Professionals also have a trick of opening windows with a long strip of wide adhesive tape.

Keep the dashboard compartment locked if you keep anything of any value in it. Otherwise it's better to leave the compartment unlocked so that the lock won't be forced and broken by an intruder who is intent on seeing what's inside.

Never leave valuables in the car—clothing, luggage, or packages of any kind—where they can be seen from outside the car. However valueless the contents may be, a package or other item is an invitation to break into the car, causing costly damage at the least. There is an illustrative story, true or not, of a man who claimed he had no trouble getting rid of his garbage daily during the sanitation men's nine-day strike in New York City. "I wrapped up my garbage in a neat, attractive package every morning," he claimed, "and left it on the seat of my car when I parked, also leaving the window open. When I got back to my car each day, the package of garbage was always gone." He was lucky that the car also wasn't gone.

It's safest not to leave your driver's license or car registration, credit cards, or anything of any value in the car. Too many people leave the licenses and credit cards in the dashboard compartment, where the thief invariably looks. If he finds your registration and is stopped by a suspicious officer, the thief produces it. If he has also found your driver's license, he can often pass himself off with your identity, especially if he has the registration in the same name. Showing the registration alone, he can say that the owner lent him the car.

Avoid packing valuables, luggage, clothing, or packages in the trunk while anyone is watching, and then leaving the car for any reason. A thief seeing you load the trunk will try to break it open and remove the contents as soon as you're out of sight.

Observe these precautions during daylight hours, too, rather than thinking that they're important only after dark. Thieves wait, watch, and often attempt to steal the car or its contents during a lull of even a minute or two when no one is watching, at any hour of the day as well as at night.

Don't buy a car, new or used, from an unknown dealer . . . or at an incredibly low price . . . or if there seems to be anything phony about the deal. It may be a stolen car, in which case you may incur a total loss of your purchase price.

Look around carefully if you return to your parked car and find a flat tire—especially in a lonely spot. If you see one or more suspicious-looking characters loitering near, keep walking and get police assistance. It's a common trick of criminals to flatten a tire, then hold up the car owner when's he's changing the tire.

Call the police if you come upon someone trying your car doors or getting into your car. He may make the glib excuse that he has the same make car and thought it was his or that he's drunk and confused, then leave in a hurry. Advise the police so they can check the area for car thieves.

Don't barge in and start a rumpus if you see several teenagers or others invading your car. It's the better part of valor to call the police and let the professionals handle the situation, rather than risk attack and injury.

Avoid parking your car in a dark spot—it's safer when parked under a street light, although this is no assurance that it won't be stolen. In any case, make sure that the car is locked up tight and that the key is in your pocket, not in the car. An officer investigating a shabby car which had been sitting in one spot for many hours found a note on the seat stating, "Owner gone abroad for good—help yourself."

Never leave all your keys in the car, on a key ring or key case, when parking where you're required to leave the car key. As previously warned, house keys on the chain could be used to enter your house or apartment while your car remains in the parking garage or lot.

Check your license plates occasionally to make sure that the fastenings haven't worked loose. If your plates drop off without your noticing, you may be stopped by police under suspicion of having stolen the car. You can be subject to a fine for driving without plates. Check any parts or devices about the car that might come loose through driving and vibration, for safety's sake as well as to prevent loss.

You shouldn't keep real valuables in your trunk at any time, since this is one of the first places car thieves look. An experienced criminal can open most car trunks fairly easily, not caring how much damage he does to the lock or the finish of the auto. With a convertible it is common for thieves to get at the trunk from inside the car, cutting the collapsible top if necessary, then emptying the trunk through a slit or hole.

Keep a flashlight in the car so you won't be caught in the dark if you have to stop your car at night. A heavy flashlight can be used as a club if you're attacked and forced to fight back (if it's a holdup, yield your valuables rather than invite violence). It's also advisable to have a "flasher" lantern in case you have a breakdown or flat tire on a dark road—to signal passing cars for help, and keep them from running into you.

Report an auto theft to the police immediately. Don't wait even a few minutes before calling in. Supply your license plate number and an accurate description of the car make, model, color, year, and any special characteristics. Speedy, accurate reports have often been helpful in recovering stolen cars (over 90 per cent are recovered in New York City) in quick time. Any delay helps the thieves get away.

If you should recover your car without police help (such as finding it abandoned near your home), be sure to notify the police at once so they can cancel the stolen car alarm on your vehicle. Otherwise you may cause the police a lot of unnecessary work, and you may be stopped for driving a stolen car even though it's your own.

Report to the police as a witness as fast as you possibly can if you see a car being stolen, or are on the scene when an accident happens. Give these essential details:

1. Location of the incident so police can get there fast.

2. Description of scene and suspects, their approximate age, height, complexion, clothing, any special distinguishing characteristics.

158

3. Number of individuals involved.

4. Direction of travel.

5. Descriptions of the car or cars involved, particularly the license numbers, then any details you may have noted—make of car, model and year, color, any special characteristics (don't be concerned if you don't get all of these, just do your best).

Never try to stop the driver of a stolen car yourself. Alert the nearest officer if there is one in sight; otherwise phone in the license number to the police as fast as possible. You are not qualified to handle a desperate car thief by yourself. You may be putting yourself in great danger, laudable as your action may be as a public-spirited citizen. Do your part, but don't take unnecessary chances.

CAR-THEFT CHECKLIST

☐ DO lock your car doors even when stopping for the briefest visit.

☐ DON'T ever leave your keys in the car; lock it and pocket the key.

☐ DON'T ever leave your motor running even if you are just dashing into a store or mailing a letter.

☐ DON'T keep license or car registration in your car.

☐ DO keep the dashboard compartment locked if it holds anything valuable.

☐ DO take valuables with you; don't leave them in the car or even in the trunk, where they can be stolen while you're away.

☐ DO call the police to handle it if you see a car, including your own, being stolen.

27

INEXPENSIVE PROTECTION
DEVICES FOR YOUR CAR

CHECK new cars for protective devices designed to help prevent auto theft—before you buy. Consider adding some such items to your present car. Here are some features offered by various makes.

• *Steering column locks* that fix the steering wheel in place so that when the key is turned and removed, the wheel can't be turned. Also, the gearshift cannot be put in gear. (Required by law on new cars after January 1, 1970.)

• *Key warning buzzer* that sounds a signal if you leave the key in the lock and then open the car door. Of course if you don't heed the buzzer, remove the key, and take it with you, the signal is of no avail. (Required by law on new cars after January 1, 1970.)

• *Plastic shields* covering ignition terminals and wires to make them more (but not 100 per cent) tamperproof.

• *Improved lock* that requires a key with more configurations and therefore a more difficult one for a car thief to duplicate. New laws in many states now forbid the sale or possession of master keys which used to be quite readily available to criminals.

Auto manufacturers are planning further improved safeguards in the face of spiraling car thefts. In the past decade, while auto registrations have gone up 45 per cent, auto thefts have more than tripled.

Consider new protective devices that you can get in auto accessory stores and other shops, or by mail order:

• *Noisemaking auto alarms* are easily installed at service stations or by yourself if you're skilled. Once you turn on a hidden alarm switch when locking your car, a blasting alarm goes off if anyone tampers with the doors or windows, with the trunk, hub caps, antenna, or other accessories on the auto. Other inexpensive alarms work on flashlight batteries; they attach to the auto door and activate a loud siren if the door is opened. The noise is usually enough to send a car thief running.

• *Electronic auto alarms* can be installed at service stations on almost any American or foreign car. When activated, the alarm system sets off a piercing siren, blows your car's horn in an attention-getting rhythm, flashes your headlights, and cuts off the ignition—an effective four-way action. The alarm is activated if a thief tries to force open the car doors or windows, lifts the hood, attempts to open the trunk or to "jump" the locked ignition. Even if the thief has a master key that fits your ignition lock, the alarms will be set off because he hasn't the special registered safety key that's part of the alarm system. Another type of electronic device keeps the hood locked until a hidden button is pressed to free the ignition system and the hood lock.

• *Electronic-key systems* open only with a unique "pick-proof" electronic key; it looks something like a plastic charge card and contains an infrared pattern which is a match for an identical pattern in the car's ignition. The built-in scrambling and decoding pattern in the system blocks the use of "hot wiring," employed in many car thefts.

• *Special parts locks* to help prevent theft of accessories are available to lock your car hood, wheels, hub caps, steering wheel, brake pedal, gas tank, and to block any attempt to jack up the car to remove wheels or for any other purpose. Gasoline thieves have been caught using an electric pump like those employed on high-powered racing and sports cars; in a few minutes the thieves can empty your tank into their own car's tank or other receptacle.

• *Stalling devices* safeguard the car by cutting off the fuel supply so that a car thief is stopped in a very short distance as soon as the motor uses up whatever gas is in the carburetor.

New developments promise even better protection against auto thefts in the future, so keep alert for them, and put them to use. Intricate locks are being perfected which operate by personal fingerprints; a photograph of a fingerprint and a photo cell are combined so that the lock can be opened only by the person whose fingerprint matches the one on the photo.

Another lock in the laboratory stage can be opened only by a "voiceprint." Each voice makes a different pattern on a spectograph, and only the individualistic sound of your voice will permit the lock to be opened—truly a modern "Open, sesame!"

Don't think that it doesn't pay to safeguard the car with special techniques just because most stolen cars are recovered by police. The fact is that most stolen cars have been damaged (if not smashed up in the frequent accidents in which such cars are involved) to an average cost of $200 when recovered— doors jimmied, windows broken, other assorted damage. Also, you wouldn't want it on your conscience if your neglect resulted in your car being used as an aid to robbery or murder.

CAR-PROTECTION CHECKLIST

☐ DO get all available protective devices on a new car, such as steering column lock . . . key warning buzzer . . . tamper-proof shields . . . more burglar-proof ignition lock.

☐ DO investigate protective auto devices that fit your personal needs, choosing from noisemaking and electronic alarms . . . electronic key systems . . . parts locks . . . stalling devices.

☐ DON'T overlook car protection on the grounds that most stolen cars are recovered, since they suffer an average $200 of damage when found.

28

HOW TO PROTECT YOURSELF IN STORES, RESTAURANTS, BARS, AND THEATERS

DON'T DELUDE yourself that robbery "can't happen here," or to you, when you're out in a public place such as a store or theater. A front-page newspaper story reads: "Woman Is Assaulted As She Leaves Store. . . . An assault and robbery described by police as 'unusually bold' was reported by a woman shopper at 12:40 P.M." in a department store parking area. "The woman lost a $5,000 diamond ring. . . ." One lesson stands out clearly here: if you want to protect yourself against robbery and assault, one of the first precautions you'll take is not to wear "a $5,000 diamond ring" out in a public place.

The thief ("middle-aged, well-dressed") saw this lady's ring flashing as she shopped. He followed her out to the parking area—even though it was a busy time just past high noon. There he suddenly wrenched the ring from her finger, grabbed her money, and sped away in a car driven up by an accomplice. The entire robbery took no more than a minute or two.

Be aware of the necessity today for increasing your precautions in public places. The need is spotlighted by a humorist who, replying to the question, "Did you get robbed today?" answered, "Only twice. First time on the parking lot and the second behind the drugstore after I stopped to get medicine. Lucky thing I cashed a check in the drugstore, or I wouldn't have had anything to give the second fellow."

Never flash money or any valuables around in a public place—store or restaurant or any place where others can see

163

and be tempted to assault and rob you or pick your pocket. Take money from your wallet and purse discreetly. It's safer to pay large amounts by check, charge account, or credit cards.

Don't put your purse or briefcase or valuable packages down on a counter in a store, bank, anywhere—unless you keep a hand on them or keep them otherwise well guarded so they can't be snatched away. This happens in stores hundreds of times daily—a woman shopper puts down her purse to pick up an item such as a scarf which she wants to examine with both hands. When she reaches for the purse again—it's gone.

Many stores and banks now have closed circuit TV cameras and other devices that reveal a crime while it's happening, but taking precautions is still your best protection against losses. The scope of the TV camera, for instance, is often limited—and the thief may get away completely.

Keep your purse in your lap, not on the floor or on an empty seat next to you in a theater. The lights go down and your purse goes out in the dark—or even in the light if you turn away for an instant. It's common also for "seat-tippers" to operate in a theater or auditorium: the criminal tips the seat in front of him; a flat purse, hat or package slides out the back into waiting hands, and you never know how it disappeared. Or he may empty your purse of money and any small valuables and slide it back, so you don't even know anything was stolen until you open your purse later.

Don't place your purse in a shopping cart. It takes only a split-second for a thief to snatch up the purse and disappear when you step over to take some cans off a shelf. Hold the purse tight to your body, preferably with the clasp facing you, not facing away (it's easy to get the habit). Or carry it looped over your arm with the purse always in plain sight, not dangling back over your shoulder.

Shout and make a fuss immediately if you see someone making off with your purse or other belongings. Don't be afraid of being impolite or feeling embarrassed. If you don't stop the thief in those first few seconds, he has a good chance to get away.

It's safer not to carry valuables with you—jewelry, papers, or other items that would be a severe loss. Even the loss of nonnegotiable documents can cause great inconvenience.

Never carry more money than you can afford to lose. Carry blank bank checks or travelers checks rather than lots of tempting cash.

Place your money in several pockets or places on your person if you must carry considerable sums. If the money is stolen from one pocket, you won't be left without funds.

Keep an eye on your charge plate, and get it back right after it's used for the sales slip. If you walk away without your charge plate, it may fall into other hands and be used by a thief.

Never give intimate details about yourself to strangers, women or men, with whom you strike up a casual acquaintance. It's one thing to be friendly and cordial, but indiscriminately mentioning your address or phone number, or describing your home may be dangerous. While you are telling all this to one likable stranger, an accomplice who was sitting nearby and listening could be heading for your house to rob it while you're chatting.

Keep your coat and hat in sight if you hang them up in a restaurant, library, courtroom, or other public place. If there's an empty chair at your table, it's safer to fold your coat and place it with your hat on the chair where no one can remove them undetected.

Be careful not to put your purse aside in a powder room, or briefcase in a men's room. Thieves find these favorite spots for grabbing a purse or briefcase or packages of other valuables which have been set down for a moment. In a flash, a purse snatcher can be out the door and lost in the crowd in a railroad or bus station or air terminal. If you hang a handbag or briefcase on the inside of a toilet door, a thief can easily remove it from the outside and get away before you can stop him.

Never leave your wallet or purse in a dressing room when you try on a suit or dress and step out to the mirror for a fitting. Hold your valuables in your hand while examining yourself in the glass or being fitted. Thefts from dressing rooms mount to higher and higher figures annually.

Be wary if the same person seems to be following you around "just by coincidence" in a store or other public place. Hold tight to your purse and watch your wallet. If you're really concerned, seek out the manager of the department and report the person. Just seeing you make the report usually impels the suspect to disappear quickly.

A man should carry his wallet in the inside jacket pocket, if he wears a jacket. It's safer there than in a hip or side pocket of the trousers. Whatever pocket you use, have a button with a tight buttonhole on it (you can have one put on) and keep the pocket buttoned when it contains your wallet, keys, or other valuables. Many wallets fit more snugly in the pocket if pushed in sideways rather than lengthways; the snugger the fit, the safer from a thief. However, a pickpocket carrying a razor blade is adept at slitting the material down the side or bottom of a trousers pocket and plucking out the wallet without your feeling anything at all.

Be careful about letting a helpful stranger take your heavy packages "to help carry them to the car"—you may never see your packages again.

Don't put your purse aside on a desk or elsewhere when you're being interviewed in an office, opening a charge account or bank account, or anywhere out in public. It can be taken while you're preoccupied even though it seems right under your nose. Keep your purse or briefcase on your lap, preferably with your hand resting on it or clasping it.

Avoid entering a laundromat late at night or even during the day unless you see an attendant or at least one or two others inside. Passing thieves look into laundromats frequently, seeking lone victims. It's safer always to go to the laundromat with a friend or two. While there, keep your purse over your arm rather than laying it aside, or carry your money in a wallet snugly buttoned in a pocket.

In Theaters, Bars . . .

Sit next to or near the aisle in a theater if you enter alone—a good rule for men as well as women. Sitting alone in a dark corner against the wall or in an area of vacant seats in the dim balcony makes you more prone to molestation and mugging. It almost appears to be an invitation to an approach from a stranger. If you're sitting on the aisle, you can quickly get up and change your seat or leave.

Inform the manager of the theater if you are molested, change your seat, and are still pursued by your assailant. Don't take a chance of "sitting it out." A criminal can knife you, rob you, and slip out of a darkened theater before anyone notices or you can summon help.

The best way to avoid trouble in an unsavory movie house, "sex show," or other public places of potential violence is to stay out of them. The same is true for your youngsters. Anyone entering such questionable premises is considered a likely target for the criminal. If you insist on going there, at least make sure you're in the company of one or more friends, although it's almost as dangerous for a pair of unescorted girls as for one.

Beware of strangers, no matter how pleasant or gentlemanly they may appear to be, if you're a woman alone in a bar. Many robberies and beatings, even murder, started with an unsuspecting or overconfident woman entering into conversation with a stranger at a bar or other public place and leaving with him to go somewhere else or to get "a lift home."

Stay with the crowds at sports events, movies, or other public functions. Don't wander off down lonely hallways or in deserted areas. Most public places are frequented by criminals looking for crime opportunities to present themselves.

PUBLIC PLACES SAFETY CHECKLIST

☐ DON'T flash money or valuables around in stores or other public places.

☐ DO hold on to your purse, briefcase, and packages; don't place them on a counter or seat where they may be snatched away.

☐ DON'T place your purse or small packages on the floor or adjacent empty seat in a theater.

☐ DON'T leave your purse in a shopping cart.

☐ DO shout instantly if someone is dashing away with your purse or other belongings.

☐ DON'T carry a lot of money, jewelry, or other valuables.

☐ DO place cash in more than one pocket or place on your person.

☐ DON'T give information about yourself to strangers you meet.

☐ DO keep your coat and hat in sight when you hang them up in public.

☐ DO carry your wallet in your inside jacket pocket preferably.

☐ DON'T enter a lonely laundromat alone.

☐ DO get up and tell the manager if someone bothers you in a movie theater.

☐ DO beware of strangers in a bar if you're a woman alone.

☐ DO stay with the crowds in public places, rather than wandering off alone.

☐ DO stay out of unsavory places where trouble might start.

29

HOW TO PROTECT YOURSELF
ON BUSES, TRAINS, TAXIS,
SUBWAYS, AND AIRPLANES

ON A bus during night hours when passengers are scarce, sit near the driver. Don't sit all the way in back, or trapped in a seat against the side of the bus. Hidden in back, you can be threatened with a knife or other weapon by a criminal passenger and robbed without the bus driver knowing or being able to do anything about it. Then your assailant can jump off the bus quickly at the next stop and disappear in the dark.

Change your seat on the bus to a safer spot if you're concerned about the loudness or threatening behavior of others sitting near you. It's always safer to get away from the possibility of violence before it erupts; don't wait or hesitate—make your move as soon as you feel at all uneasy.

Keep in mind that your best bet, aside from sitting right near the bus driver, is to take an aisle seat near an exit door so you can leave quickly if you're concerned about anything going on in the bus. If you are being annoyed, change your seat. If you are followed to the new seat, stay on the aisle—not pinned against the window—and get up to inform the driver. He'll summon police help if necessary.

Take similar precautions on a train. Sit on the aisle rather than against a window where you can't get past your seatmate readily. Choose a seat preferably near where the conductor is located—there's no harm in asking him where the safest seat is when he punches your ticket, if it's late, there are few passengers, and you're apprehensive.

It's safer not to wait for a bus in a dark spot late at night. Seek out a well-lighted bus stop, or one where several other people are waiting, too.

Look behind you when you leave a bus, a train, or the subway. If you think someone is following you, get in the light, hail a passing car and tell the driver (but don't get in), or advise a policeman if one is available.

Don't keep your handbag, briefcase, or packages on the next seat on a bus or train where someone can grab them and run, hopping off as the vehicle stops. Keep your possessions on your lap, preferably, or on the floor between your legs with at least one foot touching them, or on the side of the seat away from the aisle (but don't overlook them when you leave the vehicle).

Keep any suitcases locked, with the key in a pocket or purse, when you're on a train or bus, and place them on a rack overhead. If you must leave your seat on a train, ask your seatmate (if you know and trust him) to keep an eye on your suitcases and other valuables, such as a coat left on the seat, until you return; you'll do the same for him or her.

Don't be careless with your suitcases at an airport or railroad station. While waiting, keep your arm over your luggage and belongings on the bench beside you, or your foot touching them if you place them on the floor. At the airport, get to the luggage return area quickly so you can spot your suitcase fast when it is available, and get it before someone else picks it up and hastens away, as happens often.

Airport thefts of suitcases and other valuables are increasing rapidly as total traffic booms. Be extra careful, since the maximum liability with most airlines is limited to a few hundred dollars' compensation per passenger for losses of luggage and other valuables for which they may be liable; look for the figure in the small print on the back of your ticket.

Don't be too trustful of the stranger who seems overeager to help a woman carry heavy suitcases or packages from a train, airline, or bus terminal. Too often the man vanishes with her possessions into the crowd leaving the building or on the sidewalk. Or he may hop into a waiting car driven by an accomplice.

Take the airline limousine or bus from the airport in preference to sharing a "group taxi" with others. The taxi, handled by a dispatcher, is generally safe—except when someone sharing the cab turns out to be a criminal and robs both you and the cab driver. There's an extra measure of safety on the airline bus with many others riding along.

Check the taxi before you get in at night. Look for identification that it's a police-approved cab, a system used in many cities. For example, in New York City taxis licensed by the police bear a shield insignia on the door on the passenger side stating: "Metered Taxicab Licensed by Police Department of the City of New York, M.T.B.O.T." On the roof you'll see a roof light with the word "Taxi" on the front and the cab's medallion number on the rear. The medallion number also appears on the hood of the cab. Drivers of such licensed cabs have been investigated, before being granted the medallions, by the New York Police Department.

Be wary of cars painted like taxicabs and referred to as "gypsy cabs." They are not permitted by law in New York City to pick up passengers while cruising, as differentiated from responding to a call from a home or other place to go to a specific destination. The driver is already breaking (or at least bending) the law when he stops to pick you up without being summoned by phone.

Look at the driver's license and photo displayed in the cab as soon as you sit down. Compare the picture with the man driving. If the license or photo is missing, or if the driver's appearance doesn't match the picture, tell the driver to stop and let you out. If you feel embarrassed, you can say, "I'm sorry, I've forgotten something," or, "I must make a phone call, I didn't realize how late it is." Pay the fee and get out—it's cheaper and safer than taking a chance of being robbed or

171

assaulted. If you have a chance to take down the taxi's plate number as it moves away, report it to the police; your identity can be guarded.

Always remain wary on subway stations and in the cars late at night. Wait for your train in a well-lighted spot, in view of the person in the change booth. Stay close to the booth until the train is pulling in, then head for the doors of the car. Don't go down to the far ends of the platform where you'll be out of sight of the attendant in the booth, and probably out of hearing range as well—especially when express trains go roaring by the station.

Don't sit in a vacant subway car. Keep going to a car where there are other passengers. The safest car is probably the one where the conductor is located. Sit as near to him as possible.

Note and remember the location of the emergency cord in the subway car. Pull the cord if you are cornered and desperate.

Start yelling or screaming to attract the attention of others if you're being threatened—in a subway, bus, taxi, on any public transportation or in any public place. Noise is an enemy of the criminal.

Don't let yourself fall asleep, if you can possibly help it, on the subway, bus, train, or any other public conveyance. Professional thieves are so adept that they can rob you of almost everything except the clothes you're wearing while you remain sound asleep—even of some clothing at times. A favorite trick is for a thief to wait until just before the bus or train or subway car doors close to grab your valuables and jump out. He gets a sizable head start before you start yelling, "Stop, thief!"

Don't let a degenerate get away with molesting your person in a crowded public vehicle, elevator, or other public place. Shouting "Take your hands off me!" in a loud voice is usually enough to send your assailant away in a hurry. If you are permissive, for fear of embarrassment, there's a good chance that he'll follow you off the vehicle to threaten you further. If you're seated and being molested in an almost empty subway or train car, change your seat at once, preferably to another car. If you are followed, start calling loudly for help. Don't use violence unless you are being attacked and must defend yourself.

Keep in mind always, especially at night when few people are around, that public washrooms are often breeding grounds for criminals and degenerates. Stay out of those places. Be wary if you must use the facilities. If you see anything suspicious before you walk in, don't go in. At the first indication of any trouble whatsoever, get out of there—don't stop to argue or fight. Keep an eye on the entrance door and get out quickly if anyone suspicious-looking comes in. If you're with someone of the same sex, have him or her come into the washroom with you; ask a companion of the opposite sex to stay within sight of the door and be ready to assist and call for help if there's any indication of commotion inside or if you're in there overlong.

Avoid taking public transportation late at night alone if there's any way you can avoid it. If you're at a social affair, try to get a lift from people you can trust. When they drop you off, ask them to wait outside your house or apartment building until you're safe inside—or see you to the door of your apartment if you're a woman alone.

PUBLIC TRANSPORTATION CHECKLIST

- [ ] DO sit near the bus driver at night if passengers are scarce.
- [ ] DO change your seat to a safer spot right away if you see trouble developing.
- [ ] DON'T wait for a bus or taxi in a dark, deserted place at night.
- [ ] DO check with the train conductor for the safest seat if it's late at night and the car is practically empty.
- [ ] DON'T leave possessions on the seat where someone can grab them and run.
- [ ] DO watch your suitcases alertly in transportation terminals.
- [ ] DO check the driver's identification in a taxi, especially at night.

- [ ] DO ask the taxi driver to wait until you enter your home late at night.
- [ ] DO stay alert in subway stations and cars late at night.
- [ ] DON'T sit in a vacant subway car; find an occupied one.
- [ ] DO check the location of the emergency cord in the subway car.
- [ ] DON'T stay alone or with just a stranger in a public washroom; beware of degenerates and report any advances.
- [ ] DON'T take public transportation alone late at night if you can help it.

30

SEVEN BASIC RULES
FOR OUTFOXING PICKPOCKETS

STAY ALERT against pickpockets where there are many people —stores, sidewalks, sports events, theaters, any public function. One thief quipped, "I don't pick pockets—I take them as they come." Don't let yours "come" easily. Observe the precautions given previously to keep your wallet in a snugly buttoned pocket inside your jacket or, second best, in a hip pocket of your trousers. These tips on how most pickpockets operate will help you guard against being a victim yourself:

1. If one or two persons (pickpockets often work in pairs or even in groups to isolate a victim) bump into you hard, check your wallet or purse and start yelling if any valuables are gone. It is a common technique for one accomplice to bump into you while the other picks your pocket or purse. Many are so adept that they can strip off a watch, ring, necklace, and other jewelry or valuables without your realizing it if you're not wary. Or one pickpocket may take your wallet and slip it to his accomplice, who leaves the scene so that the wallet won't be found on the remaining thief if he's caught.

2. Keep alert if someone stops you to ask for a light, directions to an address, or any other reason. It may be perfectly innocent, but don't let him or her get too close to you. While you're busy fumbling for matches or pointing out directions down the street, he may quickly remove your wallet or some other valuable.

3. Many pickpockets use a newspaper or article of clothing over one arm as a shield to cover the reaching hand. Quickly

175

they lift your wallet or other valuables and conceal them in the folds of the newspaper or clothing. This is a favorite procedure of pickpockets in crowded buses and subway cars, stores, sporting events and parades—wherever crowds gather.

4. The most favorable opportunities for pickpockets are during work-travel periods in the morning and evening rush hours . . . in lunch-hour crowds at midday . . . with crowds entering and leaving sports events and other mass gatherings . . . in the deep night hours when people on buses and trains and in public washrooms are dulled from fatigue or drinking . . . at crowded shopping hours in stores.

5. "Handkerchief" pickpockets generally steal from inside and outside coat pockets and handbags. One hand flourishes the handkerchief as cover for the other hand, which darts in and lifts your goods. Beware of that intrusive handkerchief when a person is next to you.

6. Women pickpockets or "bag-openers" generally operate in stores during sales, especially at bargain counters. While a shopper is busy rummaging on the counter, the pickpocket—often concealing her motions with a fur piece or bulky scarf over her arm—rummages in the woman's handbag, which may be hanging loosely from her arm or placed momentarily on the counter. She uses this same technique in a crowded elevator, especially when a woman has a shoulder bag which falls a bit behind her, or lets her handbag hang down and slightly toward her back. Your foresight and hindsight can combine to thwart the thief.

7. Protect yourself in public against theft and assault by never letting down your guard. There's no need to be nervous or fearful as long as you're alert and knowledgeable about dangers that exist and might happen to you. As Ben Franklin cautioned in two words: "Forewarned, forearmed."

CHECKLIST AGAINST PICKPOCKETS

☐ DO stay alert against pickpockets in any crowd, especially at public events and when traveling.

☐ DO check your wallet if someone bumps you, particularly in a crowd; if it is gone, start yelling "Stop, thief!"

☐ DO study and guard against the common techniques used by pickpockets, as listed.

☐ DON'T ever leave your handbag open or held loosely; keep it closed, held firmly and close to your body.

☐ DO keep your wallet in a buttoned inside jacket pocket or, second-best, in a tightly buttoned hip pocket in your trousers.

31

HOW TO VACATION-PROOF YOUR HOME

NOTIFY the police, if you own or rent a house, giving details of just how long you'll be away . . . where you'll be . . . a number where you can be reached in case of trouble . . . and the name and address if you leave your keys with a neighbor. Don't skip any information that's essential. For example, if a cleaning woman is coming in once a week or so, tell the police on which days and hours she'll be there (it would be safer not to have her come in but to give her a vacation, too). If relatives are going to use the house for a few days, give police the dates.

One homeowner failed to tell the police that his cleaning woman had a key and would be in every Monday. On her first Monday in the otherwise empty house, the woman was hard at work when she was suddenly faced by a uniformed police officer who had come in through the unlocked door. Although she was able to explain her presence, she said that the fright had robbed her of ten years of life; it robbed the vacationing family of a good houseworker, since she refused to return to the job when they came back.

The police want you to inform them when you go away. Bulletin after bulletin from police departments asks people to do so, as in this typical notice distributed in the public interest: "When leaving for extended trips, notify your local precinct. The police on patrol in your area will pay particular attention to vacant homes." In one community, for instance, police ask people who are going away to fill out a "dark house card" (even though you leave some lights on). A police officer walks around your house there at least once every eight hours, checks doors and windows, listens for unusual sounds, looks into anything that arouses suspicion. Aside from the burglary protection value of this service, it often prevents extensive damage from broken water pipes and other "natural disasters" which may occur. Not all police departments are able to provide this detailed service but one very competent small-town police chief said, "We pride ourselves on serving our people like the old-time country doctor."

Tell a neighbor or close friends in the neighborhood how long you'll be away and where you can be reached. Leave them the house keys, and tell the police you are doing so in case officers need the keys to check inside the house. If anything suspicious goes on such as movement in the house, someone hovering around the door, smoke coming from a window, sounds of running water or other noises (plumbing can break, floods can hit the area), police can enter the house without breaking down the door. If asked, good neighbors are usually glad to check the inside of your house once a week for gas leaks, appliances turned on, or any other signs of trouble. If any unexpected deliveries are made, your neighbor can collect the packages and keep them safe until your return, instead of having them left by your door to be stolen or as a telltale signal that there's nobody home.

A police council bulletin advises: "Keep on friendly terms with your neighbors. Remember, the police are not omniscient . . . someone must call in the event of trouble." Cooperation among neighbors is a "must" for utmost mutual protection. It pays to heed the advice: "If you are a neighbor to a neighbor who is good, more and more reciprocal good do you both teach and learn." Consider it another way: your own safety is at stake when your neighbor's house is in flames, or burglarized. In short, "To have a good neighbor, be a good neighbor."

It's safer not to pack the car outside on the street if you can help it. A passing burglar watches for people loading up a car for a vacation trip so that when you move out he can move in and loot your home. It's safest to load up the car inside a closed garage.

Always double-check locks on every entry door and each

window in the house and be sure the garage doors are closed and locked before you leave for a trip. Don't overlook basement doors and windows and attic windows (a favorite entry of some high-minded low-life burglars). Police groan about how often an owner conscientiously locks up the entire house—except for a basement entry that is easily opened by a thief just by turning a knob or lifting the sloping doors that cover some basement entrances. This points up the value of notifying the police that you're leaving; if the police force has enough manpower, a patrol car will probably stop at your home the next day and test the ground floor and basement doors and windows to make sure nothing has been left open.

Pause at the last door as you're leaving and go back to double-check that all gas outlets, electric appliances, and water taps have been turned off. This can save some high costs from damage and will keep anybody in the family from worrying all through vacation, "Did I turn off the oven?"

Stop all deliveries—newspapers, milk, any other items that are delivered daily or regularly. It's best to arrange this in person, by phone or by mail; a note left in a milk bottle, "Stop milk delivery for two weeks," can be spotted by thieves who look for such clues, particularly during vacation periods. Pile-ups of newspapers and milk bottles are common signals for burglars that the family is away and that the place can be entered and looted at leisure. Arrange with your neighbors to check deliveries after a day or two and to stop them if you've overlooked doing so; then you'll do the same for your neighbors when they're away.

Tell your mailman or the post office to hold your mail at the post office for you to pick up when you return. Or arrange for delivery to a cooperative neighbor if you prefer.

Leave at least one light on, preferably two, so that lights appear at night both at the front and back of the house or apartment. In the apartment, leave a light that will show at the front entry through the crack below or around many doors, or if someone eases the door open a trifle; do the same for the back entry door and room. Use a light regulator switch that turns the lights on and off rather than leaving them on day and night; different types of automatic switches have already been discussed.

Consider a burglar alarm system of some kind, ranging from inexpensive devices for a door or window to costly arrangements which signal an alarm in the house and at the nearest police station when a burglar enters. Read details on the various possibilities, elsewhere in this book.

Never leave small valuables out in the open in your house. Transfer all possible costly items to a bank vault, or perhaps to a friend's house. Out-of-sight is safest for such valuables.

Have your lawn cared for if you're going to be away more than a week or ten days. An uncut lawn, with grass growing tall and straggly, is a clear signal to the criminal that the house occupants are away for an extended time. It's a lot cheaper and more relaxing to arrange for the lawn to be cut each week while you're gone than to cope with a burglary when you return (it's healthier for the grass, too).

Arrange to have the snow removed from walks and driveways when you're away in winter. The house will look occupied, and you won't be blocked by snowdrifts when you return, nor will you be fined by your town for leaving snow on sidewalks outside your home.

It's best not to draw the shades and blinds all over the house. This, too, signals the burglar that the occupants are away and the house is closed and empty. He likes to enter such premises and loot at leisure behind drawn shades. Lock up tight, but leave an appearance of normal living going on in the house or apartment.

Avoid publicity about your travel and vacation plans. In spite of repeated warnings, too many people still advise the newspapers or local society editor that they're off to Europe or around the world or whatever. You'll be safer on your safari if it's not printed in the papers scanned by criminals alert to just such items and the opportunities they offer. You might as well take a paid ad: "Burglars, attention! The family at (address) will be away between July 1 and 15, so the house will be empty. Walk in and help yourself." Tell the editor *after* you return, and you'll even be able to supply a photo of your family sunning and smiling at the vacation resort.

Better not disconnect your phone service while you're away unless you have a special reason. A burglar who suspects the occupants of a house are away for a while may get the name from the mailbox or lawn sign, look up the phone number, and call. If the line is reported as "temporarily out of service," it's a pretty good tip that the people are away. You can arrange with the phone company to have your calls transferred to the number of a friend if you wish.

Tell the phone answering service, if you have one, *not* to inform callers how long you'll be away. Just have them say, "Mr. Brown will be in touch with you after August 15," not "Mr. Brown will be out of town until August 15."

It's safer not to have your phone bell close to the entry door where a burglar could hear it from outside. Professional criminals, hearing a phone ring many times without anyone picking it up, know that there's no one at home. It's safer to turn the phone bell down or off entirely than to leave it at "loud" if it can be heard from outside. This is especially important in apartments.

Don't leave any easily moved articles on the porch or lawn, in an unlocked garage, or anywhere outdoors. Lock them up in the house, basement, or garage. Not only criminals but even youngsters or passers-by might take such articles if it's apparent that there isn't anyone around to watch from a window and see them.

Never talk to strangers about your vacation plans. Smooth-acting crooks, female as well as male, often try to strike up conversations on a bus, in a store, wherever there is an opportunity. He (or she) will talk about their own travel or vacation plans, leading you into telling them when you'll be away: "Don't you prefer early August to July at a resort?" The potential thief then follows you home, or learns otherwise where you live, and plans to help himself to your property when you've left with those overloaded suitcases. It helps you enjoy a vacation from worry when you zip your lip, outside of telling friends and neighbors, of course. They will keep an eye on your place, and will report anything suspicious to the police.

Notify the building superintendent, if you live in an apartment house. He'll pass the word to trusted employees, and they'll all keep closer watch for anything suspicious around your apartment—unexpected noises, lurking strangers, and so on.

It helps to leave a small radio playing while you're away on vacation, as well as when you're out just for the evening. The sound fosters the impression that someone is at home. The cost in electricity is small for the comparative safety margin you gain. If you have an automatic timer, you can have the radio turned on and off according to your normal listening patterns.

You'll enjoy a vacation that's more worry-free and lighthearted if you've taken all possible precautions to safeguard your house or apartment.

VACATION-PROOFING HOME CHECKLIST

- ☐ DO tell the police the exact dates you'll be away and how you can be reached.
- ☐ DO leave information and keys with a neighbor (or building superintendent) for emergency use in case of fire or break-in.
- ☐ DO double-check locks on all entries, doors, windows, when leaving.
- ☐ DO stop all deliveries—newspapers, mail, any others.
- ☐ DO leave lights on with an automatic timing device.
- ☐ DO have your lawn cared for as usual, or arrange snow removal.
- ☐ DON'T draw all shades and blinds; leave the home looking occupied.
- ☐ DON'T tell strangers about your vacation plans, address, and so on.

32

HOW TO HAVE A SAFE VACATION

DO NOT DISTURB—that little sign on your hotel or motel door will give a thief a laugh but won't give you much protection. "He that travels much knows much"—the experienced traveler learns that observing simple, basic precautions as you go can add much to your peace of mind without detracting a bit from your pleasure. When you're careless and your possessions are stolen or you or your family are assaulted by criminals—that's when the joys of travel diminish or vanish completely. You needn't be overly apprehensive as you travel, thus spoiling some of your enjoyment; just take the simple, fundamental precautions and stay alert rather than fearful. Prevention is better than cure.

Before you go traveling, reread the pertinent recommendations in other chapters which apply here . . . protecting your home while away . . . protecting your youngsters . . . protection on the street . . . safeguards for driving . . . protection on public transportation and in public buildings, and so on. For example, the recommended safeguards against pickpockets apply perhaps even more to foreign countries; pickpockets are more numerous and bolder in many areas than at home. Some tips are necessarily repeated, but you'll profit by checking through other categories, too, before you travel in this country or abroad.

Never carry a lot of cash, neither domestic nor foreign currency. If you insist on carrying a mass of bills, keep a minimum number in your wallet so you don't show a load of money when you pay a bill. Keep the rest of your cash in different pockets or in a locked suitcase, but never concentrated in one batch.

Use travelers checks or credit cards, as you prefer, rather

than cash. Keep an up-to-the-minute extra list of your check numbers, denominations, and so on, noting the details each time you give a check. Do the same with credit cards. Keep the extra list somewhere other than with the checks themselves—in another pocket, purse, suitcase, with your wife or husband, or in the hotel room. The list facilitates recovering your money quickly if the checks are lost or stolen; it can make the difference between compensation and total loss. Read the fine print on instructions with travelers checks and credit cards and follow the directions precisely, or you may incur serious losses. Ask advice at the bank, too, or wherever you get your travelers checks.

Consider wearing a money belt if you must carry a lot of cash or small valuables such as jewelry. For the ladies, small garter-wallets are available for carrying extra large bills, but the practicability of those depends on whether the length of the skirt conceals or reveals the hiding place.

Lock your suitcases out of sight in the car; keep them locked on public transportation, in hotel rooms, or wherever you leave them. If the locks on your luggage are flimsy, you can get extra suitcase locks for an extra measure of protection. If your hotel or motel room has a closet with a lock, put the locked suitcases in the closet when you go out, then lock the closet and take the key with you.

Don't take valuables with you if you can help it. Flashing costly jewelry as you travel marks you as a likely victim. Not only do you stand to lose your valuables but you also invite possible violent attack.

Deposit valuables, if you must take them along, with the hotel or motel manager. They are safer locked up there than carried on your person or left in your room. If you deposit jewelry that you want to wear to a gala dinner or affair, it's worth the extra trouble to redeem it from the hotel safe as needed, then redeposit it when you return from the evening out. Don't be lazy about this if you return to your hotel late, since a thief who has noted the jewelry on you during the evening might take a chance of entering your room and stealing it while you're asleep.

Consider carrying an extra lock specially made to wedge

easily into a hotel or motel door while you're inside. Even a chair tilted up between the floor and the door handle provides extra protection, since the noise of someone trying to push the door in after picking the regular lock tends to drive a thief away. You might consider placing obstacles in the path of an intruder entering your dark room, a chair or suitcase that he would stumble against noisily. Realize that innumerable people who occupied the room previously had an opportunity to duplicate the key for later illegal use.

Take along a small alarm device; different types are available for only a few dollars each. They attach to the room door from the inside and make a loud ring or buzz if the door is pushed open. You can also keep a small, lightweight alarm at your bedside; you ring the device by pushing a button, activating a lever, or pulling a string—the noise drives an intruder away as it summons help. Most such items operate on ordinary flashlight batteries.

You can improvise a "burglar alarm" by hanging a few empty metal hangers over the doorknob inside, or anything that would rattle noisily when the door is opened. You might prop up a book or two against the door, a couple of glasses piled atop each other, or any heavy object that will fall over and make a noise if the lock is picked and the door is opened.

Always see your youngsters safely back and locked into the room if you are returning from dinner and are on your way to a night on the town. Don't just drop the kids at the entrance to the hotel or motel, as plenty can happen between there and the room door.

Teach your children to double-lock the room door when alone, and not open it to anyone but you—not to a voice saying, "I'm the maid" or "hotel manager" or anyone else. Instruct them to pick up the phone and tell the room clerk if they're frightened or concerned about anything at all. Their safety is worth more than your possible embarrassment about false alarms. Similar precautions apply to you—not to open the door to strangers and to make sure that the voice announcing "bellboy" really belongs to him.

If you have a roommate, take this precaution when there's an unexpected knock at the door: you go to the door to inquire who is there while your roommate goes to the phone, ready to make a quick call for help if needed.

Double-lock the door (most rooms now have an inside bolt of some kind as well as the regular door lock) every time you're in the room, and when you go to sleep. If there's a place for the key in the lock inside the room, leave the key there after you lock the door.

Write down the local police number on a slip of paper by the telephone as soon as you get into your hotel or motel room. Also, carry a slip of paper with local emergency numbers. If you want the police in a hurry, you don't want to go fumbling through phone books for the number when quick action is needed. Of course, the operator can always get the police for you, but if you're in a foreign country you may have difficulty making her understand (hasn't it happened with you?). It's a good idea to learn the word for "police" in the language of each country you enter.

Check the address and phone number of the official U.S. representative in the city, or the nearest one available. In case of trouble, you can usually get help there—and at least you'll be understood. Certainly taking simple precautions beforehand will aid in keeping you out of trouble.

It's risky to go into dangerous places such as a red light area or a dingy nightclub that you wouldn't risk in your own town— just because it's in a strange city or a foreign country and you don't know the real dangers. Criminals thrive on trusting or careless tourists and are eager to steal from anyone regardless of nationality. Think twice before you enter a dive. Well-heeled men and women who have been assaulted and robbed in a nightclub in a far-off city often admit, "I wouldn't be caught dead in a sewer like that one in my home town."

Be wary of wandering down "that cute little dark alley" in a foreign country at night, or even by day if it has a deserted look, particularly if you're alone, or one of a pair of unaccompanied women. Abroad, too, there's safety in numbers, or in being accompanied by a trustworthy guide, not a pickup guide who may purposely guide you into danger. Rates of crime and violence are rising all over the world, so don't proceed on the theory that any place is safer than your home town or a big city in the U.S., or that Americans are left unmolested in foreign places. The opposite may be true; "the rich American" may be a prime target for thievery and attack.

Recheck the recommendations in this book about riots in this country, and follow the same protection rules abroad. Riots are a world-wide disease, more prevalent in some other countries than in the United States. Remember: *go away* from there—*stay away* from there—at any slightest sign of a crowd commotion that may erupt in violence.

It's unsafe to buy "bargains" from strangers on the street, or those you encounter in hotel lobbies, bars, other public places. The jewels, wristwatches, articles of clothing, souvenirs usually turn out to be just about worthless when bought in shady encounters. You're much safer dealing with legitimate merchants.

Be careful about trusting strangers when traveling—in a foreign country or anywhere else. Be friendly, of course—meeting people in their home environment is one of the pleasures of traveling. But there's a difference between being friendly and going all out in trustfulness. Don't wander off into a lonely or dark place with a stranger. Don't give the number of your room which an accomplice could be looting while you chat with his friend at a bar. Observe a little more than "reasonable caution."

Take special care to keep valuables safe when you find yourself sharing a room with strangers, as may happen on a cruise or at a resort. Your roommates are probably as trustworthy as you are, but you'll be safer, and it's fairer to them, if you're not careless in leaving money and valuables out in the open. If you feel apprehensive about a roommate, for any reason, try to have your accommodations changed before trouble happens.

It may be dangerous to join a "friendly little game of cards" with strangers on a cruise or other vacation gathering if the stakes are higher than you can afford. Well-dressed, well-spoken card sharks (cheats) who look like nice ordinary people prey on friendly travelers who are seeking fun and companionship. Don't be lured into betting more than you should. If the stakes are too high and you're losing too much, don't hesitate to drop out for fear of being a poor sport. There's no sportsmanship on the part of professional crooks who cheat others out of their money. A common pattern is to lead the sucker on by feeding him winning cards, then suddenly to clean him out in a few high-stake manipulated rounds.

If you see evidence of out-and-out cheating in such a game, don't start a quarrel. Leave the game quickly and quietly and report at once to someone in authority with the ship, hotel, resort, wherever you may be. Let the authorities take over to gain justice and compensation for you.

Never pick up hitchhikers on strange roads whether driving here or abroad. Many drivers have suffered attacks from hitchhikers in any language. Don't let down on any of the safe-driving precautions listed in preceding pages; in fact, you should be more careful on unfamiliar highways and byways. Never forget the warning: "Always drive as though your life depended on it." It does.

Keep an extra list of the serial and model numbers of your cameras, binoculars, or other costly equipment. Keep such items locked in a suitcase or motel room and then in a locked closet, if possible, in your hotel or motel room. Don't leave those items or any valuables (certainly not money!) scattered around on tables or bureau tops where the cleaning woman, bellboy, or anyone else will be tempted to take them away. Out-of-sight is out-of-temptation when you're traveling or on a vacation.

Don't attempt to smuggle "a little something" through customs to try to avoid duty or "just for the fun of it." At worst you can get into serious trouble; at best you'll encounter aggravating inconvenience and delay. Customs officers know all the tricks, including false bottoms in suitcases, just dropping an extra wristwatch into your jacket pocket. With skilled professional smugglers being caught every week, you have little chance as an amateur to get by.

For example, a professional crossing the southern border in his car thought his scheme was foolproof. He took a dirty, grease-marked block of wood he'd used under a car wheel, hollowed out a pocket inside for $100,000 worth of drugs, then plugged the opening and disguised it so that the joining was "invisible." He tossed the block of wood carelessly into the trunk of his car, mixed with the auto tools. Customs officials first passed it by, then double-checked it and arrested the man on a charge of smuggling. Your own naive little tricks would have little chance of succeeding.

Realize, too, that the person who sells you the merchandise you intend to conceal may report you; he'd get not only his profit from the sale but also a percentage of the fee when the property is confiscated. It's not uncommon for customs officials to receive such advance information and to be on the lookout for the would-be smuggler.

Never get careless with your credit cards just because they're not "cash" in themselves. The safest place for a man to carry such items is in his inside jacket pocket, not in a side or trousers pocket. It is estimated that about 200 million credit cards are in circulation in the U.S. There are about 1½ million lost annually, of which about 300,000 are stolen. Dollar losses are estimated to run between $50 million and $100 million a year. Credit card holders are bearing a considerable part of the losses. If your card is lost or stolen and someone runs up big expenses with it, you can be in trouble; with some cards you will be liable for the whole amount or part of it.

Liability differs with different cards, so check the rules carefully, especially before you go traveling, in order to know exactly what you're responsible for and how to report loss or theft. If you've lost the rules that go with your credit card, call the company and find out *now*. You certainly don't want to have to cut a trip or vacation short because of loss of a credit card that you're counting on to cover much of your cost.

You should not worry excessively about thievery spoiling your vacation or any trip. Taking precautions helps to give you the confidence that things will go right. The worst blow is when things are stolen and your vacation ruined because of your own carelessness or ignorance. Your vacation is saved, rather, by following the basic precautions such as distributing your money about your person in different pockets and perhaps in a money belt—then if one pocket is picked, you still have enough else-where to keep going. You'll find that you're much better off and see much more in total when you're *before-sighted*. Bon voyage!

SAFE-VACATION CHECKLIST

☐ DO check all other chapters on safeguarding yourself and possessions indoors and outdoors, everything that applies also to vacationing.

☐ DON'T carry a lot of cash, jewelry, other valuables; use travelers checks or credit cards (of course, report immediately if you lose them).

☐ DO keep your luggage locked always.

☐ DO deposit any valuables with the manager of the hotel or motel.

☐ DO carry and use small lock and alarm devices.

☐ DO instruct your children to double-lock the doors and keep people out of the place when left alone.

☐ DON'T venture into red light areas and dangerous or lonely places where you wouldn't go at home.

☐ DON'T buy "bargains" from strangers, or reveal intimate details to them.

☐ DO keep an extra list of numbers of cameras, binoculars, other costly equipment.

33

HOW TO KEEP FROM BEING CHEATED

THE FIRST word in protection against frauds is "DON'T." If you're at all suspicious about signing a "contract" with a doorbell-pushing salesman, or for a suspect bargain at a store, installment purchase, insurance scheme, anything at all—*don't*. If you're uneasy or uncomfortable or even slightly worried about a deal or a purchase, chances are that there's something wrong with it and that you may be defrauded. When the chance to get a "once-in-a-lifetime buy" tempts and yet concerns you, remember that you managed well before the "fantastic opportunity" came along. Opportunity knocks many more times than once. The poor man's philosopher, Elbert Hubbard, wrote: "The actual fact is that in this day Opportunity not only knocks at your door but is playing an anvil chorus on every man's door, and then lays for the owner around the corner with a club."

Never give a confidence man either your confidence or your cash. One warning against a fraudulent offer, which applies 99 times out of 100, is that when it seems too good to be true, it probably isn't true, or worthwhile, no matter how trustworthy it appears on the surface. Always check and recheck before you buy. The legitimate offer welcomes investigation; the fraudulent seller usually vanishes when you say you want a few days to check thoroughly.

As just one example, hundreds of residents of a Canadian city were cheated out of more than a million dollars in a short period of time. A well-organized group of confidence men offered high-paying bonds connected with what seemed to be a worthy cause. The bonds presumably were to help a popular church center right in the city. The certificates looked very official, imprinted with the names of the center's manager, a highly respected citizen, and others.

Buyers were assured that there was absolutely no risk, because the bonds could be cashed in at the center at any time if a refund was wanted. Only after a few buyers tried to cash in their bonds did they learn that the center had no knowledge of the proposition and that the certificates were as worthless as scrap paper. The significant lesson for you is that not one purchaser had bothered to call the center to verify the offer before investing his money. A phone call or a brief visit to investigate would have exposed the fraud right at the start. It seems that Montaigne was right when he wrote despairingly, "We seek and offer ourselves to be gulled."

Investigate every questionable charity before you make a contribution. Instead of just handing out your money in response to an appealing story, say that you want to look into the matter first. Get the address of the main office, and ask others about the charity before you give. Don't just call a phone number given to you by the solicitor; it could be a set-up with the person at the other end primed to give you a glowing report about a complete fake. It is estimated that fake charities collect about $100 million annually from well-meaning but careless contributors who thus cheat not only themselves but the worthy causes to whom they would otherwise have given the money. As with any kind of offer, the worthwhile charity welcomes your investigation.

Thoroughly destroy credit cards that may be sent to you through the mail as an offering for you to sign up for the service —if it's one you don't want. Also get rid of credit cards that have expired, or that you don't use any more. Tear or cut up the cards into small pieces; otherwise problems may arise from some unauthorized person using a credit card bearing your name.

Don't ever use merchandise you never ordered. In this common fraud, items arrive by mail or other delivery, along with an invoice. You open up the package to see what it's all about, then realize that it arrived unsolicited. Your first safeguard: *don't*

193

use the item. You never have to pay for such merchandise if you don't use it. The shipper has the responsibility to come and take it back. The recommended action is to rewrap the item, write across the front of the package, "This merchandise not ordered—return to sender," and drop it into the mailbox; no postage is required from you, the shipper pays the return costs.

If a package arrives C.O.D. and you never ordered it, refuse to accept it; it will be returned to the sender at his expense. Most people pay the C.O.D. charge if it's $10 or less rather than argue with the delivery man, who leaves immediately. When you open the package you may find a paper-wrapped brick, or something else just as worthless. Once you've paid the C.O.D. charge, you'll probably never get your money back. If it arrived through the mail, ask your local postmaster for assistance. The mail-order gyp either refunds your money in order to be able to continue using the mails or, too often, goes out of business and you're stuck.

There are many honest and worthy mail-order businesses which serve the public well. They welcome legitimate complaints and fulfill their obligations. If you feel cheated over something you've ordered by mail and are refused refund or other compensation, advise the seller that you'll seek justice through the U.S. Post Office, and then do so if necessary. The Post Office Department can cut off mailing privileges from a firm that cheats via the mails, and the gyps know and fear this.

Beware of hasty installment purchases from a salesman at your door, or from a retail store, by mail, or from any other source. Make sure to read the printed order (which is a contract) in full detail, before you sign. Tell the seller that you want to take along the blank form for a day or so, in order to check the deal thoroughly, and to talk it over with your husband or wife or a knowledgeable friend.

Note particularly such facts as exactly how much the installment payments will amount to over the entire term of the deal; sometimes people are fooled by small early installments which then become bigger and bigger until they're paying astonishingly large sums.

Check the period of time in which you can return the merchandise without obligation if not satisfied. If the time period is a week, for instance, be sure to send written notice that you wish to return the item, postmarked within seven days of order date. Otherwise you may be stuck for it, involving much harassment and perhaps litigation if you don't pay.

Find out whether the sales order you sign can be sold to a finance company for collection. Such businesses, which are primarily collection agencies, may apply escalating penalties when payments aren't made exactly when due. You can find yourself obligated for much more than you intended to pay for an encyclopedia set, a television set, or whatever it may be.

Beware of gyp retail stores that offer what seem to be miraculous bargains for purchase on the installment plan, but make peculiar demands such as that you must make a cash payment even before examining the merchandise available (this is true of some stores which prey on residents of ghetto areas particularly).

In spite of improvements in protective legislation, many frauds in the installment areas are being perpetrated by brash operators. Don't let them get away with bilking you—fight back. If cheated, get in touch with your local Consumer Protective Bureau; many exist under different names in sizable communities. Or check with your State Attorney General's office or local District Attorney.

Don't hesitate to ask for information and possible help from your local Chamber of Commerce, administration offices, and such organizations as the Better Business Bureau. If they can't intercede directly for you in the particular instance, they usually know where you should go for help. While the Better Business Bureau is often of specific assistance in helping you to get your money back on a fraudulent sale and in checking evil business practices, unfortunately it has no real enforcement power. However, the Better Business Bureau can tell you where to seek effective assistance. It can also advise you, if you ask before buying, whether a specific firm has an unsavory record, and will add to its records any trouble you may report.

Never borrow money except from the most reputable sources, and then check interest rates carefully so that you're not cheated. See that payments for the loan remain the same throughout, or at least are not small at first . . . then ballooning to impossible amounts.

Don't be fooled into thinking that an annual rate of $7.50 per $100 on a personal loan means the same as 7½ per cent interest on a home mortgage. The 7½ per cent you pay on a home mortgage is the actual interest you pay on the *balance* of the money you owe, so the interest proportion of payments decreases along with the diminished total amount you owe. However, the $7.50 per $100 on a personal loan is figured on the original total amount of the loan, even as you pay off, and comes to an annual interest rate of almost 15 per cent. There's no fraud involved; it's just mathematical fact, but too often one of the obscure facts of loans in your life.

Never borrow from questionable lenders at high interest, no matter how desperate you are. You may fall into the hands of loan sharks whom you must repay on their terms or else possibly be crippled or killed—and certainly nothing is worth risking that.

Recent laws help protect you from exorbitant interest rates by recognized loan companies, but the criminal lender is operating outside the law right from the start. You might borrow $500, keep up with the weekly payments until you pay back $400 of the original loan plus interest of 25 per cent or more. If you miss a payment then, you find that as a penalty your remaining obligations are doubled, so that you finally pay back $1,000 or more for the original $500 you borrowed. Or else you miss payments, penalties pile up, and you never seem to be able to catch up but, under meaningful threats, you keep paying. Don't ever put yourself in that awful situation, risking life and limb.

You can't possibly underestimate the dangers and horrors that may come from dealing with loan sharks. In spite of increasing legal safeguards, loan-sharking crimes are usually withheld from the police, unlike other types of crimes. The reason is that loan-sharking, in contrast with a burglary or other common criminal attack, results from agreement between the borrower and lender, generally two willing adults. One party doesn't force the original agreement on the other; on the contrary, the borrower often begs for it. As a result, when the borrower gets into difficulties, he hesitates to go to the police or other law enforcement agencies, because he entered the mess willingly, even eagerly.

The horrifying fact is that, with penalties for late payment, interest rates when dealing with loan sharks run up to 700 per cent. It is estimated that the Mafia gets at least $30,000 a year back on every $10,000 it lends, and the spread is expanding. Strong-arm tactics are the usual course if the lender doesn't pay off promptly. In a common instance, a man finally reported to the district attorney's office that he was taken out in a boat, stripped of his clothing, and threatened with being thrown overboard to man-eating sharks unless he paid the loan sharks.

Even worse than a beating perhaps, the delinquent borrower may be coerced into helping the loan sharks in their other illegal activities. For example, if he is in the meat business, he may be forced to buy and then sell to his customers loads of stolen or tainted meat. If he is in the trucking business, he may become an inside man for the racketeers, keeping them informed in advance of valuable shipments for easy hijacking. People dealing with loan sharks have lost not only their lives, but their souls; many find that the loan sharks have become permanent unwanted partners in their businesses. It's far better to face the music at the start, no matter how fearsome the problems, than to become involved with the loan sharks who operate outside the law.

Keep alert to truth-in-lending laws, which allow the buyer to back out of certain legal transactions in three days (sometimes more, depending on the state law), avoiding all obligation and cost. As one example, this applies when you have put up your house as security for credit. Various states have additional safeguards in their laws. In every case, your speedy action is required. If you regret making a deal the same day, or a day or two later, act *immediately* before your legal cancellation rights run out. Ask a lawyer, local legal aid groups, or your local government authorities. But don't delay, or you lose out on protecting yourself and your home and family.

Never take the word "guaranteed" for granted. If the details of the guarantee are not clear, then ask for an explanation before you make a purchase. Are you guaranteed full money refund if not satisfied 100 per cent? How long does that refund privilege last? An offer that "guarantees your satisfaction" but doesn't spell out what happens if you're not satisfied is no guarantee at all. Remember, too, that a guarantee by a company or an individual that hasn't the resources or ability to fulfill it isn't worth the paper it's written on.

Beware of insurance frauds often practiced by fly-by-night operators. Such gyp companies may claim or indicate that they are backed or underwritten by government agencies, or have government approval. They may provide policies for high-risk cases that well-known insurance companies turn down. They may quote extremely low premiums, comparatively. But if an insurer can't meet your claims in case of damage or loss, then every penny you are paying in premiums is, in effect, stolen from you. In such cases you're paying not for protection but for a worthless sheet of paper grandly printed up as a policy, possibly embellished with "seals of approval" and impossible "guarantees." The swindlers will promise anything, because they know that they won't be around if called on to make good.

Companies that write policies for people who have been turned down as too high a risk often amass a good deal of money from premium collections, then go bankrupt or dissolve into nothing. The U.S. Post Office Department investigated one case of a bankrupt company that left about 5,000 holders of auto insurance policies holding the bag for some $1 million in unpaid claims, after paying their premiums regularly. This is far from being an isolated instance.

The safest course usually is to get your insurance from one of the major or known companies. There are some legitimate mail-order insurance companies that offer lower rates, may take higher risks, and do back up their policies. Before you sign, check with your state insurance department, or state commissioner of insurance, to find out whether the company and policy you are considering is legitimate and dependable. Be especially suspicious if rates are much lower than those offered by the major companies.

Be cautious of any notice in the mail or by a caller at your door advising that you are a "contest winner," when you're not even aware of having entered any contest. In the fraudulent "contests," you have to purchase something else, perhaps an expensive service contract, or pay "a fraction of the cost" because you've gained special privileges as a contest winner. Invariably the end result is that you're gypped by paying out money for shoddy or overpriced merchandise. A typical case is that of "winning" a tract of land which involves overpayment in building a home on the land. When you sign a paper signifying yourself as the owner of the land, you may find that the small print obligates you to make payments for "upkeep" or "improvement," or for other reasons.

Beware of the "test-marketing" racket and its variations. Basically you are told that you are able to get something at "small token cost" because you've been selected to test-market the item and then report your results. Either the item never arrives, or it's not worth nearly what you pay for it. If you investigated, you'd undoubtedly find that anyone who would pay the fee asked would be acceptable as a "test-marketer."

Choose reputable local firms for home repairs and property improvements. There are many operators who offer tempting "bargains" in home improvement of one kind or another, with easy payment plans which must be read thoroughly beforehand, including every word of fine print. Otherwise you may find you've signed the equivalent of a second or third mortgage, which you must pay off on time or lose your home by confiscation.

There are itinerant termite inspectors who carry some termites with them to prove that you need a costly termite control job right there and then. Purveyors of siding, roofing, or other materials tell you they're overstocked and will give you a bargain —in what turns out to be inferior merchandise and workmanship. Whenever you're offered something for nothing, you usually wind up with less than nothing. For any kind of major repairs, get written estimates from local outfits, then go ahead with a firm proved responsible in your area.

Learn the plain unvarnished facts, and play safe accordingly. For instance, the Better Business Bureau of Westchester County in New York State reports that repair gyps cheat homeowners in that one suburban area out of more than a million dollars each year. Hundreds of men and women representing themselves as handymen, contractors, roof repair companies, landscapers, driveway repair specialists, and others ring doorbells after driving up in a truck or car. They offer "super special" bargain prices if permitted to do the job right now "as long as I'm in the neighborhood working for other satisfied customers."

The head of one local Better Business Bureau advises: "Make it a practice to deal with reputable local firms that stand behind their work. If someone comes to your home offering to make repairs or do work, tell him that you want to check first with the Better Business Bureau (listed in the telephone directory)—usually the phony caller will be gone before you hang up the phone."

Be suspicious of "home freezer" plans that promise food delivered to your home at such low prices that you soon will make up the cost of the freezer. In many cases, deliveries cease as soon as the freezer is paid for. In another version of this freezer offer, the meats and other items are of inferior quality. The freezer may also be of cheap construction, involving costly breakdowns and bitter dissatisfaction.

Watch out for "bait" advertising that operates in many fields, especially in gyp stores. An ad offers an armchair for the "incredibly low price of $29.95 for this quality." The fact is that the price is so incredibly low that you can't even find the chair in the store. However, the ad brings you in, and it's then up to the high-powered salesmen to talk you into buying a chair for $49.95 or more. In an instance where a customer threatened to report to the Attorney General's office at once, he finally walked out with the chair at a $29.95 purchase price—and the salesman was fired for not being able to make the sale at the higher price.

Sometimes stores make honest mistakes in advertising such as pricing an item too low through someone's error. It is where a pattern develops of repeatedly printing a low price as "bait," then refusing to sell that item to a customer, that the authorities take action against the store.

Avoid all "astounding bargain" lures such as offers for an auto repair of a particular type at half the going rate. Gyp shops often make this kind of offer in order to get your car into the shop and take it apart. Then they tell you that, lucky for your safety, they found this or that part, or others, faulty to a dangerous degree; these they replace at high cost to you. Your safest course is to patronize a local automotive repair shop that wants to get and keep your repair work year after year.

The same caution applies to itinerant workmen who ring your doorbell and offer a "free inspection" of your stove, refrigerator, vacuum cleaner, or other appliances. A swindler will find something wrong, or will break a part, resulting in a costly repair.

CHECKLIST AGAINST BEING CHEATED

☐ DON'T sign a contract or buy an "unbelievable" bargain before thorough investigation; resist that buying urge or impulse.

☐ DO examine every questionable "charity" before contributing.

☐ DO destroy credit cards offered in the mail if you don't want them.

☐ DON'T ever use merchandise you haven't ordered; don't pay for it.

☐ DON'T enter into high-pressure installment purchases.

☐ DON'T borrow money except from the most reputable sources, and even then check interest rates over the entire loan period exactly.

☐ DO check how long you have to cancel a deal or return a purchase, and observe the time period carefully.

☐ DON'T take a "guarantee" for granted—learn the exact terms.

☐ DO beware of insurance frauds, especially high-risk policies.

☐ DO deal with reputable local firms, not with itinerants.

☐ DO be very careful about buying a "home freezer" plan.

☐ DON'T be fooled by "bait" advertising offering bargains you then can't find in the store.

34

YOUR SAFEGUARDS AGAINST FRAUDULENT OFFERS

DON'T FALL for phony funeral plans requiring payment in advance. There are endless fraudulent variations in this racket. You pay a sum that you are led to believe covers "everything." Then it turns out that a costly casket or certain required services aren't included in the price you paid. The plot of land that you sign for may turn out to be quite inaccessible or unusable for the purpose. In many cases, between the time a person invests in a funeral plan and his death years later, the company that sold the plan and collected the money has gone out of business or simply evaporated. The family is left holding the bag.

Carefully preinvestigate schools that guarantee to provide you with a job after you graduate from the course, either in classrooms or by correspondence. Few institutions can do this, since they cannot tell in advance how many students will be employable in the skills they are seeking in the courses. Employers hire workers based on their proved abilities, not just because they completed a certain course. In the face of such guarantees, make the school authorities prove their promise before you pay, or arrange to pay them *after* they provide a satisfactory job. It usually turns out that the phony school merely provides the names of employers where you can apply, after the course is completed and you've paid your fees. In many cases the prospective employers never heard of the school and have no job openings. Once you learn a skill well at a legitimate school and can perform it well, your chances are good of getting a job without outside help when openings are available.

Be very careful about franchise offers. Look into the situation thoroughly and become firmly convinced that the proposition is right for you. There's a great temptation to get out of an unsatisfying job and invest your savings in a business that practically guarantees that "you can be your own boss and earn $250 and more a week. . . ." Whether it's a food business of some kind, a dance or other school, a motel, or an operation in any field, don't jump in and invest your money without taking the time *beforehand* to find out if the promises are true. It's worthwhile to do a little traveling around to talk with a half dozen or more operators of such franchises in other cities, finding the locations and making inquiries yourself rather than going to places the salesman specifies.

Government investigators are constantly warning against fraudulent offers of dealerships and franchises. In one instance, a company advertised that an investment in radio and television tube testing devices which would be placed in hardware, drug, and variety stores would quickly bring in a net income of $100 to $500 per month for an investment of under $4,000. Investigation by the Federal Trade Commission showed that few of the distributors earned even close to $100 monthly the first year. In another instance, a chain of hamburger-pizza drive-in restaurants with a trade name and trademarked products as part of the deal promised that an investment of under $10,000 would bring in a net income of about $30,000 a year. Looking into the actual experiences of franchisers who had gone for the proposition showed that *all* the promises made were enormously exaggerated, and investors suffered severe losses.

There are many legitimate franchise operations which produce excellent profits for the investor, but there are also gyps who grab a person's lifetime savings and then slam the door on him. Take your time, investigate thoroughly, refuse to be rushed.

It's dangerous to put your money down on what seems like a terrific money-making scheme where you pay comparatively little to get in on the ground floor and are supposed to pay the rest over a long period of time. An example is the gypster's land development scheme. Too often the investors find that the salesman was out to collect only the first payment, since the land, or whatever is offered, isn't worth even half that sum. Insist on seeing what you're getting before you buy, then read the fine print on the bill of sale before you sign and pay. Again, don't be rushed. Talk over the proposition ahead of time with family, friends, and an officer at your bank (frequently the bank will look into the matter for you as a service). Be suspicious when you're offered any terrific buy at "pennies down—years to pay."

Don't be frightened out of your money by collection agencies with official-sounding names who try to make you pay for something you were sold under false pretenses or that has proved unusable or unsatisfactory. In one case, complaints from a number of people caused the Federal Trade Commission to stop a company called the Intrastate Credit Control Systems from using a letterhead printed "State Bureau of Credit Control." Their forms stated, "We MUST hear from you within ten days or this account will be turned over to State Bureau of Credit Control." Some forms were signed by an individual's name with the title "State Collection Supervisor," and included imposing comments such as "referred to file of County Collection Supervisor." When people being dunned complained to state authorities, they were told that the "State Bureau of Credit Control" had no official connection whatsoever.

Never take it lying down if you've been cheated and are being pressured. Don't be fooled by demands from the "U.S. Collection Bureau" or other such official-appearing names. As advised previously, ask for help from your local District Attorney, State Attorney General, or Bureau of Consumer Fraud (or Consumer Affairs, or whatever such an agency is titled in your area; your local city, town, or village authorities can tell you).

Telephone solicitations are risky. Unless the telephone caller can identify himself or his organization to your satisfaction, the safest course is to say, "We have a rule against telephone solicitations"—then hang up. If you're interested in a telephone offer, be sure to check it, not hastily but over a period of time. In looking into the matter, don't call the number given to you on the phone, but look the company up in the phone book and call the number listed. If there's no listing, drop the whole matter. Visit the address of the company to make sure that this thriving big business isn't in a barren, little, temporarily rented office.

Take heed of this actual case: a telephone solicitor interested a lady in a get-rich-quick scheme involving investment "right away." He suggested that she check "Mr. Henderson" at her local bank, and gave her the number. She phoned that number, "Mr. Henderson" answered and said that the offer was a great one, perfectly legitimate, that he had invested heavily in it himself. A few minutes later the telephone caller rang her doorbell, left with her sizable check, then made a beeline for the nearest bank and cashed it. A week later, the lady became concerned about not hearing further. Looking up the bank in the phone book, she noted that the number was different. When she called the bank, she was told that there was no "Mr. Henderson" working there. The money she had paid out was gone forever.

It's best to turn down get-rich-quick schemes flatly. It is astonishing how often seemingly intelligent individuals walk into a police station and tell how they have been gypped by being incredibly trusting and overeager. There are hundreds of variations of money-switching tricks where the con man takes money, puts it in a bag or package, returns the package over some double-your-money pretext, followed perhaps by an argument. The swindler then leaves; the sucker opens the package to remove the money he had put in and finds that the bills have been switched for bill-size pieces of scrap paper. Though you may not believe how many people are so stupid as to be hooked, such schemes have been worked so often that the police have names for them, such as the "handkerchief switch" or "Spanish handkerchief switch" (often used to cheat Spanish-speaking persons).

Don't you or your family become victims of a smooth-talking, well-dressed stranger, or an attractive weeping woman, or even a broken-down old man or woman—people who work confidence games come in all sizes and guises. "Confidence men," or "con men" (including women), earned the name because their first goal is to gain the victim's confidence in their honesty. From there on, the con man just cashes in on the confidence he has built and leads the victim to the slaughter.

Never buy from a stranger on the street. People are cheated every day by strangers who approach and lure them into buying everything from mink skins to miniature cameras and miniskirts at "a fraction of the cost." An exquisite watch is shown; it is purchased; then the victim finds that a switch has been made without his knowledge and that his watch has no works. "Genuine mink skins" turn out to be a cheap imitation. Again, when greed takes control, the buyer's brains lose control.

Keep remembering that the hand is quicker than the eye when it's a swindler's hand. A case in point: a smooth talker offered a diamond ring "worth over $500" to an acquaintance he'd met in a hotel lobby. He asked only $200 for the ring because he said he needed cash desperately. He gave the prospective purchaser the diamond ring and said he'd wait in the lobby while the buyer-to-be walked out to the nearest jeweler and had the diamond appraised. A legitimate jeweler nearby said that the diamond was worth over $1,000. The sucker hurried back eagerly to pay the $200, and the seller took the ring with an amusing gesture to "kiss it goodbye." The buyer gave the "$1,000 diamond ring" to his wife, who said she was sure it was glass. They both went back to the same reputable jeweler, who said that this "diamond" *was* glass, not the one he saw the first time. In "kissing the ring goodbye," the swindler had switched the genuine diamond ring for the worthless one, and the victim had kissed his $200 goodbye.

Never pay fees in advance except to legitimate businesses and establishments, and on the premises. An example of the advance-fee swindle is the real estate cheat who rings your doorbell or phones and says that he has a prospect who passed your house, loved it, and will buy it right away at a price so high that you find yourself willing to sell—even though you might not have thought much about selling up to that time. Or, you might have advertised the house for sale.

The operator says he'll need your check for a specific

amount, usually 10 per cent of the alleged purchase offer, in order to bring the buyer "next weekend" to close the deal. If you hold back giving the check, the swindler shows you a form; he and you sign it, and he convinces you that he'll hold the check, not cashing it unless the deal goes through as promised. Of course he cashes the check at once and leaves the area. Or, if he remains, you find that the fine print on the form states clearly that the fee is given only for *trying* to sell the house for you— and you're probably stuck, since he has a signed paper, and now it's his word against yours. (Contact your local District Attorney anyhow.)

A legitimate real estate agent doesn't demand such fees in advance. Nor does he ask you to sign forms until the sale has been made. You're safer dealing with established real estate brokers, with offices long in the area. If you're doubtful about a real estate salesman, check him through the local Chamber of Commerce or Real Estate Board.

Avoid advance fees or cash deposits on any such offers except by legitimate establishments. That includes bargain offers of sewing machines, vacuum cleaners, other household appliances, anything. Similarly, beware of giving advance payment on cut-price cruise tickets, vacations, other bargain offerings, unless offered by established businesses on which you have checked beforehand.

Never trust a stranger to hold your money for any reason. A typical example of how you can lose all your cash is this oft-worked swindle: a man starts chatting with you at a bar, on a bus or train, or any place where it seems so natural that you don't even remember later whether you started the conversation or he did. Without your realizing it, he is probing for information about you, ingratiating himself until you soon have the feeling that he is an old, trustworthy friend.

Something comes up such as the purchase of a watch. He says he knows a wholesale jeweler from whom he can get you a beautiful brand-name watch like his, which sells for $200 (his watch is the genuine $200 article), for $100, "exactly what I paid for mine." You want that great bargain, so you're hooked.

It seems reasonable that you wait outside the building while he goes in with your $100 to get the bargain "as a personal friend of the manager." The only trouble is that you wait for him to come out, and you wait and wait and wait. He never does come out of the building, since he has walked right through to the rear exit. You never see him or your $100 again.

Count your change whenever you make any kind of purchase or payment. There are "short-change artists" working in practically every kind of business, often at the cash register of legitimate restaurants, stores, and other establishments where the owner or manager knows nothing about his customers' being short-changed. The simplicity and swiftness of the cheat's maneuvering fools many people.

The short-change cashier may give you change of a ten-dollar bill by putting down a five-dollar bill right on the change plate in front of you and piling on a couple of singles and silver. Unless you count your change carefully, you'll never know that the operator slipped out the original five-dollar bill from under the others and palmed or pocketed it. Later in the day you find that you have five dollars less than you thought, but you have no idea what happened to it, and you dismiss the whole thing. If, in counting your change, you had pointed out to the cashier that he or she had short-changed you, you would have been handed another five with a flustered apology so seemingly genuine that you would have believed every word.

Be especially careful about being short-changed when you're traveling, notably in foreign countries where a different kind of currency compounds your confusion. Don't think you'll be short-changed or overcharged only in small establishments— some of the biggest and fanciest places have practicing gyp artists fouling up the premises. The bigger the bill the bigger the profit in adding a little something extra.

Don't ever let yourself be rushed in handling money. When you get your bill, and then when you are given your change, add it up carefully, consult the printed money-exchange scale that you should be carrying, and make a fuss if you find yourself cheated. Correction will be made with profuse apologies and horror-stricken groans of "how could this happen here?" The louder you complain, the quicker you'll get restitution, as they don't want other customers to hear. If you find an overcharge on your bill, don't tip the waiter or captain. At least that may help discourage them from overcharging on the next dinner check.

It pays to check weights and sizes when you buy meats and other items. Watch out for the thumb on the scale which adds to the price of your purchase. Also look for a string attached which may mean a foot on the scale: the string dangles down to a loop where the clerk puts his foot and pulls down; the numbers on the scale register more than the items weigh. If you think you were cheated, weigh the item on your scale at home and report repeated overweights to your local Bureau of Consumer Protection, District Attorney, or other authorities.

Watch out for shopping frauds of all kinds, and report them to store management. If you don't get satisfaction, contact the authorities listed previously. Don't put up with being cheated by use of false-bottom baskets of fruits and vegetables, or "pint," "quart," and "gallon" bottles and tins that hold a lesser quantity. Remeasure yard goods if you suspect a shortage at all; look out for a common trick where the clerk uses a yardstick with an inch cut off the end so you get only 35 instead of 36 inches (often found in "bargain stores"). Don't accept egg boxes that aren't stamped with the grade—they're inferior grade but mixed in with higher-priced eggs to fool the unsuspecting shopper. Tell your sharp-eyed youngsters to watch and report to you any such fraudulent tricks when they're shopping with you or alone.

It isn't safe to discuss your finances or any money matters with strangers. This goes even for people who aren't asking you for money but seek information in the guise of survey takers or bank representatives, or in other seemingly reasonable disguises. Don't answer their questions, whether you're approached in person, on the phone, or by mail. Such information may be used by a swindler who shows up later, even weeks or months later, to try to take your money away from you by one scheme or another.

Be suspicious of the corroboration of another person you don't know. Confidence men often work in pairs or groups, including men and women. Swindlers have used this kind of gyp successfully time after time: a man tries to sell you a "$5,000 mink coat," for example, for $500 cash. His reason may be something like the claim that he has a great job opportunity in another city but has to get there that day or lose out; he needs the cash to rent a car and make the trip, so his wife has agreed that he can sell her brand-new coat.

A well-dressed woman walking along is stopped by the seller who offers the coat to her, telling her the same story, probably even boosting the price to $750 or $1,000. She admires the coat, and says that it's one of the most beautiful minks she has ever seen; she would buy it herself at this terrific bargain price except that she already has such a coat. She leaves, the sucker is convinced, pays the $500, learns later that the coat is made of fake fur and worth less than $100. What the pigeon (buyer) never realized is that the seller and the woman who seemed to be a stranger meet at a prearranged place an hour later and split his money, since they have worked together for a long time. Instead, the fall guy probably tells his wife that a wealthy woman who was offered the coat was also fooled, so that he's not the only one and shouldn't be blamed.

Never buy a disguised "genuine" article. Hundreds of thousands of dollars a year are spent by suckers who buy what is offered as the genuine article, in disguise, at a fraction of the regular cost. Typical in this racket is the offer of well-known perfumes in blank packages. The seller tells you that the perfume is really a famous brand such as Joy, "the world's most expensive perfume," which sells for perhaps $25 a tiny bottle at the department store. The sucker is told, "You can verify that yourself, sir." However, he'll let you have it for $5. He says he can do this because he has managed to buy a load of it in France and brought it in by one mysterious (and questionable) means or another.

He opens the package, and sure enough the label is printed "Joy." The bottle, label, and perfume are all fake, and you pay

$5 for a few cents' worth of toilet water . . . if you are a patsy like hundreds of thousands of others. The racket is worked with watches and other costly merchandise. Even if the item is genuine, it may be stolen or smuggled, and you can get into trouble because "he who profits by crime commits the crime."

Help protect the elderly especially from shameful frauds which seek them out as prime targets and ruin them, frequently cheating them out of their life savings. A large percentage of such victims are in their seventies. Often they are lonely and respond to kind words from confidence men or women: they open up their hearts and then their pocketbooks. In many instances they have turned over all their money to swindlers to "invest" at high interest or for quick profit turnover—and never see their savings again.

Warn elderly relatives and friends about such criminals who prey on old people. Make them promise to let you know, or to discuss the matter with an officer at the bank, in person, if they are approached with any scheme that involves their giving money over to someone. Then you call the police to check on the individuals concerned.

Point out to them as an example that in New York City alone, police officials estimate that the elderly are swindled out of over half a million dollars annually by fraudulent operators. Criminals often pretend to be working for the Social Security or Medicare offices, and say that they've come to collect a refund on an overpayment. Then they talk the trusting elderly individual into turning over all the cash in the house as payment on the refund. The intended victim can usually get rid of the swindler by saying, "Wait outside while I call the local Social Security (or Medicare) office to double-check." When the locked door is opened again, the crook is gone.

You must stay alert at all times to avoid being cheated. Avoid phenomenal bargains from anyone, especially those offered on the street, by phone, or under any unusual circumstances. Understand without question that you cannot outswindle a swindler, so don't try—that's his racket, not yours. Stay away from suspect offers in merchandise, services, anything.

Although there is nothing much you can do against an armed thief, you *can* prevent being taken by a swindler simply by staying wide awake, not making any advance payments to anyone you don't know, refusing to deal with anyone except those whom you are certain are established, reputable, and absolutely reliable. Patronize those who are in business locally to stay.

CHECKLIST AGAINST FRAUDULENT OFFERS

☐ DON'T fall for phony funeral plans requiring payment in advance, or for any questionable propositions involving advance payment.

☐ DO double-check "schools" which guarantee a job with the course.

☐ DO investigate thoroughly any franchise or dealership "opportunity."

☐ DO be very wary of any get-rich-quick schemes and offers.

☐ DON'T be frightened by collection agencies with phony official-sounding names.

☐ DO get government and other authoritative help if cheated, as advised.

☐ DON'T fall for telephone solicitations; investigate thoroughly.

☐ DON'T buy from a stranger on the street—anywhere.

☐ DO stay alert against short-change experts; always count your change carefully, taking all the time you need, in foreign lands, too.

☐ DO watch for shopping frauds, as described, and notify authorities.

☐ DON'T buy disguised articles offered as "genuine."

☐ DO warn elderly relatives and friends particularly; they are prime targets of fraudulent operators.

☐ DON'T trust strangers making offers just because they are well-dressed, well-mannered, and ingratiating.

35

ESSENTIAL TIPS FOR PROTECTING
YOUR BUSINESS
UNDER TODAY'S CONDITIONS

EVERY business, large or small, needs protection. Losses from illegal practices are staggering, and they are increasing. An estimate of total crimes against property, covering only burglary, larceny, and robbery, figures close to 300,000 such crimes in 1970, *at least 50 per cent of them against businesses.* This number does not include the crimes of embezzlement, fraud, arson, auto theft, forgery, and counterfeiting, which would boost the total far higher.

Burglars display great ingenuity, as in an unusual theft by vacuum cleaner in a west coast city. Thieves picked the door lock of an inadequately protected office where they knew lots of loose currency, collected during the day, was stored in a safe. With a key they opened the outside door of a floor safe, revealing a narrow slot at the top of the inner safe, through which paper money was dropped as collected. Unable to open the inner safe, the burglars placed the nozzle of a vacuum cleaner against the slot and "cleaned out" the safe by sucking up the loose bills.

According to one police department survey, burglars enter most places of business in the following ways: 22 per cent break front windows; 16 per cent break front door glass; 14 per cent break rear or side windows; 14 per cent enter through basements, coal chutes, or other openings; 13 per cent force rear door locks; 10 per cent break rear door glass; 9 per cent force front door locks; 2 per cent enter through roof or skylight. Although this is only one survey, and the statistics may not apply to your area or structure precisely, the information is food for thought about particularly vulnerable spots that require extra protection.

Proper precautions beforehand foil many crimes. A suburban bank was held up by a bank robber who handed a teller a sack and demanded, at gunpoint, that he fill it up with paper currency. Prepared for such a situation, the teller swept money into the sack and, along with the bills, a tear-gas cartridge (permitted in that state) unnoticed by the robber. Fifteen minutes later, police arrested the bank robbers, two men and two women, with remnants of tear-gas on their clothing; one of them had suffered tear-gas burns and was weeping. The loot, over $1,500, was recovered.

In another bank robbery, holdup men pulled batches of bills from drawers that had been rigged to activate cameras when the bills were withdrawn. Using the clear, detailed photos of the lawbreakers taken by the cameras, the police tracked down and apprehended the three holdup men. In other instances when bills are picked up in a batch, just lifting the weight triggers an alarm system, including special cameras.

If you have a small business establishment, you'll find that many of the recommendations for protecting homes, autos, and people in the preceding chapters may apply to your business protection also. Other specific advice given later for guarding larger types of businesses can also be adapted to the requirements of smaller firms.

If you have a medium-sized or big business, professional protection companies will make a survey of your premises and operations and provide you with specific recommendations. In most cases, as you have undoubtedly learned, businesses suffer heavy losses from a small percentage of untrustworthy employees on the inside, and criminal forces on the outside. A security plan and program tailored to your individual situation and needs can provide the maximum protection needed.

General Business Precautions

Keep any cash registers empty and open at night, to avoid losses as well as damage to locked units. (To repeat, don't ever leave large sums on the premises overnight.) The professional burglar will open a locked cash register with tools or by forcing, and it is one of the first places he checks out for loot.

Provide adequate lighting outside and inside the premises at night. Keep lights on near any entrances or exits visible from the street, the rear or sides of the building, so that police officers and guards can easily spot a lurking or entering figure. Keep these lights on all night long in areaways, vestibules, and halls, since intruders tend to shun the light and much prefer the concealment of darkness. Don't make the mistake of turning off your night-light protective system on weekends and holidays—a favorite time for burglaries.

Keep a light on near the safe if it is visible from the entrances or through windows. The thief hates to tamper with a safe under the spotlight.

Inform police authorities of your lighting arrangements and keep them consistent, day after day. If lights that are supposed to be on are out, police officers making their rounds when the premises are closed are instructed to investigate. Statistics show that 95 per cent of burglaries in business establishments happened in places which were poorly or inadequately lighted.

Never leave the premises until you check all windows and doors, grates, grills, and so on, to be sure that they are locked or firmly secured from within.

Report to the police at once any individual or persons who arouse your suspicions by their actions—repeatedly entering or surveying your premises, loitering, parking outside for long periods. If a car is involved, report the license number.

Always place valuables and currency, also blank checks and check protectors, in a strong safe at night. It is better if safes are not movable. Do not leave valuables in cash registers or flimsy containers.

Check such places as rest rooms, storage areas, basements,

under counters, in closets, or other possible hiding places to make sure that no one is concealed inside when you lock up at closing time. Be watchful of unknown persons such as salesmen and others entering who may linger and hide, or may tamper with locks, alarms, cash registers or safes.

Beware of flimsy construction of doors, windows, or other possible entries. Door frames should be made so that frames cannot be pried off or hinges removed if they are outside hinges. Basement doors should have sheet steel on both sides. Glass bricks in windows are safer than plate glass where ventilation, light, or see-through effectiveness are not necessary. Steel bars and protective barriers that can be locked at night and cannot be readily lifted or pried off are helpful. Check again that all doors have pin tumbler locks or stronger ones, and that glass doors which could be broken have double cylinder locks requiring keys both inside and outside.

Investigate special doors and windows that offer considerably increased safeguards against easy entry for a burglar or vandal. Overhead doors that roll down on fixed tracks when the establishment is closed and are rolled up when open give excellent protection; the doors should be locked by dead bolts fitted with pick-resistant cylinders.

Heavy shutters for doors and windows that operate from within and don't allow tampering from outside are good safeguards. Heavy-duty crossbars set from within on deep, strong, specially constructed hooks, held with pins or thumb screws, afford good, simple protection where attractive appearance is not essential.

Guard against easy access from fire escapes, utility poles, manholes, alleys, roofs, sewers, loading docks, or other possible entry spots which are often overlooked in protection measures.

Keep a record of serial numbers and other helpful identifying details on business equipment and other items that could be carried away by burglars.

Examine the outside premises carefully with an eye for shrubbery, weeds, debris, anything that offers concealment to a burglar; arrange attractive landscaping without places for a burglar to hide. Have adequate and revealing lighting on at night wherever possible, or lights that go on if the alarm system is activated. It may pay you to call in lighting engineering services for a survey of your premises and subsequent detailed recommendations. Local light and power companies may supply a survey and recommendation service without charge.

Notify police beforehand if you will be handling large sums of money on special occasions; some police departments like to be advised of regular payroll deliveries and other frequent handling of large amounts of cash.

Know and inform your personnel about what to do in case of a holdup. Above all, warn them, don't be a hero! It is best to follow the holdup man's instructions, realizing that your life is more valuable than any property. Try to stay calm and trigger an alarm, but only if it can be done without revealing the action. Try to observe details as much as possible to help the police later—time, description of holdup man (see other chapters for details), any distinguishing features such as a lisp or scar. Remember places he touched that might reveal fingerprints. Note how he makes his getaway, license number and any details about the getaway car, make, color, people in the car. *Don't touch anything,* but call the police as soon as possible and prevent anyone from touching or disturbing anything meanwhile, keeping them away from the scene of the robbery.

Keep valuables in a sturdy, burglar-resistant safe or money chest, rather than in a safe that is merely fire-resistant.

Don't fail to set the alarm system, if you have one, whenever closing up the premises for the night, weekend, or holiday. Police officers often find that business establishments have been looted when the alarm system was not in effect because of someone's carelessness. One individual and at least one alternate should have the responsibility for setting the system. A good idea is to have a check-out sheet near the exit door to be initialed daily by the last person to leave or the person charged with setting the overnight alarm system.

Business Locks and Keys

Reread earlier pages on this subject, but realize that the business firm will do best to call in security experts or locksmiths experienced in serving business premises. They can best tailor the locks and keys to your individual problems and needs.

Although key locks are the commonest types in use, they are also the most vulnerable and are relatively easy for the professional burglar to open. The stronger and more complicated the lock, the greater problem it presents to the burglar. Yet too many businesses permit the use of the flimsiest, simplest, old-fashioned locks to "guard" entrances. Don't rely on size, weight, or price in choosing your locks. Consult a locksmith who handles all types of locks, not just one brand, so he can choose from a variety exactly what is best for your business. If you call in a security company, the experts will probably recommend improvement in your locking system as a first step to more effective protection.

Consider the wide range of locks available to help choose the right lock for the particular purpose.

Skeleton key locks offer little if any barrier to the professional burglar, even to the poorly skilled. At best they simply lock the door against honest people who are stopped by any locked door; they are totally ineffective against thieves who want to get in.

"Warded" or *"notched"* *padlocks* which are opened with a simple notched key offer little protection against the burglar who has the slightest skill in picking locks. They are useful as a sign to others that "this door is locked," but not as protection of anything valuable.

Disc-tumbler and pin-tumbler locks provide a greater degree of security, although they are far from burglar-proof (nor is a bank-vault lock completely burglar-proof). Pin-tumblers particularly are more complicated and more burglar-resistant. Although not considered adequate to protect valuable documents, classified information, or large amounts of money or other valuables, pin tumbler locks are adequate for most doors, gates, files, and other common uses. Various types are available in differing shapes and qualities; generally the costlier they are, the more complicated, and the stronger the materials used, the more protective they are. Choose according to your need, the costs involved, and the locksmith's advice.

Combination locks, lever locks, double cylinder locks, alarm locks, specially constructed bolts, other costlier and more intricate types of locks offer still greater protection. More recent promising developments include electric and time locks to thwart burglars. There are pushbutton combination locks that don't require keys. You should examine through a qualified locksmith or security expert what is available and usable for your doors, windows, grates and grills, cabinets, closets—wherever protection is required. Locks should be inspected at least annually against deterioration.

Remember that a lock is no more effective than control of the keys to open it. A former bank employee who looted the bank of $80,000 still had in his possession keys to the bank doors and the night depository. Naturally the fewer duplicate keys used, the safer the lock. A baggage handler arrested for thefts at Kennedy Airport had in his possession keys for many terminal doors and even some security rooms.

Double-check for precision fit of keys, for just as tightness of closure and aperture is essential in installation of locks, so keys should be precision-close in operation. Depending on turnover of the people who have keys, it is usually desirable to change keys and lock mechanisms at intervals.

Examine the range of keys available, as well as locks. There are flat keys, round or barrel keys, master keys that open a whole system of locks, corrugated, and other keys. For large operations, sophisticated computerized key systems are available. Again the choice depends on individual needs; the costliest locks are not necessarily the best.

Alarm and Security Systems

You shouldn't be without an alarm system if you feel that you have anything on the premises at all worth safeguarding. If you have no system now, call in at least several alarm system companies, or a security organization, to make a survey and to tell you exactly what you require for your business. Before ordering installation or service, be sure to check references with other firms in your business serviced by the system. There are many types of alarm systems to be considered: inside systems that sound alarms loudly; silent alarms that notify police headquarters or a central security office; step-on alarms under rugs or mats; alarms with foot switches, door switches, window switches, or other connections; photocell systems triggered by any movement in an area; radio-frequency alarms operating on radio wave systems; noise-alarms triggered by sounds and vibrations from drilling and other tools, for example; ultrasonic and electromagnetic systems; others. One company stresses "the electric watchman: automation on guard [via] invisible light, unheard sound, vibration detection."

Look into *electric-eye systems,* in which an invisible beam of light crosses a point of entry or other area of a room. A person passing between the light source and receiver breaks the circuit and triggers an alarm. *Foil tape* carrying an electric current may be applied around windows, doors, and other apertures; opening the window or door activates an alarm signal. *Sonic alarms* are triggered by sounds, and *vibration alarms* by movement. *Other systems* are operated by the heat of a body entering a room, or by changes a person causes in room pressure upon entering the area.

The choice, range, cost, other considerations in choosing an alarm system must be based on the needs of your establishment. But don't let time go by until you look into the subject, lest you suffer an expensive burglary, fire, or other damage. Keep in mind that insurance premium reductions are often available to businesses with adequate alarm systems. Thousands upon thousands of burglaries, fires, and other disasters are prevented annually by good alarm systems.

An alarm system should cover every possible opening against burglary and vandalism—not only doors and windows, but also skylights, roofs, ventilators, air conditioning units, coal chutes, any opening. It is often vital to wire side walls too, lest burglars break through from the next room or building. Have the night lighting system connected to set off alarms if tampering occurs.

Look into the advantages of large office and plant security communications systems utilizing electronic phone dialing setups, infrared beam units, spot fire detectors, emergency "hot lines." Other ingenious devices available are "panic buttons" which can be carried in the pocket on business or home premises where radio-controlled alarm systems are installed; even while obeying an order by a holdup man to lift his hands above his head at gunpoint, an individual can press his pocket and activate a radio beam which silently dials a central control point or police headquarters, thus reporting a crime under way at the particular point.

If a company has many employees and needs strong protection, especially in the manufacture of valuable military and industrial items, a security card which is inserted into special key interlocks to gain admittance can be distributed to each employee; audio and video devices which aid surveillance can be used (but beware of items which involve "invasion of privacy" and may be illegal); many other types of security and surveillance plans are available but are best discussed in detail to fit your corporation's needs by qualified companies specializing in office, store, and plant security.

Using Television Protective Units

Investigate closed-circuit television as an aid in safeguarding your business. Available for only comparatively few years, the possibilities for improved usage are unlimited, although current use is limited by the field of vision of TV cameras if installed inadequately. The seeing eye, activated automatically, can transmit pictures to guards at a central point. They can see anyone entering gates, rooms, or any vital security areas manned by the cameras. To be effective, installation must be done by security experts in that field.

A midwest manufacturing company called in a security

agency to check on dock losses. Experts strategically placed closed-circuit TV cameras to cover the dock, centered on a large mass of merchandise piled there as bait. Detectives monitored the sets. Just before the end of the day's work, a truck pulled up and the driver loaded eleven cartons on his truck. He then went to the other end of the pile and took four more cartons and placed them on the truck. His orders had called for only eleven cartons. Arrested when he left the terminal, he professed to be surprised that he had fifteen cartons and claimed it was an "honest mistake." When detectives pointed out the TV cameras, he started yelling for his lawyer.

TV surveillance doesn't provide total protection. Rather it is an excellent part of a total protection plan for the business where it fits in. As with other machinery, such as computers, protective TV cameras are only as good as properly planned installation and attention by humans make them. Weather elements such as rain, sleet, snow, and fog reduce the effectiveness of outdoor systems. If a guard doesn't pay close attention to simultaneous closed-circuit TV scanning, he can readily miss the agile thief slipping past the camera's eye. Also, the field of vision may be limited, and there must be sufficient light for humans and objects to be seen clearly.

Television closed-circuit camera film strips, taped quickly, have led to many arrests and convictions. In Queens, New York, security camera photographs were a major factor in the arrests of three men who had held up four different banks for a total of over $50,000. The manager of the bank noted that thanks to the efficiency of the TV cameras, as publicized in newspapers, "It's the holdups that haven't happened that make us happy . . . but we can't measure those." However, in some establishments where the alarm system was inadequate, burglars have managed to enter through skylights and other apertures, avoiding the cameras, and loot safes successfully. This points up again the need for a *total* security system.

Professional Investigators

Here are just a few of the reasons that professional investigation by an outside company is beneficial for the sizable business.

1. Outside investigators, highly experienced with many types of businesses, provide impartial judgment and reports on what goes on inside as well as outside the premises. Their findings help deal with solving such problems as theft, pilferage, sabotage, low employee morale, break-ins, and many other worrisome and costly phases of office, store, and plant protection.

2. A staff of women as well as men, with a wide range of skills, usually focuses on your problems, weaknesses, and strengths. Undercover people who operate discreetly are provided by reliable security agencies when needed.

3. Qualified professional investigation services know criminal approaches and techniques and use a large variety of scientific and other equipment in investigating faults and recommending improvements in your protection system.

4. Such investigations frequently uncover leaks and losses which you may not have known even existed. This can effect considerable savings in your operations. If court actions become necessary, the investigators often qualify as expert witnesses.

5. You are the final decision-maker. You study the reports and recommendations made by a qualified investigation concern that has seen your business situation broadly as well as close up. Then you decide whether to adopt the protection recommendations or not.

Investigate the security firm thoroughly before hiring, as if you were taking on a senior employee in your business. Your trade paper can give you names of leading protection companies in your area. If feasible, interview more than one to compare services offered and the kind of personnel who will do the work for you. Check with their other customers in your vicinity. If your protection now is inadequate, much can be gained as losses are stemmed. On pilferage alone, estimates of losses in sizable businesses run as high as an average of 75c or more per employee per day (a conservative figure). With hundreds or thousands of employees that can be a dead loss drain of tens of thousands of dollars a year in that category alone in one company, many millions of dollars industry-wide.

Use your common sense, whether your business is large or small, in deciding upon your own protection needs. As in most business judgments, "common sense," as Emerson noted, "means the shortest distance between two points." (A cynic has commented, "Common sense isn't.") If you are not completely confident that your protection arrangements are adequate, don't delay in having a protection survey made by your own people or an outside company.

It's unwise to let your judgment be distorted by the "scare statistics" some unreliable protection services may throw at you. On the other hand, don't let matters drift so that you continue to suffer hidden or obvious losses through all kinds of leaks. The safest and most profitable course is to make a protection survey at least annually (this becomes quicker and easier once services are established), and put an efficient and effective protection plan and program into operation. While many sizable businesses have strong protection programs, it is astonishing how many do not, thereby continuing to suffer heavy losses year after year.

Safeguards Against Hijacking

Never underestimate the problem of hijacking if your business does considerable shipping by truck. Particularly in the large cities, well-organized gangs seize trucks loaded with all kinds of merchandise—television sets, liquor (as in the legendary prohibition days), cameras, suits, dresses, coats, furs, electrical appliances, and other valuable items. Any merchandise easily disposed of becomes a likely target. It is estimated that the annual nationwide hijacking toll at this writing is about $600 million and is on the increase. Official investigators believe that much of this loot moves smoothly through what is known as

225

legitimate business, manufacturing, distributing, and merchandising industries controlled by the underworld. If you are the victim of hijacking, work closely with police, and discuss with security experts how to provide better safeguards against street and highway raids with more effective convoy systems and other controls.

Join with other heavy truck users or truckers in checking losses through hijacking. In addition to hiring security experts, cooperating companies have learned to use special methods—having private cars as convoys following selected trucks, having armed guards or private police accompany some trucks, painting trailer-license numbers on truck roofs so stolen vehicles can be spotted by police helicopters and radio station traffic observers. Many companies believe that the hijackers often check from the inside so well that they know exactly what is on the trucks they stop, and even have the goods sold before they steal them. In England, it is reported, a shoe manufacturer adopted a unique method which discouraged hijackers; one truckload that was stolen and then abandoned contained $28,000 worth of shoes—but all those in the truck were for the left foot. The hijackers apparently despaired of intercepting the load of matching shoes for the right foot; they left the merchandise intact.

Here are some official guidelines to help prevent hijacking and larcenies of trucks:

1. The trucks most often stopped by hijackers are the large van or tractor-trailer types.

2. Most hijacks occur when the truck is at a dead stop. That's the time when the driver should be especially alert.

3. Warn drivers to watch for a car or panel truck with three or four men inside, persistently following the truck. If suspicious, they should stop near a policeman or police car to have the suspected vehicle investigated. If the needed police car is traveling in the opposite direction, the driver can attract its attention by flashing his lights on and off. It works in daytime also.

4. Don't hesitate to seek the cooperation of police, since hijacking has grown into one of the major criminal problems. In

many cities police have been alerted to check transfer of goods from one truck to another on the street; to investigate upon seeing an unusual type of merchandise such as liquor at a transfer point where only fashion goods are handled normally; to question drivers stopped on the street, roadside, or near transfer points, wherever anything appears suspicious, and to check bills of lading and stocks; to enforce laws requiring drivers of trucks (and other vehicles) to remove keys from the ignition even while parked in a seemingly "safe" place, as outside a diner.

Prior to big shopping holidays such as Easter and Christmas, particularly strict precautions need to be taken. Although hijackings occur every month of the year, they tend to peak up at holiday shopping seasons.

Investigate special locks, keys, alarm systems, and other security devices developed especially against hijacking. These include special driver switches and control units for doors; two-way radio devices; loud alarms with automatic transmitting units which go on if any doors, including the motor housing cover, are opened, except by the driver. There are available special anti-hijacking alarm systems, with self-contained electronics and heavy-duty batteries, which sound a siren audible a quarter-mile away if anyone tries to move or break into the trailer or tamper with the alarm.

BUSINESS-PROTECTION CHECKLIST

☐ DO check the listing of most vulnerable break-in spots and take recommended action to safeguard them.

☐ DO keep cash registers empty and open at night.

☐ DO provide adequate protective lighting inside and outside at night.

☐ DO cooperate with police and other authorities for best protection of your premises.

☐ DON'T permit flimsy, unsafe construction; investigate special doors, windows, shutters, gates, fencing, other safeguards.

227

☐ DO keep a record of serial numbers of equipment which could be taken away.

☐ DO plan beforehand for protective action in case of a holdup.

☐ DO install a sturdy, burglar-resistant safe.

☐ DO check all locks and keys, and replace if necessary, as recommended.

☐ DON'T be without good alarm systems, choosing from types suggested, to suit your specific needs.

☐ DO consider television protective units if they fit your requirements.

☐ DO consult professional protection companies for a plan tailored to fit your individual business needs.

☐ DO take safeguards recommended against hijacking, if needed.

36

HOW TO STOP STEALING BY EMPLOYEES

THE OVERWHELMING percentage of employees are honest, so enlist their support for programs to help stop stealing by others. Such thievery reduces profits and ultimately affects salaries and wages. The watchful employee who will report anything overt or suspicious is a big help in stopping leaks. In a typical case, a salesman for a tile company noticed their product displayed for sale in a store which was not a customer for the item. His report alerted security guards, who followed a company truck and saw the driver make a delivery to the dealer without an authorized order. The driver's confession implicated a platform checker and foreman at the plant, stopping an estimated loss of thousands of dollars a year. Similarly employee cooperation can turn up thievery in this sensitive area.

It pays to consider professional screening, utilizing modern methods and equipment, before hiring key employees who will be in positions of trust. This kind of screening checks a man's or woman's references and background thoroughly without causing embarrassment. One company figures that they cleared up inventory losses of more than $100,000 annually by replacing suspected employees with others checked and passed by the screening service.

Install new shortage control systems in your business if you suffer unusual inventory losses consistently. Professional consultants and security advisers will check your systems and recommend methods and protection which can save a business far more than the cost of the service. It's worth looking into.

Reports reveal that in American business, "the man in the blue or white collar," according to a business journal, presents companies with their major theft problem, "not the man with the mask and gun." In one year, statistics just for banks show that staff pilfering cost banks almost $14 million, compared with losses to bank robbers totaling $7 million, or just about half. Estimates run as high as four billion dollars a year in business losses due to dishonest "fringe benefits" taken by employees. "Like charity," a newspaper columnist commented, "law and order (and protection) begin at home."

No person likes to be considered cheap or penny-pinching. The owners and managers of a company don't like it either. And it would be nice to be able to consider employees as honest adults instead of as petty-thieving children. But a company is in business to make money and it must control how it spends it.

A small company can usually control internal security matters in an informal way rather than with rigid controls or professional protection services. The outgoing mail, for instance, should be checked for non-company envelopes, and company envelopes should be spot-checked to make certain that the postage meter is not being used extensively for someone's personal benefit.

In most cases, keeping an accurate record of how much stock (pencils, paper, etc.) is used in a month is all that is needed in a small company. But if more stock is being used than seems logical, it is a good practice to have employees sign for each item—or even make out an order form for the needed material.

Personal phone calls (especially long-distance) can cost a company an exorbitant amount of money. No system seems to be perfect, but requiring all employees to log their long-distance calls—and the purpose of each—helps. The telephone company can also arrange the installation of phones so that only the switchboard operator can dial long distance. This keeps the control in one spot. A more complicated system offered by the telephone company provides each employee with a code number which he must give to the operator before a call is completed.

Then in the monthly telephone bill long-distance calls are broken down by employee code numbers.

Some corporations have had unpleasant difficulties with check forgeries. One small company (20 employees) discovered that checks it was paying out were not reaching the people intended—yet the checks were being cashed. They were cashed in the issuing bank on the same day they were made out, so the theft had to be internal. The forged checks were for various people, but each signature was written in the same shaky style. Working with the bank officials, the company set a trap and caught the employee. Then it issued check-cashing cards to each employee, and thereafter when checks were drawn they were mailed by the responsible accountant who prepared them. In this case the bank was partly at fault for not requiring proper identification, but the company should have insisted that the bank require it—for the sake of all the honest employees. A good lesson was also learned: the fewer people who handle checks, the less chance of problems.

Read the advice in the other chapters on eliminating thievery —especially the chapter on the retail store. These recommendations often apply to internal security, although extra care must be taken not to hurt labor-management relations.

CHECKLIST AGAINST EMPLOYEE THEFTS

☐ DO enlist the help of honest employees (the overwhelming majority) against internal thefts.

☐ DON'T overlook the value of having prospective employees screened by professional consultants.

☐ DO install shortage control systems to spotlight internal thefts.

☐ DO issue check-cashing cards for employee identification at the bank and make certain the bank requires this identification.

☐ DO consider using long-distance telephone logging systems or other plans offered by the phone company.

☐ DO bring in outside professionals if losses through employee thefts are sizable.

37

HOW TO KEEP YOUR BUSINESS
INFORMATION CONFIDENTIAL

MEMOS which are tossed into wastebaskets after reading, but which might contain information of value to a competitor should be treated more carefully. Some years back a cartoon appeared in a business magazine showing one office cleaning woman saying to another, "I make extra money by saving the contents of the wastebaskets here and selling them to the firm on the floor below." Soon afterward a supply company started manufacturing electric wastebaskets that shred the paper contents into narrow strips. New devices are being offered for "confidential records destruction," like one desk-top electric shredder unit about the size of an electric typewriter. It is "capable of handling paper, tissue, carbon paper, newsprint, and card stock . . . up to 200 pounds of paper per hour, including clipped or stapled sets."

Destroying records by electric shredding or other means is just one small step in a program of combating what is generally known as industrial espionage. The dictionary defines the term as the "gathering of information of varying degrees about products, manufacturing techniques, processes from manufacturing concerns that wish to keep these matters secret for their own use." The need for such protection goes beyond manufacturing concerns; it applies equally to such businesses as advertising agencies, planning engineers, architectural firms, and others.

If a records security program is required by your business, plan it carefully. Call in security consultants who are expert in this field and can set up for you simple systems which have

233

worked for other businesses like yours. Each plan must be tailored to the individual company needs, of course; an advertising agency would probably require different procedures from an engineering or manufacturing concern. In general, here are some vulnerable areas that must be safeguarded:

Employees should carry identification cards, for use particularly when entering or leaving the premises after hours, and they must return the cards when leaving the company's employ. New employees (including secretaries and others) should receive printed instructions relating to the firm's security methods and be advised of specific procedures and regulations applying to their work. Individuals leaving the company should turn all their material back to a department head, who should check what is returned against a list of what was given in the first place. Security instructions should include emphasis on not talking about confidential business matters to others, either in other departments or outside, on elevators, public conveyances, at home, anywhere.

Entrance and exit controls should be strict and as foolproof as possible. Persons entering or leaving before or after normal hours should be checked in and out, along with any guests or visitors. During office hours, receptionists should maintain firm control regarding where people go in the establishment, with visitors escorted to and from inner departments rather than left to wander freely. The same applies at packaging, receiving, and shipping departments, where passes are often required as a security measure.

Confidential information, memos, plans, other documents, should never be left exposed on desks or tables or carried openly from office to office. All employees involved with such material should be reminded of security needs again and again (circulating a monthly security bulletin is helpful in large businesses). Printed or processed papers containing anything of even a slightly confidential nature should be checked at every stage against leaks, in internal departments and outside plants, such as printers. Important information should be stamped "Confidential" and conveyed carefully in "Confidential" envelopes. Only a minimum number of copies should be prepared. Discarded matter containing even slightly confidential items should be destroyed rather than discarded carelessly in wastebaskets or bins. All strictly confidential figures should not be printed but should be written in by hand on copies conveyed to the limited number of individuals for whom the information is intended.

Offices should be locked as much as possible, as well as conference rooms or any rooms containing materials of value, certainly after hours, during lunch hours, or when the occupant is away for any considerable length of time. The same applies to desk drawers, files, cabinets, closets, any place where the contents have any confidential nature at all.

Security management should be entrusted to one qualified person, assisted by as large a staff as required by your company scope and needs in this range of operation and control.

Look into every possible area of security if your business is vulnerable to information leaks. Often it is essential to check regularly against "bugged" telephones and sophisticated listening devices planted in your offices and other areas. You'll learn from discussing your situation with outside or inside security specialists, if you have few or no controls in operation now, that losses and leaks can occur in many directions. "Spies" hired by competitive companies may be planted in your concern as employees in high or low positions; this accents the importance of careful screening in hiring practices. Unguarded conversations between employees and with outsiders, sometimes by loose-tongued top executives, must be prevented. Outside suppliers—advertising agencies, printers, legal and other consultants—must maintain security precautions on your business and materials. Offices and conference rooms, even restrooms, may be "bugged," and should be checked where necessary. Hiring away of employees, often at executive levels, in order to gain confidential information must be guarded against as much as possible.

BUSINESS-SECURITY CHECKLIST

☐ DO guard against business information falling into the wrong hands, even discarded material—notes, memos, miscellaneous records.

☐ DO call in consultants if needed in your particular business to plan a tight, lasting records security program, checking the various recommendations made.

☐ DON'T overlook any possible area of security leaks if your business is vulnerable, including sophisticated listening devices planted in offices, on telephones, other places noted . . . industrial spies . . . employee leaks . . . outside suppliers.

38

HOW TO PROTECT THE RETAIL STORE

MANY of the measures applying to other businesses, homes, and individuals can be helpful in safeguarding the retail store. In addition to the information covered elsewhere, here are some points of special concern to the security-conscious store owner:

Keep adequate lighting on all over the store whenever it is closed at night, on weekends, and holidays. Patrolmen are instructed that they should investigate and report the fact when premises that are usually well lighted are darkened, indicating the possible presence of burglars. Keep plenty of inside light on exits and entrances, emptied open-drawer cash registers, and safes.

An adequate alarm system is an economy. It can more than pay for itself in helping to prevent costly burglaries. Don't be without one.

Consider the construction of gates and grates in front of windows, doors, skylights, in fact any aperture through which a man could wriggle. You not only help reduce break-in losses but may save on insurance costs as well for glass breakage, vandalism, and thefts.

Don't litter up windows with so many signs and posters that patrolmen cannot see into the store on their rounds. The same applies to high displays which block a clear view into the store.

Always make nightly deposits after the store closes, as cash and checks are safer in the bank than in your closed and empty store.

Notify the police if you close the store for a day or more

for vacation or for any other reason. Arrangements will then be made for extra attention to your store during daylight hours as well as at night.

Make up at least three cards with the names, addresses, and phone numbers of the people who should be called in case of break-in, vandalism, fire, or other emergency. Post one card on the inside of the front door so it is visible from the street, another on the back door, and give the third to your local police.

Never cash a check unless you are sure of the identity and reliability of the individual. It's a good rule when a person offers a personal check for business dealings, even though it may be someone local you think is trustworthy, not to let the check exceed by much, if anything, the value of goods purchased by the check. For identification, do not rely on business cards, addressed envelopes, or any other item which can be made up, found or forged. Insist on a driver's license or valid credit card that bears a signature. Be sure that signatures and endorsements are signed in your presence, even if you must have them signed again. If in doubt, most retailers find it safer in the long run to lose profit on a sale than to suffer loss of the full value of the merchandise involved.

It's risky to leave valuable merchandise in windows or on counters if you can possibly prevent it. If you must have valuable items on display when the store is closed, be certain that the premises are protected electronically and by every other means practicable.

Arrange a cooperative alarm system with adjoining stores in case of holdups. Many arrests have been made through such a system where one retailer can press a silent alarm button concealed behind the counter which rings an alarm next door (and preferably at police headquarters also). The person in the adjacent store immediately alerts the police. Each cooperating retailer is also advised, as soon as he notifies police, to have someone watch at the door or through a window for a description of the robbers and the license number of an escaping car.

Keep a close check on possible employee theft. Estimated retail losses by employee theft, $4.7 billion, are just double the estimated losses through shoplifting, $2.35 billion. In a large retail operation, employee theft cannot be controlled properly except by special security personnel, either an inside staff headed by a qualified executive, or outside security forces.

Most employees are honest, but a small percentage will stray. Measures which supervise all personnel properly are welcomed by honest employees as safeguarding them against false suspicion. Only dishonest individuals in any situation criticize and defy fair safeguards. Here are some protection checkpoints against employee thefts:

• Check each applicant carefully *before* he becomes an employee; many dishonest people would never be hired if checked out properly beforehand.

• Good pay, worthwhile incentive programs and rewards for excellence in performance, pleasant employment conditions all contribute to getting a better class of honest, able employees.

• Realize that most internal thefts occur because the opportunity is present. A system of proper supervision closes up leaks.

• When losses occur, professional investigators hired as clerks or in other positions generally detect those who are stealing cash or merchandise in fairly quick time.

• Close inventory controls soon reveal it when quantities of merchandise are being taken. Physical inventory should be checked often against inventory records, or losses may continue for a long time without being detected.

• Keep close checks on all related operations—receiving sales, transfer, delivery, inventory—and on collusion between sales people and customers. Each should be checked against the others, for efficiency and to prevent and rectify mistakes, as well as for prevention of dishonesty. Set up interweaving systems for your own operations. Make sure that different employees check others, rather than let one do all the checking. Each cash register should be checked and cleared at least twice a day, with properly signed records kept.

• In cash operations, registers should usually be the responsibility of one individual for each register, with keys held by supervisory personnel (checked in turn). Each clerk must account for each slip in his possession or allocated to him. Cashiers should stamp slips paid in the customer's presence at the time the sale is made. Each day's receipts should be checked against sales as soon as possible, as delays encourage stealing.

• All incoming checks should be marked immediately "for deposit only." Checks should not be held long, but should be deposited the same day as received (usually involving night deposits). Bank deposit slips should be checked with daily receipts every day to find any discrepancies without costly delay.

• All canceled checks should be examined carefully for any evidence of change or alteration of any kind. The same should be done with bank statements, and a duplicate requested from the bank if anything appears suspicious such as erasures or alterations.

• Disbursements should be made by checks and not by cash, wherever at all practicable. The refund system should have careful checkups. Petty cash withdrawals should always have a supervisory signature of approval. If any mistake at all is made in preparing a check, it should be voided clearly and immediately, on the spot.

• In any shortage, look closely for any possible collusion between individuals, such as those in receiving, trucking, shipping, sales, account-keeping.

Tracking down "mysterious" losses is important. For example, a large department store caught an ingenious thief who posed as an employee, even wearing an identifying employee name tag. He would accept money from customers for purchases, then walk off with the money and the item as though to wrap it up and get change, but would never return. When the item was to be sent, he would keep the money and return the item to stock when the purchaser left. The store changed its employee-identification system.

Another enterprising thief worked a "merchandise refund" racket from which he said he made his living for several years.

He would enter a department store or drugstore, unobtrusively pick up items worth under $50, and place them in a paper bag he'd brought along. Then he would approach a sales or exchange clerk and ask for a cash refund on the items. He would explain that his wife had bought the items and asked him to return them for a refund, but that the sales slip had been lost. Since the items had the store's price tags and the man looked like a young, attractive, well-dressed husband, the cash refund was usually given quickly, without any trouble. When finally caught, he boasted that his usual take had been $50 to $80 per "working day"—but not worth the jail sentence.

You'd be surprised how reluctant some store owners are to put in certain safeguards—especially if they involve hiring an internal security guard or an outside security service until they compare the cost of their actual losses in a year against the cost of needed help. Obviously, if the cost of inside or outside help is less than the losses, the store owner will be ahead if he hires the help. But sometimes he will also be ahead if the out-of-pocket costs of security are equal to or are even greater than the amount of loss; this is because the unseen costs of losses, the cost of hiring a new employee, the cost of ordering, restocking, etc., when added to the actual loss from pilferage or theft, may clearly swing the balance in favor of protection. In addition, think of the headaches missed.

Look into shopping services which provide sharp-eyed, experienced investigators who act as customers and report whether sales people are providing prompt, courteous service. They also may spot cheating and stealing activities by individuals in your employ.

RETAIL STORE CHECKLIST

☐ DO recheck precautions in other chapters, many of them helpful to retail stores, too.

☐ DO keep adequate lighting on at night, indoors and outdoors.

241

☐ DO install dependable alarm systems.

☐ DON'T overlook protective gates and grills for show windows.

☐ DO inform police of all special openings and closings.

☐ DO observe the recommendations about cashing checks.

☐ DON'T leave very valuable merchandise on counters and in windows after closing time if possible—or even when open.

☐ DO have a plan to prevent or cut losses due to holdups.

☐ DO take recommended precautions constantly against employee thefts.

☐ DO get a professional security survey and outside staff if needed in addition to inside security people.

☐ DO consider adding shopping services with skilled investigators from outside to check personnel and customer cheating and stealing, as well as quality of service.

39

WHAT TO DO WHEN YOU
SPOT A SHOPLIFTER

IT IS estimated that one out of every sixty persons visiting a store is a shoplifter. Crimes in this category have increased more than 93 per cent over a seven-year period, according to the FBI, which calls shoplifting "the fastest-growing larceny violation in the nation." This bureau also states that the average value of goods stolen in the average store through each shoplifting is about $28; the average store is losing through shoplifting or internal or other theft about $1.50 out of every $100 worth of merchandise it stocks (the percentage is higher in department stores than in specialty stores.)

Losses can run much higher per theft. In one instance, two professional shoplifters took four mink stoles valued at $9,000 by unlocking a display case right out in the open. A woman said she had stolen 1,900 men's suits in a single year, with a male accomplice; while he tried on clothing, she stole as many as four suits at a time by folding them and placing them between her knees under a full skirt (this would hardly work with miniskirt fashions).

Kleptomania (an irresistible impulse to steal, especially when economic gain is not the prime motive) does not account for a significant percentage of shoplifting, although "I'm a kleptomaniac" is often used as an alibi by the apprehended shoplifter.

Many types of people may be shoplifters. One analysis of about 10,000 shoplifting arrests showed about the same percentage of females as males; 21 per cent were juveniles (other estimates run as high as 50 per cent, perhaps more). Most

243

thefts were between noon and closing. Friday and Saturday are the biggest shoplifting days; the rest are about even. Months were about even in shoplifting losses, with peaks at gift holiday seasons.

Potential shoplifters may be carrying lunch pails, musical instrument cases, briefcases, extra-large purses, large bags or sacks uncommon to the store, bulky books and magazines (flat items are slipped in and hidden between pages), bulky umbrellas (merchandise is tucked in between the folds)—or wearing out-size clothing, especially with large slit pockets.

Those pushing loaded baby carriages, especially with large purses, sacks, or knitting bags, may be suspect. People loitering in a department or making repeated visits without apparent reason and refusing service when approached should be watched carefully. Persons acting nervous and looking around frequently, pushing goods off counters "accidentally," are suspect. Making fast selection and going to fitting rooms without help of a sales-person, especially when taking bags along, should arouse suspicion. Making frequent trips to locker rooms and restrooms, anywhere out of the way, merits surveillance. Placing hands in pockets often while near counter of small items, handling items quickly and nervously—all such actions may be tipoffs.

Pay special attention to large and odd packages being carried. One shoplifter was caught using a neatly wrapped package with a large bow on top. The bow was self-adhering; when lifted, it revealed an opening in the package into which the thief would slip an item, then quickly replace the bow over the slot. Shop-lifters may carry large hollowed-out books or similar articles into which small, valuable items can be dropped.

Peepholes, closed-circuit television, still and tape cameras, observation points, one-way mirrors, convex mirrors that see around corners and in many directions, all are useful in catching shoplifters. In a typical instance, a cashier watching the TV monitor saw a man pick up a shirt and hide it under his jacket; she alerted a guard. When caught, the defendant groaned, "I didn't realize I was on camera." A woman returned a sweater her little boy had brought home; he told her where he had stolen it, and she said she was afraid that his picture might have been taken by the store's cameras; it had. Use of mirrors and cameras will also serve as a deterrent; a shoplifter prefers not to risk getting caught in a protected store when so many are without these helpful devices.

Keep close supervision of washrooms and fitting rooms. These are favorite places for shoplifters who will put on several sports jackets under a bulky overcoat, three skirts under a billowing dress. In the cubicles, thieves use the opportunity of privacy to attach items snugly and securely to hooks inside the coat and on belts and waistbands. Rather than taking off weight as is fashionable (and healthful), shoplifters enter washrooms and fitting rooms slim and trim and come out inches bulkier all over—unless your investigators see and detain them.

Don't leave unused checkout aisles open, a too-common practice. Shoplifters carrying concealed items under their clothing can slip out of these aisles swiftly.

Maintain extra coverage at peak shopping hours. The more customers in the store, the more watchful eyes you need. Knowing that one out of sixty is a shoplifter, you have to spot the one.

Keep small, expensive items in locked cabinets or out of easy reach of grasping hands as much as possible. This precaution is especially essential near checkout counters, where a small item can be grabbed and concealed in a flash.

Keep checking infrequently used doors. If they are securely locked, a shoplifter can't open one swiftly in order to slip out loaded with stolen goods.

Publicize your anti-shoplifting measures in the store and to your employees. Display posters telling customers that cameras and investigators are ever-watchful for shoplifters in your store. Inform employees regularly about what to do when they see a shoplifter stealing goods, and when they recognize known shoplifters in the store. The publicity won't disturb anyone other than the shoplifters.

Use all possible safeguards in marking items to make it difficult for shoplifters to get away with an excuse when caught, as they often claim that the items aren't from your store. To help prevent label-switching, consider using tamperproof gummed labels which rip into pieces rather than come off in one yank when someone tries to remove them . . . conceal extra price tickets around the item, especially useful with fashion goods . . . use distinctive staples on price tickets, with a pattern different from other stores . . . use hard-to-break plastic string and tough-to-tear tags on merchandise so tags can't be yanked off in a flash.

New Developments To Prevent Shoplifting

Keep up with newest developments as they are offered, in order to stay one step ahead of shoplifters. As soon as you install another precaution, these thieves try to find a way to get by it. One of the most promising, relatively new ways to stop and foil shoplifters is the "electronic dot" system. Through this modern method, invisible dots—smaller than a sharp pencil dot—are placed on labels and price tags of selected items. If the dot is not "deactivated" at the checkout counter, alarm systems start flashing or ringing, and the person involved (who is carrying hidden items while checking out others and paying for them) is quickly detected.

The system is quite simple, as employees learn quickly how to handle the sensitized labels and deactivator units. Customers can see no difference in the labels. In a department store without checkout counters, the deactivators are strategically placed to trigger alarms when labeled stolen items are taken through exit doors. The system can be adapted to help prevent employee pilferage also.

Another new system uses an "electronic wafer"—a device securely attached inside the folds of a garment or other item. Unless the "wafer" is deactivated, when the shoplifter tries to take the merchandise from the store, it emits a signal that triggers a variety of receiving instruments and alerts store security people. The systems are claimed to be harmless in respect to radiation or other injurious effect.

Penalties Increase in Severity

Check with local authorities, your retail merchants association, and your attorney regarding the laws in your state governing the questioning and arrest of suspected shoplifters. Most states now have special "shoplifting laws" which minimize the chances of suits or other penalties for "false arrest" (up to now the cry of nearly every practicing shoplifter when caught with or without the goods). For example, a typical law permits an official to make an arrest "when he has reasonable cause to believe a crime has been committed without being liable for false arrest." In one state after a similar law went into effect, arrests for shoplifting rose sharply; in the first seven months convictions were obtained in 87 per cent of the cases, and value of recovered merchandise more than doubled.

The National Retail Merchants Association, in explaining the trend toward more severe punishment, wrote: "Many of the laws follow a pattern in which a police officer, merchant, or store employee, believing he has probable cause for suspecting that the merchandise has been unlawfully taken, may take the suspect into custody and detain him for a reasonable amount of time in a reasonable manner for the purpose of recovering the goods. This action will not make the retailer or his employee liable for false arrest, false imprisonment, or unlawful detention."

In one state, punishment at this writing runs as high as a fine of $10,000 and ten years in jail, depending on the amount stolen. As the facts of life about the severe penalties possible upon detection and arrest for shoplifting hit the amateur, particularly "noncriminal" men, women, and especially juveniles, their activities outside the law are likely to decrease.

First offenders, when caught and faced with severe punishment, usually stop the activity and never go back to it after being released. A knowledgeable sociologist explains her findings: "Apprehension for shoplifting is a very frequent first brush with the law for young people. The experience often has a traumatic (shocking, lasting) impact that may have real significance in their lives. If the young shoplifter can believe he has a great deal to lose by continuing to steal, he stops."

Don't hesitate to prosecute offenders. The best laws and security don't work if those who break the law feel confident that they will go free without any punishment.

CHECKLIST AGAINST SHOPLIFTING

☐ DON'T shrug off the huge losses due to shoplifting; take needed precautions now.

☐ DO understand that many types of people may be shoplifters, from young juveniles up.

☐ DO particularly watch as potential shoplifters people carrying the sizable receptacles listed, and odd-shaped packages.

☐ DO consider use of peepholes, closed-circuit TV, cameras, special mirrors, and other devices.

☐ DON'T bypass close supervision of washrooms, fitting rooms, all exits, unused checkouts, similar outlets for shoplifters.

☐ DO arrange extra coverage at peak shopping hours and seasons.

☐ DON'T keep small, valuable items where they can be pilfered readily.

☐ DO publicize your shoplifting precautions to scare off potential thieves.

☐ DO employ safeguards in marking items to incriminate shoplifters.

☐ DO look into new systems against shoplifters, such as "electronic dot" methods and others.

☐ DO check with authorities for local regulations on questioning and apprehending suspected shoplifters.

40

HOW TO SPOT COUNTERFEIT MONEY AT A GLANCE

NOTE THE differences between counterfeit and genuine money so that you can check a bill that comes into your possession if you have any qualms about its authenticity. There is usually a clearly detectable difference, since good money is made by experts using specially designed machines, and printed from steel plates produced by the finest engravers. Counterfeit money usually looks and feels different because the bills are generally made from notably defective plates, printed with inferior ink on cheap paper, and made with poor equipment by less competent workmen.

One of the unique cases in counterfeiting involved a fourteen-year-old boy in Michigan who was arrested for using home-made bills to get change from a money changer in a laundromat. He created his bills by making copies of one-dollar bills on a copying machine, cutting the copies to size, and pasting the two sides together.

Compare a genuine bill with one that you suspect, observing these points: the *portrait* on a genuine bill stands out distinctly from the oval background, the eyes appear lifelike, and the background is a fine screen of regular lines; the portrait usually merges into the oval background on the counterfeit bill, it is dull, smudgy, or unnaturally white, and the oval background is dark with broken, irregular lines. On the *colored seal,* the genuine bill has even, sharp sawtooth points around the rim; on the counterfeit the points are generally uneven and broken off.

Serial numbers on the counterfeit bill are poorly printed, uneven in appearance, and badly spaced; but figures are even and strong and well spaced on the genuine bill. The distinctive *paper* of a genuine bill has tiny red and blue threads scattered on the surface, although not always noticeable if the bill is badly worn and soiled; a counterfeit bill usually imitates the actual red and blue threads with printing. *Slight differences* can be a giveaway; on one counterfeit $20 bill, the flag on top of the White House on the back of the bill was flying straight out at right angles to the pole, while on the genuine bill the flag is waving at a downward slant.

You can't recognize a counterfeit bill by rubbing it on a piece of paper to prove it isn't genuine. Ink can be rubbed off genuine bills as well as counterfeit ones.

Check coins you suspect to be counterfeit by a few simple tests. Dropped on a hard surface, genuine coins give off a bell-like ring, but counterfeit coins usually sound dull. When you feel a counterfeit coin it generally feels greasy to the fingertips, unlike genuine coins. Look at the corrugated outer edge, even and regular on a genuine coin but usually crooked, uneven, and with some ridges missing in spots on a counterfeit coin. The edges of the bad coin can usually be cut easily with a sharp knife, while genuine coins resist the knife blade.

Consult a bank officer, or check with the police, if you think you have been given counterfeit bills or coins; they have the experts who can make a real determination. To supply needed information, try to remember how and where you received the suspected money.

Heed the warning of the Treasury Department that "not all strangers are counterfeiters, but all counterfeiters are likely to be strangers."

COUNTERFEIT MONEY CHECKLIST

☐ DO learn the main differences between counterfeit and genuine money by look and feel.

☐ DO check particularly the portraits, colored seals, serial number printing, paper with telltale threads.

☐ DO note counterfeit coins by difference in the "ring" when dropped on a hard surface, feel of the material, the corrugated edges.

☐ DO check with a bank officer or the police if you think you have been given counterfeit money.

41

HOW TO PROTECT THE STORE
DURING RIOTS

BE PREPARED in case of riots if there is any threat in your area, especially in larger cities. Ask local police and other authorities for their recommendations. Qualified business groups can also probably give you very specific advice for your locality. For instance, the alert Retail Merchants Association of Detroit, a division of the Greater Detroit Board of Commerce, has issued basic "Riot Precautions" as part of a campaign to educate and prepare retailers in order to lessen harm to people and premises.

It's risky to be caught unprepared even if you are quite certain that riots affecting your establishment, employees, and customers are not imminent. Knowing what to do "just in case" is informative at the least, and at most can save lives, help prevent injuries and property damage. Here are some basic guides to consider:

Make your riot-action plans in consultation with civil authorities who are the experts and have the ultimate responsibility.

Name a responsible executive in charge of riot precautions and controls, and give his name and phone number, business and home, to the police. He should create a plan of action, and designate personnel who become part of an "emergency guidance squad." Include a watch on roofs and other strategic points but not at dangerous outside positions.

Your plan should provide procedures for evacuation of customers and personnel from the store in case of riot if deemed advisable. It should include emergency transportation possibilities, first-aid facilities and training, identification by badges or arm bands, arrangements for food, adequate communications between members of the emergency squad.

Arrange for property-protection measures such as covering or hiding possible weapons, hammers, knives, and guns . . . removal of valuable merchandise from display windows . . . installation of protective gates and grills . . . arrangements to board up windows . . . special guards inside store . . . cash removal from registers with empty register drawers left open . . . removal of valuable merchandise to better protected locations . . . proper bright lighting, including display windows, to discourage looters, who prefer darkness for their activities . . . fire extinguishers readily available . . . safe places for records . . . emphasis on personal safety as most important.

Review insurance coverage on riots. Coordinate your plans not only with police authorities but with other businesses. Establish public relations policies and make plans to establish sound community relations; notify customers and personnel about store reopening; consider other problems faced by your store in your community, depending on size, location, other factors.

Work closely with the police before, during, and after any riot activity. Advise everyone never to interfere with police and other public officials in performance of their duties. Discourage the spread of rumors and false information.

Take precautions to remove or shelter trucks and other vehicles. Keep elevators stationed above the first floor to block easy access by rioters. Check carefully that locks are in place, grills secured, any other protective equipment in operation, but realize that ordinary locks and grills furnish a deterrent rather than sure security against riots and rioters. Remove flammable material as much as possible.

Include nearby store warehouses, storage areas, and any other structures in your riot precautions and plans.

RIOT-PROTECTION CHECKLIST

☐ DON'T be caught napping—help prevent considerable damage with sound riot-precaution plans in cooperation with local authorities.

☐ DO name a responsible executive in charge of riot precautions.

☐ DO arrange for proper evacuation of customers and personnel, property protection measures, other basic necessities.

☐ DO look into adequate insurance coverage for riots.

☐ DO work closely with the police on riot plans and handling.

☐ DON'T overlook protection for trucks and other vehicles.

☐ DO include precautions for warehouses, storage areas, parking places, other spots that are your responsibility.

☐ DO work with other local businesses and authorities to help prevent and curb riots, to improve the community, to ward off riots before they begin.

42

HOW TO SAVE LIVES AND PROTECT PROPERTY AGAINST FIRE

FIRE PROTECTION starts with proper safeguards built in at the time a home is constructed. In an apartment house, fire department construction and inspection regulations are intended to assure maximum fire protection, with proper installation of sprinkler systems and other safeguards. In a house purchased years after it was built, you take what you get. It is desirable to have a qualified expert look over the house and suggest fire protection safeguards practicable for that dwelling.

Give serious consideration to the values of a fire alarm system in your home, especially if you are in the country and quite far from help. A farmer in New Hampshire whose home was miles from any fire department apparatus installed a simple fire alarm system which awakened his family of eight when a blaze began in the kitchen after bedtime. He credits the alarm with saving all their lives, as the wooden structure went up in flames only minutes after they had escaped outdoors.

Fire alarm systems for private homes (and even apartments) are becoming commonplace. Most units are designed to be hung on a nail near the ceiling of a room. They are activated by heat rather than flame, which means that the fire needn't reach the units to set them off. A blaze in any part of the room will usually generate enough heat to set off the ceiling-high alarm.

You'll need an alarm in any room which might catch fire, especially at night: one for each child's bedroom, one for your own bedroom, one in the attic, and one in the boiler room or basement. Also remember that a stairwell can act like a chimney flue, and fire can race up it in an instant. That's why you should have an alarm on the wall at the highest point of any stairwell that goes from one story to the next.

The best units are those that are not connected to the electrical wiring of the house (in case the wiring goes out, or is burned through). The units should act independently of each other. Most good units have a container of highly pressurized gas, which is released by a special "trigger" which melts at a certain heat level. The best units also have a visible gauge which shows that the gas is still under pressure, so that if pressure is lost the unit can be recharged or replaced. Units are available from a modest cost of several dollars each to the permanent, guaranteed (and more expensive) kind, which will be replaced with new units free if the gas pressure ever lessens. Some companies also make a policy of replacing any unit that goes off because they collect the used units that saved lives.

The important thing to remember about these alarm devices is that they emit a very loud sound for some minutes, alerting everyone in the house to get out before the house is engulfed in flame. These alarms can also be heard by nearby neighbors.

If you have a second or third story in your home, you need not only an alarm system that will alert you to fire anywhere in the house but a way of getting yourself and your children out of a second or third story bedroom if the stairs are blocked by fire or smoke. Rope ladders are less expensive than metal ones, but remember that rope burns. It may also rot in time, which metal won't do. Flexible aluminum ladders are good because they last and they are light in weight and so can be used by a woman or child, if necessary. These are designed to hook onto the window sill on the inside and be thrown or dropped outside the window so that one can climb down them to the ground. Be sure the escape ladder you buy is long enough to reach the ground. They come in two-story and three-story sizes. These ladders should be kept permanently in some location near the window that is likely to be used. If you've got to escape from a fire on short notice, it's no good to have to go hunting in a closet (or another room) for the escape ladder.

256

It's risky to try to control all small blazes with water from a bucket or hose. While small fires from paper, rags, and wood can generally be controlled with water, flaming gasoline or even grease require stronger smothering action with foam or dry-chemical fire extinguishers.

Have a fire extinguisher handy, more than one if necessary, depending on the size of your house or apartment. Extinguishers of about five pounds or less are small enough to handle quickly and easily, and are available at stores for a few dollars, the price depending on size, quality, and other factors. Be sure the one you buy has a seal from Underwriters' Laboratories or Factory Mutual. (Carbon tetrachloride extinguishers may give off toxic gases and are not recommended for the home.) Follow instructions with the extinguisher for mounting in a conveniently accessible place (not in a crowded closet, for example, where you may have to fight your way in to grab it). Keep the extinguisher high enough so that small children can't reach it, as it is not a safe "toy." Do have it clearly visible in a hallway, laundry room, some place where it won't spoil the looks of the room but is out in the open to keep reminding you of its availability, and can be seen readily by neighbors or others who may come to your aid.

Practice with the extinguisher when you get it (if possible with your model), and test it about twice a year to make sure it is in good working order. In actual use, aim for the *base* of the fire where the flames originate. If the fire is in a receptacle like a pail or deep pan, start at the brim and work downward. Remember that heat rises, so stay as low as possible in fighting a fire. Always leave yourself a clear way out.

Try to turn off the house current if you know that a fire has an electrical origin.

Keep inflammatory materials such as piles of paper, rags, wood, and waste items at a minimum in your home, checking frequently.

Follow these guides if fire breaks out in your home, apartment, or other building:

DO REMEMBER: Get out fast. Don't underestimate how fast a small fire can spread. Use stairs, not the elevator. Close all doors behind you. Don't panic. Once you are safely out, call the fire department—dial "Operator," or use alarm box. Don't go back in.

If a fire breaks out in your home, get out fast—with your family. A fire can spread faster than you can run. Even if you just smell smoke, get out. If you escape through smoke, stay near the floor where the air is better. Take short breaths, breathe through your nose. If you are trapped in a room, follow all the tips on the right side of this page.

Make sure children can open doors, windows and screens to escape routes.

If you find smoke in an open stairway or open hall, use another preplanned way out. Teach your children how to use the phone to report a fire if they are trapped. If they can get out, they should know where the alarm box is in the neighborhood.

Make sure your family knows the quickest and safest ways to escape from every room in the house. Close doors behind you. Keep a flashlight in all rooms to help escape at night.

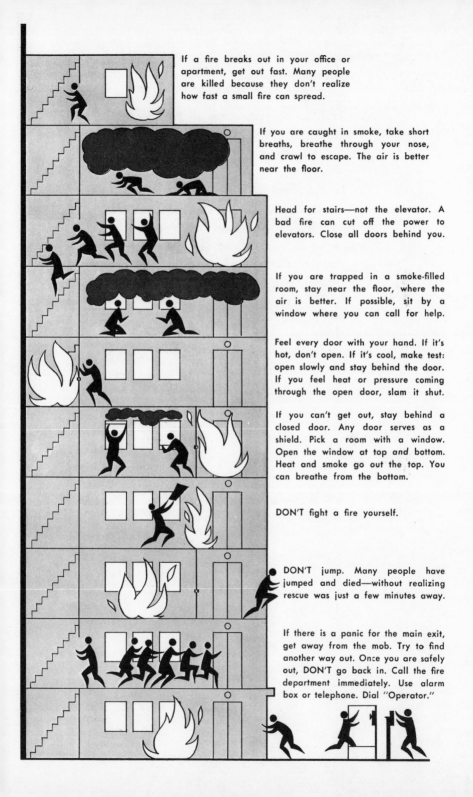

If a fire breaks out in your office or apartment, get out fast. Many people are killed because they don't realize how fast a small fire can spread.

If you are caught in smoke, take short breaths, breathe through your nose, and crawl to escape. The air is better near the floor.

Head for stairs—not the elevator. A bad fire can cut off the power to elevators. Close all doors behind you.

If you are trapped in a smoke-filled room, stay near the floor, where the air is better. If possible, sit by a window where you can call for help.

Feel every door with your hand. If it's hot, don't open. If it's cool, make test: open slowly and stay behind the door. If you feel heat or pressure coming through the open door, slam it shut.

If you can't get out, stay behind a closed door. Any door serves as a shield. Pick a room with a window. Open the window at top and bottom. Heat and smoke go out the top. You can breathe from the bottom.

DON'T fight a fire yourself.

DON'T jump. Many people have jumped and died—without realizing rescue was just a few minutes away.

If there is a panic for the main exit, get away from the mob. Try to find another way out. Once you are safely out, DON'T go back in. Call the fire department immediately. Use alarm box or telephone. Dial "Operator."

FIRE-PREVENTION CHECKLIST

☐ DO investigate fire protection in construction and alterations.

☐ DO look into fire protection and alarm systems for your home.

☐ DON'T depend on water to fight small blazes; have a fire extinguisher handy, kept safe from young children.

☐ DO turn off the house current in a fire of electrical origin.

☐ DO have an escape plan for fire, with windows and doors easily opened.

☐ DON'T panic, don't jump, get out fast; if trapped, follow the instructions to avoid smoke inhalation, using stairs instead of elevator, closing all doors behind you.

☐ DO call the fire department quickly, after first getting out of the burning building; dial "O" for "operator," or emergency number 911 if in effect in your area.

43

WHAT YOU SHOULD KNOW
ABOUT THE CRIMINAL MIND

DON'T EVER trust any criminal to be like the usual person you encounter. His thinking is different and his actions are unpredictable. And your life may well be in danger. That's a basic point you must never forget in safeguarding yourself and your family from those outside the law. Remember this always in any dealings with the criminal element. As warned earlier, if faced by an intruder, give up your money instead of resisting. Don't try to fight back or to struggle physically under usual circumstances, no matter how mild or "nice" or "reasonable" your antagonist may appear on the surface.

It must be emphasized: never forget that the criminal is not a "normal" person. A lifetime of dealing with many differing people on all levels unfortunately doesn't qualify you to handle the criminal mind, which has more twists, turns, and inconsistencies than a mangled corkscrew. Police records often establish the M.O. of a given criminal (the "modus operandi" is his or her usual method of working), which can be very helpful in tracking down individuals after a crime. However, it is also true that any criminal may suddenly and surprisingly deviate from that M.O. A quiet, usually mild burglar may after years of working nonviolently change for no good reason and become more dangerous than a rattlesnake in attacking or striking back.

Don't ever be fooled by a lawbreaker into letting your guard down against him because outwardly he conducts himself as a worthy citizen, seems to "love his family," is "good to his mother," and displays other such merits. If he is an active burglar, racketeer, loan shark, confidence man, fraudulent operator, or any other type of criminal who preys on others, don't be put off by his gentlemanliness or his concern for his own family. He'll have no compunctions about robbing, cheating, or injuring yours.

Once a person helps himself to your property, and justifies himself for doing so, he is outside the law and there is no limit to how far his criminal actions can extend. Don't believe or trust him for an instant, or you'll fail to protect yourself and your family properly. "But I didn't know . . . he seemed so nice" is a common lament of those who have been victimized. Now that you know, you can't have that excuse in relation to crimes within your control, such as avoiding loan sharks and gyps.

Never lower your guard against a burglar or other criminal with the thought that you can reason with him because of some theory you've read or may have about handling offenders. Stories appear in the press regularly, discussions abound on television and radio, about the "soft" approach to the criminal or the value of being "tough." Some have contended that it may not really be the lawbreaker's fault because he (according to one newspaper story) was influenced by "the extra Y chromosome, or XYY pattern, necessarily related to antisocial or criminal behavior." Just keep in mind that you are not a qualified scientist—your responsibility is to safeguard your family and yourself as well as possible. Simply handle the immediate situation carefully by giving up your valuables, as advised; don't try to placate, argue, or arouse your assailant into a physical attack.

Don't let yourself be persuaded by alibis into refusing to report or prosecute a crime against you. Let the authorities be the judges of the criminal action. When caught after breaking into homes, offenders may come up with the wildest excuses, such as these actual recorded alibis: "I had a killing headache and just came in through the open window to get a couple of aspirin tablets" . . . "It was pouring and I have a heavy cold, so I only came in to get out of the rain." A man apprehended right inside a home which he had entered illegally said that he had an attack of sugar diabetes and broke into the home to call a doctor. Emphasizing that this is no laughing matter, a leading authority on the criminal mind stresses: "A burglar is a burglar, whether he is a $5 burglar, a $50 burglar or a $50,000 burglar; we worry about them." That's a good tip for you, that a $5 "petty thief" can react as dangerously as the criminal who is after the big money. Stay cautious and unbelieving of any offender, and you'll stay safer.

You should know that repeaters (recidivists, habitual criminals) commit a major part of the crimes that are on the increase. Most of these are "career men" in criminal fields. Even though caught and jailed, they are likely to continue their lawbreaking activities time after time when released. An FBI analysis of over 30,000 criminals who repeated crimes shows an average six arrests, three convictions, and two imprisonments each over a ten-year period. The survey further shows that criminals don't believe in the biblical warning, "Use not vain repetitions." Forty per cent of auto thieves and 48 per cent of check forgers were repeaters. Of almost 20,000 prisoners released by the federal criminal-justice system in one year, 55 per cent were rearrested for new crimes within the next two-and-a-half years.

The narcotics problem accounts for a big portion of the increase in the number of crimes each year. There is no question that addicts are responsible for the bulk of crimes today, particularly burglary and muggings. Some police departments have reported that as many as 90 per cent of the individuals they have arrested for burglaries in a recent year are narcotics addicts. They will do almost anything in their desperation for money for more drugs. Their crimes are often unpredictable, even by the offenders themselves; they sometimes take impossible gambles, perhaps on the spur of the moment. They are dangerous assailants to cross.

Tragically, there are wide inconsistencies. To support his habit, the narcotics addict will sell what he steals for practically nothing at times. In one reported burglary, a narcotics addict arrested for breaking into a wealthy home took jewelry, furs, and other loot valued at $5,000—and sold them for $100, a

263

fiftieth of their value. He wanted money in a hurry to buy drugs, and rationality didn't enter into the transaction any more than in the conduct of his daily life. You must realize that you can't afford to take chances in fighting a criminal who starts by taking such reckless chances himself.

CRIMINAL MIND CHECKLIST

☐ DON'T consider any active criminal to be like a "normal" or "usual" person. He is unpredictable and dangerous.

☐ DO realize that a criminal's M.O. (modus operandi, method of working) can change suddenly, so that one who has been nonviolent for years can strike without warning.

☐ DO convince yourself that it is usually safer to give up your valuables readily than to risk a deadly reaction.

☐ DON'T ever let your guard down against any active criminal.

☐ DO report any criminal action, and let the authorities be the judges.

☐ DO understand that a high percentage of crimes are by repeaters (recidivists, habitual criminals).

☐ DON'T trust narcotics users who, when desperate for a "fix," will do almost anything to get money for drugs.

44

THE KINDS OF CRIMINALS
AROUND TODAY

DON'T THINK that all criminals are alike. They differ in appearance, habits, work methods, and all other details, just as average citizens do. You'll be misled if you proceed on the assumption that there is "a criminal type" and "a normal type." Among burglars, as just one category, there are a number of specialists, including these:

The "doorshaker": he rings the doorbell of a house, or door after door down the hallways of an apartment building, or knocks on the doors of rooms at hotels or motels. If no one answers, he tries the doorknob, enters if the door is unlocked, and starts gathering loot. If someone answers the door, he asks a quick question such as, "Is Mr. McGillicuddy there?" Then he apologizes that he must have the wrong address or room number and goes away to try to shake down another entrance door. Door-shakers, who may be men or women, often drug addicts, laugh over the fact that in the course of each day's work they find many doors left unlocked by people who are "asking to be robbed." The burglar is only too glad to oblige; one said that he considered an unlocked door a welcome mat inviting him in to "clean out the premises."

A survey made in the morning hours by the New York City Police Department confirmed the shocking carelessness of citizens who then tend to blame the authorities or somebody else, anyone but themselves, for their own negligence. Checking some Queens apartment houses, police found that one out of every

265

six apartment doors was left unlocked—25 out of 150 apartment doors covered in the survey.

The "loid" man: he earned his name originally by using as his lock-opening device a thin, stiff piece of celluloid, like the little pocket calendars that banks and others give away. He simply works the strip of celluloid, tin, plastic, or other stiff, thin material through the crack of a door to force the bolt of a spring-lock back so he can just turn the knob, open the door, and walk in. He proves that ordinary spring locks provide little protection from a "loid" man, or even a reasonably adept amateur crook.

The "pick" man: he picks open a variety of locks with a special tool with a little hook at the end, or even with a shaped piece of ordinary tough wire. The "pick" man often considers himself a craftsman, superior to other types of burglars. Like an artist, he may leave his own distinctive marks (M.O.), or lack of them, as a particularly careful craftsman, which can eventually lead to his capture by the police.

The "punch-and-grab" burglar: he forces a lock by differing methods, punching out the cylinder, jimmying the lock open, unscrewing the mechanism with specially fashioned tools, or other methods involving pressure of one kind or another.

The "sneak thief": he generally does a quick in-and-out of large offices or other buildings employing many persons at desks, benches, cubbyholes. His favorite time is the lunch hour or the standard coffee-break periods in midmorning or midafternoon when people gather in the company cafeteria or canteens. The sneak thief moves swiftly through the empty areas, pretending to be a messenger, delivery man, salesman, or service man. He may wear overalls or an apron or other garment with large pockets for loot, or a delivery service cap, or other commonplace camouflage. He snatches purses, watches, earrings, other jewelry —whatever personal valuables are left on the desk or in quickly accessible drawers. His prey is the careless individual who leaves a purse or other valuables around instead of locking them in a drawer or locker.

"Aerialists": some of these are as adept as human flies. They swing into houses or apartments by climbing an adjacent tree,

266

dangle from a rope hung from the roof to let them down to a top apartment window, jump across from a fire escape to an unprotected window, taking risks often far beyond what the results warrant in loot. Some of the most acrobatic of the "aerialists" have been killed or crippled falling from a high apartment window while engaged in burglary that would have netted only a few dollars at most.

There are many other categories of burglars, and variations within the variations. One super-specialist chose, oddly enough, to steal only new locks from hardware and other stores, which he sold to one steady criminal buyer day after day, week after week —"a nice, steady business," he said smugly. Police officers who have long worked in the burglary squad can often examine the scene of the crime and tell not only what type of burglar did the job but sometimes the specific individual M.O. They then set out to watch the particular thief carefully and to catch him on another job or with evidence to arrest and convict him. Frequently the lawbreakers can be traced through many kinds of stolen articles—jewelry, clothing, art objects, TV and radio sets, suitcases, and even telephones which they sell to a "fence" (professional receiver of stolen goods) for $5 to $25 or more.

Don't be caught off guard because you think of criminals and their activities in terms of stereotypes. The unexpected can always happen in crimes—and often does. Most citizens questioned about murder, for example, will suppose that the greatest numbers of murders are committed with firearms. Actually other often-used weapons for murders turn out to be knives, hammers, heavy ashtrays, or other handy blunt instruments, since a great percentage of murders are done on the spur of the moment. Such fatal crimes of sudden passion are caused by arguments, fights, flaring of tempers, or when a criminal feels himself forced into the final act of desperation.

Most criminals don't have brilliant minds. They are not impossible to catch. Pessimists may say, "There's no sense in reporting a burglary or other such offense," but this is foolish. Always make your report to the police; the records show even the toughest lawbreakers can be apprehended.

Much can be learned from reading case histories. There was, for instance, the first woman placed on the FBI's list of ten most wanted fugitives, sought in a kidnapping. She was arrested when applying for a position as a nurse at a hospital. Her application required fingerprinting, a process she went through without protest. The FBI, on the lookout constantly, matched the fingerprints, although she was using another name. The officials acted quickly and arrested her. Apparently she was either unaware or overconfident about being identified by fingerprint comparisons—or simply didn't care any more. It has been noted by some psychologists that criminals at times seem to have an "inner wish" to be caught and punished for their sins against society.

Another example: a pair of thieves had "carefully" planned a bank robbery in the Southwest. They pried open the back door, which wasn't adequately protected by an alarm system or other surveillance, and raided the cashiers' drawers, only to find them empty. Then they used a compressor drill to break into the main vault, but instead found themselves in a storage room which didn't contain any valuables. Next they forced their way through a wall where they figured the vault was situated; they found themselves emerging outdoors on a main highway—and were apprehended.

Stupidities abound among criminals, clever as they may think they are. One burglar's M.O. was leaving his tools behind him at the scene of the crime. When arrested, he said that he felt he'd been very canny to leave his tools behind: he could never be caught when a job was finished because of carrying a set of burglary tools. He hadn't bothered to realize that he could be traced by the tools themselves.

Crime-fighting profits from the fact that criminals as a class tend to be less than brilliant, figuring they can get away with the stupidest stunts. One prisoner returned from an outside work detail with his face puffed out and mouth bulging, claiming that he had the mumps. A guard ordered him to open his mouth, and dragged out a chain over a foot long which he had tried to conceal in his mouth for use in an escape attempt.

Criminals don't generally "get away with it." News reports are perhaps more dramatic and therefore more widely noted about the criminals who got away with it than the many who either miss the haul completely or are caught. Don't believe that it's almost impossible to convict the lawbreakers these days, because of changes in the interpretation of the laws. A popular cartoon showed a disgruntled police officer reporting to headquarters: "By the time I protected his civil liberties, informed him of his constitutional rights, and made up my mind whether to shoot when he ran, he got away." Factually and fortunately for you, that's an exaggeration.

The power of improved police techniques, detailed effort and follow-up, and some luck combine to catch a high percentage of lawbreakers. A detective stepped into a phone booth just outside a store and was dialing his number when he saw a holdup man running from the store with a bag of loot; the detective dropped the phone and grabbed the runaway before the thief even knew what was going on.

Three officers chasing a purse-snatcher followed him into a nearby building and ran into a narcotics peddler handing a packet to an apartment dweller in his doorway. Snatching them both, the officers found and arrested three more users in the apartment, along with a supply of drugs valued at over $50,000. The solutions of most cases are not that easy, usually requiring painstaking efforts over an extended period.

Never envy the criminal for living off others rather than working steadily for success. A noted police authority, from his experience with the burglary squad, spotlighted the lawbreaker's lot in describing "pick" men: "[These nervous men] work under tremendous tension. They might look smooth and talk calmly, but you'll find that noise disturbs them . . . the slightest thing will set them off. . . . They are suspicious, superstitious and sick . . . they have no real life. They have a tendency to move around a lot. They stay away from their neighbors. . . . And when they are finally caught, they are worn out inside. Right down to nothing. They've eaten up their own insides. They're hollow."

The next time someone remarks that the criminal has "the easy life," tell him about a lawbreaker acknowledged to be an expert among criminals who finally, past age seventy, has turned legitimate and is helping the police, as a consultant, to trap others. He now calls himself "the biggest fink in America" because he is assisting those on the right side of the law. In spite of the eminence he achieved in the criminal world, he admits that he spent thirty-five of his seventy years "up to now" in prisons for burglary, bank and train robbery, safecracking, assault, manslaughter, and assorted other crimes. As he puts it at this late date, he wasted thirty-five years of life in what he calls "government service."

CHECKLIST OF CRIMINAL TYPES

☐ DON'T think of a standard, recognizable "criminal type"—lawbreakers come in all sizes, shapes, ages, characteristics.

☐ DON'T be caught off guard; expect the unexpected in criminals' actions.

☐ DON'T think that criminals usually "get away with it"—a high percentage are caught, and police methods are constantly improving.

45

UNUSUAL STORIES ABOUT CRIME AND PROTECTION

YOU SHOULD take crime and protection seriously but don't forget the gift of laughter which can help you handle adversities. Here are a few oddities that may be interesting or amusing and certainly prove one thing—that in crime the unexpected should always be expected.

A burglar who was a scholarly type was caught inside a public library trying to break open the safe in the main office. Police were alerted by a silent alarm which went off at headquarters when the safe was opened after hours. It was found that the burglar was using a stolen car in which he had hidden a loaded revolver, a carbine rifle, $600 worth of stolen clothing, and a book stolen from a library. The volume's title was *Blue Book on Crime,* detailing methods used by police to block and trap lawbreakers. Apparently the burglar hadn't yet gotten around to reading the book.

A bank robbery involved "frozen assets." When FBI agents tracked down one of the thieves, his female companion admitted that she was hiding some of the loot. She removed a package of chopped meat from the kitchen freezer, boiled the meat, and when it had thawed removed from the center another foil-wrapped package. It contained $2,000 of the stolen money.

The doctoring of pay books, tracked down by fraud detectives, was not totally unexpected. It occurred at a prison where inmates handled the records for the prison store.

In an office burglary, two of the items missing occasioned some surprise—two tickets to the annual Policeman's Ball.

A sign outside a hospital warns: "Trespassers will be prosecuted to the full extent of the law. [signed] The Sisters of Mercy."

When news spread in Rio de Janeiro that a criminal was robbing and then disposing of street beggars by drowning them, some beggars subsequently appeared on the streets wearing life preservers.

When a Charleston, South Carolina, store selling firearms was burglarized, the *Saturday Review* reports, the dealer ran this newspaper advertisement: "Will the persons who removed thirteen rifles, shotguns, and pistols from our shop after we were closed please come by and fill out Federal Form 4473 to comply with the Gun Control Act of 1968? All guns *must* be signed for and proper identification given."

A woman who had a record as a habitual criminal was arrested in Iowa for violating parole and passing forged checks. Being seven months' pregnant, she claimed that authorities who had placed her in jail were holding her unborn child illegally. Prosecuting attorneys replied that they would gladly release the child if the woman would produce it. The judge ruled against the woman's plea, stating that "pregnancy cannot be allowed to become a sanctuary for illegal practices."

In Blantyre, Malawi, Africa, a 25-year-old man was arrested and given a three-year term at hard labor for a theft. It was revealed that he had stolen the equivalent of 69 cents. The presiding magistrate, in meting out the severe sentence, said that this was "the worst robbery case in Blantyre this year."

A police officer attempting to arrest a 34-year-old man caught disturbing the peace encountered a bewildering attack as he advanced on the belligerent individual. The man raced away a short distance, stopped, pulled off his leg, and hurled it at the officer, who ducked in the nick of time, avoiding possible serious injury. The wooden leg was returned to the assailant, who was then booked for drunk and disorderly conduct.

An avid reader whose friends admired the mass of books in his home was understandably upset when a missing library book was traced to him by an investigator. He admitted that he had been stealing the volumes from libraries and book stores for the past fifteen years. It took eight truckloads to remove the books.

A cartoon contains valuable advice in case you are ever a witness testifying about a crime. Prosecuting attorneys tend to endorse the recommendation wholeheartedly. The picture shows an irate judge shouting to a determined woman in the witness box: "Madam, just tell the truth, the whole truth and nothing but the truth—and then shut up!"

Two men carrying a TV set out of a home were stopped by a neighbor. They said they were taking away the set for over-haul and repair. They agreed to take the neighbor's set also. Neither set was returned; the men were thieves.

A drunk who claimed to have a gun robbed a cab driver after midnight. As he lurched away, the driver followed cautiously and, turning a corner, saw a police car at the curb. He told the policeman about the robbery, then looking at the back seat, shouted, "There's the crook!" A moment before, the drunk had stepped into the patrol car, thinking it was a taxi. He sobered up in a jail cell.

Licensed florists complained to police in a South American city that street venders were stealing flowers from graves and selling them from their carts at cut-rate prices.

A sign on the entrance door of a California store reads: "This door is alarmed. Do not open."

CHECKLIST OF UNUSUAL CRIMES

☐ DO take crime and protection seriously.

☐ DON'T, however, forget the gift of laughter in handling criminals.

☐ DO expect the unexpected.

46

WHAT YOU SHOULD KNOW
ABOUT POLICEMEN

THE POLICE are sworn to be on the side of the law-abiding individual, and against those who break the law and infringe on the rights of others. The policeman is basically a "law-enforcement officer." If you are a law-abiding citizen, the policeman is on your side. His role is to protect you, your home, your family, your business—so long as you are on the side of the law. To the criminal he is an ever-threatening, relentless enemy.

Policemen are "people." As in every large number of people, there are varying degrees of character, ability, and types of individuals. In every large group, there must be some "bad apples." For many reasons, including intensive screening, the overall caliber of policemen in most communities in the United States is high. In spite of loud outcries from a comparatively few people (many of whom are in opposition to the law) against the police and "police brutality," public opinion in broad polls turns out to be overwhelmingly for the police as an essential protective force in this society. In spite of criticism, a percentage of which may be justified, and the never-ceasing drive for improvement, the role of the police is to serve you, aid you, and protect you.

As a law-enforcement officer, a policeman sometimes has to enforce a law that is antiquated or no longer necessary. In such cases, in a democracy citizens can change such laws and should. They should not expect the policeman to ignore such laws (though they often do) because that makes him a law-ignoring

274

rather than a law-enforcing officer. A judge can consider extenuating circumstances, and a policeman often will—though he shouldn't, according to the rules of his job. A policeman is not a judge. He is not allowed to interpret laws loosely or severely; he has to interpret them exactly, according to his instructions.

There is a recent case of a suburban couple who decided to spend their anniversary night at a hotel in a nearby big city. They left their car overnight at their suburban railroad station and took the train in. The next morning they found a ticket on their car for overnight parking. The fine was $2 and could be paid by mail if the man pleaded guilty. But the man decided to go to court and present his case, which was that there were no signs in the village station parking lot prohibiting overnight parking. He inquired at the police station and found out that the ordinance was in effect from October 1st through April 30th for good reason—in case of snow, the parking lot had to be cleared by morning and this could not be done if any cars were parked overnight. But notice of the ordinance had been published in the local paper many years previously, before this particular couple had moved to the village.

As a result of spending an hour in court waiting (his case was dismissed) and then writing to the Town Board about it, there are now conspicuous postings of the local ordinance in the village parking lot. Ignorance of the law is no excuse, but proper notice of any somewhat unusual law is necessary to create respect for the law. The officer who ticketed the car parked overnight was doing his duty. But the citizen who took the time to state his case—instead of taking the easy way out and paying the nominal fine by mail—was doing his duty also. While this case concerns a comparatively trivial matter, it is really illustrative of both the police officer's and the citizen's responsibilities with regard to laws in a democratic society.

Because a policeman is a law-enforcement officer, he sometimes enforces laws which are on the books but which some citizens resent. For instance, most citizens strongly approve of local speed limits and laws prohibiting driving while intoxicated.

275

But the individual who is apprehended while speeding or driving while under the influence feels resentful not of the law which he broke but of the policeman who apprehended him.

Sometimes a policeman has to enforce an unpopular law or local ordinance. For instance, many communities have now banned the burning of leaves because it contributes to the air-pollution problem. Most people are opposed to air pollution— in fact, there is no sane reason to be *for* air pollution—but stuffing leaves into plastic bags is a lot more work than raking them into piles and burning them. The ordinances against leaf-burning are thus not terribly popular, but they are necessary if the will of the majority is to be supported with regard to air pollution. In fact, no other groups are really damaged by these ordinances. Nevertheless, when a man gets a summons for burning leaves illegally, he steams with resentment of the ordinance, but mostly he hates the policeman who caught him. Obviously, some of the work policemen have to do is necessarily unpopular.

Most police are overworked and underpaid, as compared with many others in private and even public service. The policeman works long hours and is never really off duty. His work, protecting you and your home and public institutions against criminals and lawbreakers, often puts him in danger. Nevertheless, the policeman as an individual derives much pride from his work of protecting the public; his position as a guardian and helper of others uplifts him and sustains him. That is one of the reasons why, in spite of the dangers and hardships of police work, items such as this keep appearing in the press: "A Boston police sergeant was smartly saluted by seven fellow officers when he retired after 38 years of service. The seven fellow cops were his seven sons—all policemen." In fact, father-and-son in police work is a tradition.

Many community police departments are understaffed because of tough working schedules and conditions linked with inadequate pay. The police chief of the Los Angeles police department said, "We just haven't the manpower to keep crime in check. We need 10,000 men, but we can't even fill our authorized strength of 5,383." This is a national problem, affecting every area. A vital factor is that to build up a department to maximum strength and efficiency, the police must have the moral and economic support of the citizenry. This is especially necessary at a time when small groups have singled out the police as objects of abuse and physical attack when they are really opposed to the laws the police are obligated to enforce.

A task force of the President's Crime Commission witnessed 5,339 "police-citizen encounters," during 850 eight-hour patrols, and found only twenty cases in which police were felt to have used unnecessary force. A newspaper columnist noted: "That is a record of satisfactory performance in 99.63 per cent of the sample under study. What other occupation or profession boasts a better record?"

You can't always recognize a policeman by his uniform. In big cities some may wear false wigs and skirts, the black garb and (fake) beards of Hasidic rabbis, hippie rags, doormen's uniforms, other disguises. A patrolman described what happened when "several youths brandishing sticks" closed in on another policeman and himself who were disguised in false beards and black robes as rabbis. He said that when the two officers lifted their robes and showed their badges and weapons, "I'll never forget their looks of amazement. They didn't try to run. They just stood there—stupefied." The result is shown not only in arrests but also in deterring crime by making hoodlums feel insecure and confused when they learn that "policemen come in various shapes and forms."

Protection with Nonlethal Weapons?

Don't jump to conclusions, strongly for or against nonlethal weapons, until you know something about the subject from all angles. Because of conflicting facts and theories, firm conclusions cannot be drawn at this writing. Probably the leading category of nonlethal weapons now is the tear-gas type of product bearing such names as Chemical Mace, Federal Streamer, and others.

277

There is a large and sometimes angry difference of opinion between those people who are for the use of tear-gas products and those against. Proponents say that the stinging, incapacitating effects are temporary, and in the end harmless. Opponents of the use of tear-gas products insist that there can be lasting, harmful results including severe skin damage, serious eye injury, even death.

The purpose of nonlethal weapons is to reduce the use of billy clubs and firearms by law enforcement officers, of any weapons which can inflict drastic injury, crippling, and death. The problems have worsened as riots and other confrontations between segments of the public and law enforcement personnel have increased. The ideal solution could be nonlethal aids which enable law enforcement officers to stop lawbreakers instantly, and subdue rioters, criminals, anyone disturbing the peace, for a sufficient length of time, but with only temporary physical effects.

One commentator put it this way: "To preserve our free way of life in an orderly society, it is essential that *riots be controlled without violence.* The new riot-control tools which use temporary discomfort instead of shooting and clubbing are democracy's answer to this problem." Another authority acknowledged this but noted, "In all recorded history, man has searched for the 'Philosopher's Stone' that would turn lead into gold, or riots into peace, in our analogy. But no one has yet discovered a magical answer for Instant Peace."

Special problems are involved in controlling a riot or "civil disorder." Public buildings, police stations, churches, schools, stores, and many other establishments can be destroyed if the violence gets out of control. Rioters don't go by any rules. Fair play is ignored. A mob is governed by mass hysteria, hatred, and impulse. The longer the riot continues, the more destructive the situation grows. Each violent step leads to greater disaster and chaos. When prevention fails, there is no alternative to quick, effective measures by official control forces.

Nonlethal weaponry is not limited to tear-gas devices. Energetic research is going on in many laboratories to try to produce an effective tranquilizer unit that will turn a raging rioter into a meek lamb instantly. The troubles up to now have been many-faceted. Tranquilizers have not worked in a few seconds; instead a raging criminal, for example, even after being struck by a tranquilizer dart, maintains energy for enough time to keep attacking an officer or anyone else, and to inflict fatal injury before the tranquilizing chemical has sufficient effect to render him quite harmless. (In one case, a police sergeant fired regular bullets at an assailant plunging toward him with a knife; the bullets killed the criminal but his forward momentum drove the knife into the sergeant who died from the wound.)

There is another big problem with tranquilizer weapons—the difficulty of figuring out and using the correct dosage in the split-second timing often essential. A dose large enough to subdue a violent 250-pounder may kill a 150-pound attacker, while the dosage sufficient to tranquilize the small man might have little effect on the big one. The law enforcement officer, holding the tranquilizer gun and about to be brutally attacked, has no time to measure out the proper dosage according to the size and weight of his assailant. Furthermore if his attacker is using a gun with lead bullets, he can shoot and kill the officer long before a tranquilizer dart, no matter how well aimed, can have any subduing effect. As another consideration, even a mildly dosed tranquilizer dart may kill if it pierces an eye or other vulnerable spot, or it may induce a fatal heart attack in a person who has a weak heart. Obviously, there are no easy solutions.

Other nonlethal possibilities advocated by some people have their serious faults. The use of fire hoses against an unruly mob may, if it does not subdue the attackers sufficiently, arouse them from what started as noisy shouting into violent counterattack. The same is true of dyes and stenches added to water sprays; fierce anger and violent reaction may result in a nonsubdued crowd inflamed by the smell and by the disfiguration of skin and clothing. Another factor is the indignant reaction of storekeepers and others whose store fronts, buildings, and interior premises may be marked in indelible dye stains and made unpleasant by

279

lingering offensive odors. Even gadgets that generate "harmless" high-volume foam covering up to 50,000 cubic feet in a few minutes can do more harm than good; being covered with foam may antagonize rather than control a crowd.

Research in nonlethal weapons continues, however, and better methods will probably be found eventually. One rather astonishing approach is the development of an electronic item which gives out a strange vibration tone that results in loss of control of the bowels among those hearing it. An obvious, difficult problem which has arisen in this area is in making the tone rigidly directional so that it doesn't affect anyone except those who are to be subdued. Nevertheless the electronic scientists involved have high hopes.

Tear-gas products are in use by the forces of law in many communities. Other developments are being studied, tested, and even used, but primarily aerosol units are the major part of the "nonlethal weapons" arsenal at this time. The range available includes pen-size sprays, carried in the pocket by a clip or attached to an officer's belt or kept in the squad car; units which form part of a police baton, billy, or night stick, so that an unruly crowd simply sees the officer carrying the night stick, and he need only turn the baton to use the tear-gas end if necessary in his judgment; larger aerosol containers under nine inches long and less than three inches in diameter, usable in one hand, with a spray range of up to thirty feet, average contents of sixty sizable half-second bursts, and "guaranteed against leakage or functional failure for four years from date of manufacture."

According to a leading manufacturer of such nonlethal weapons, "Some [police] departments report assaults on police officers have been cut in half [by their use]—others report police brutality complaints have been cut by 80 per cent." A magazine article quotes a policeman who used a tear-gas spray during a riot as reporting, "A man may be trying to wipe up the sidewalk with you. You give him a little squirt, and he sits right down in the street and cries. For half an hour he is as helpless as a newborn baby. After that he's OK."

On the other hand, another publication reported that a

"disabling riot-control spray . . . is coming under increasing criticism from the medical profession." It cites the case of a teenage boy sprayed in a riot whose doctor said that the boy "spent five days with excoriations [redness and bruises] about the entire eye" and that "skin peeled from the youth's face and from around the eye. . . . The doctor said that it [tear-gas spray] endangers people with rheumatic heart trouble or a congenital heart condition" or with "bronchial troubles such as asthma."

All sides agree that effective nonlethal weaponry is highly desirable and badly needed. A report of the President's Commission on Law Enforcement and Administration of Justice notes: "Police use of firearms to apprehend suspects often strains community relations or even results in serious disorders." The Commission recommended usage of firearms "*only* when the officer believes his life or the life of another is in imminent danger, or when other reasonable means of apprehension have failed to prevent the escape of a felony suspect whom the officer believes presents a serious danger to others." There is general agreement on all sides with this view.

Don't use tear-gas devices yourself as a private citizen if it is against the law in your state and community, as it is in many areas. Before you buy a device, check the legality with local police or other law enforcement authorities.

CHECKLIST ON POLICEMEN

☐ DON'T forget that policemen are on the side of law-abiding individuals.

☐ DO understand that policemen are "people," varying in types, character, and ability, mostly of high caliber as a result of detailed screening, but including some "bad apples," of course, like any body of individuals.

☐ DO realize that most police are overworked and underpaid compared to people in private industry, and that most departments are understaffed.

☐ DON'T believe in exaggerations about "police brutality"— the facts refute these.

☐ DON'T be one-sidedly for or against nonlethal weapons; first study the detailed facts pro and con.

☐ DO understand that the prime purpose of nonlethal weapons is to provide control without use of clubs, guns, and other death-dealing weapons, and that improvements are being sought and developed constantly.

47

WHAT YOU CAN DO TO HELP THE POLICE HELP YOU

COOPERATION with law-enforcement authorities by you and others can make the crucial difference in effective protection for the individual and his property. A newspaper report shows that cooperation with the police is an important factor in putting law-breakers behind bars, as in these few specific instances cited:

High school boys eating in a restaurant noticed three men at the telephone booth, two blocking the door while a third worked on the coin box inside. As the men left, the boys followed discreetly, took the license number of the car in which the men drove away, and passed it on to the police. Arrested later and identified by the boys, the men were found to be involved in organized coin-box thefts which had robbed the telephone company of about $15,000. The boys received rewards.

An alert citizen heard a man who was carrying a shotgun mutter that he was going to "get the Thompsons." He informed a policeman, who found the Thompsons' house nearby, caught the man inside the house, and disarmed him before he could murder the family.

A woman became suspicious that a burglary might be taking place in a neighbor's house, because of a car parked for a long time near the house. She called the police, who caught two men who admitted to a string of 170 burglaries in two states.

The police can't do the whole job required all alone. They need the constant help of an alert, involved, cooperative citizenry. As stated earlier, don't be concerned that your tip may be a "false alarm." Police realize their responsibility to investigate all tips and are fully aware that many may be false alarms. On the other hand, if one life is saved, one crime prevented, the time spent on the investigation of tips, whether real or mistaken, has not been wasted.

The police can be highly effective against criminals in spite of crimes which may get the spotlight. Here's an example detailing what happened, step by step, in a bank holdup in late afternoon in a southern city:

1. A bank was held up at gunpoint. The bank's holdup alarm went off in police headquarters, and a police alert went into effect.

2. A lady, suspicious of activities around the bank, took down the license of the getaway car. She gave the number to police officers as they arrived at the robbery scene.

3. Within minutes, the possible escape routes were cut off by police setting up roadblocks.

4. The runaway car was wrecked trying to run one of the police roadblocks, and the arrest was made—34 minutes after the robbery attempt began.

Recognize the wide scope of a policeman's responsibilities and actions in trying to protect the citizenry in all kinds of situations. Here are a few examples from limitless numbers of cases:

Responding to a call that a baby was choking, two radio car partners entered the home and found a seven-day-old infant gasping for breath, clearly in an emergency condition. They rushed the infant out to the car, and as one officer drove the other applied mouth-to-mouth resuscitation. Doctors said that the infant survived only because of the emergency actions and treatment by the officers.

An off-duty patrolman, driving home after a long tour of duty, saw flames leaping from the windows of a small hotel. He stopped the car, jumped out, shouted to someone to sound the fire alarm, and entered the building by climbing the fire escape. He made three trips into the burning hotel, rousing and leading out eight persons, saving their lives. Overcome by smoke, he was pulled to safety by other police who had arrived on the scene.

A probationary patrolman, a member of the police force for just one week, was home asleep after an exhausting day in his new work. He was aroused by his mother, who heard noises from the closed tailor shop under their apartment. He gathered up his shield and gun, went downstairs quietly, and arrested two men who had broken into the shop. A police official commented, "All in the day's (and night's) work."

Policewomen also are important for keeping your family and home safe. They perform many functions which can de done best only by a woman, as cited in a cartoon showing two convicts in a prison cell. One disgruntled convict explaining his capture grumbles to his cellmate, "She was blonde, petite . . . and a bluecoat."

The police department youth programs to combat juvenile delinquency are very worthwhile. If at all possible you should participate. Activities differ in small, middle-sized, and large communities. New York City has a system of youth councils with police and private citizens helping young people.

One small town concentrates on a police department drum and bugle corps. According to the local superintendent of police, this activity "keeps approximately eighty youngsters busy twelve months of the year, practicing, drilling, and competing for trophies." In addition, he points out that "a three-man youth bureau provides assistance to other boys and girls with their problems. Often the youngsters are more frank with a policeman than with their parents."

The key aim here has been, as it is with police departments everywhere, to prevent crime before it happens, and to stop youths from becoming criminals. Many police heads, along with cooperating citizens, report that such activities have "substantially reduced the incidence of juvenile crime."

Volunteer auxiliary police forces exist in many cities. Most of the volunteer men and women are unpaid and unarmed; they serve about four hours a week on police duty, usually under instructions from their own precinct. They wear uniforms similar to those of the regular police, but with a special sleeve patch inscribed "Auxiliary Police." Asked why he had volunteered, a father of three gave a typical explanation: "When you have a family, you feel that when a family goes out, they want protection. I felt my duty as a citizen is to protect them." The auxiliary police are given training and have proved helpful in many aspects of safeguarding people and property. In New York City the assistance of the auxiliary police helps to supplement the work of the regular police in handling crowds and parades, directing traffic, and general patrol on the streets, parks, elsewhere when needed.

POLICE-COOPERATION CHECKLIST

☐ DO realize that cooperation with the police can make the crucial difference in effective protection for your family and property.

☐ DO participate in worthy police department youth programs.

☐ DO consider joining the volunteer auxiliary police force if it exists in your locality.

48

HOW TO GET COMPENSATION IF YOU ARE EVER A VICTIM

IF YOU are the innocent victim of a violent crime, you should make certain you get all the compensation coming to you. Check police and local and state government officials about the situation in your state, for not all states provide compensation. New York State Governor Nelson A. Rockefeller explains that the program in his state was created "to provide compensation for the innocent victims of violent crime. . . . The plan was the outgrowth of an intensive study by a distinguished committee . . . after the tragic murder of a young man in a subway that left his widow and child to face a life of destitution."

Get details locally in order to file a claim properly. In New York State, for example, here are some of the specifications:

Eligibility: You can file a claim if you sustain personal injuries and (a) are the victim of a crime; or (b) are a surviving spouse or child of a victim of a crime who died as a direct result of such crime; or (c) any other person dependent for principal support on a victim of a crime who died as a direct result of such a crime. If the claimant is a minor, the claim may be signed by his parent or guardian or the person with whom he resides.

Provisions: The crime must be reported promptly to the proper police authorities, preferably within 48 hours or sooner after the crime took place. You must prove that you suffer serious financial hardship as a result of the loss of earnings or support and out-of-pocket expenses.

Compensation: You must have (a) out-of-pocket expenses

for medical or other services of at least $100 not reimbursable from other sources; or (b) loss of earnings for at least two continuous weeks. Maximum award for loss of earnings is $100 per week; if weekly earning is less than $100, compensation will be based on actual earnings. Monies paid by other sources will be deducted from your allowance for loss of earnings.

Filing Claim: Claims must be filed within 90 days after the occurrence or death (may be extended if for good reason, but not after one year after date of the occurrence). Inquire from local authorities where claims are to be filed (in New York State, claims are filed with the Crime Victims Compensation Board, Albany, N.Y. 12206).

VICTIM-COMPENSATION CHECKLIST

☐ DON'T overlook the possibilities of compensation if you are a crime victim, now provided by some states.

☐ DO check local authorities for claim possibilities in your state, and ask for details on filing a claim.

☐ DO act quckly if you are a crime victim, as claims must generally be filed within a limited time after the occurrence.

49

HOW TO CLAIM TAX DEDUCTIONS FOR THEFTS

BE SURE you get all possible tax deductions available to you in case of losses from theft or other crimes. Your accountant or local tax information office can advise you. It's quite likely that you can save some on taxes if you have suffered loss or damage due to a crime against you.

You can often take a tax deduction on a loss due to vandalism (deliberately mischievous or malicious destruction or damage of property). Such loss is caused by persons or forces outside of your control. It is deductible if the damage or destruction is sudden and unexpected.

Deduct for stolen or embezzled property held for personal use. Your theft loss should be figured as (a) the fair market value of the property stolen or embezzled, or (b) its adjusted basis, that is, including increases or decreases of the value of the property since you acquired it—whichever amount is smaller. This sum is then reduced by the amount of insurance or other money received or expected to be received. Finally, a $100 minimum is applied. If the property should be recovered, the initial loss figured must be reduced by the fair market value of the item at the time of recovery.

For example, let's say you bought a movie camera for $185. Three months later it is stolen, and you are advised by a camera dealer that its fair market value at that date is $135. You reported the theft to the police but the camera was not recovered. From the fair market value of $135, you can now deduct the $100 limitation, and your deductible loss is $35.

In a theft of one or more articles, the $100 limitation is applied to the total loss. For instance in the theft of the $135 camera, a projector with a market value of $165 was also taken. The total loss was $300, minus the $100 limitation, resulting in a deductible loss of $200.

If a husband and wife file a joint tax return, they are treated as one individual in applying the $100 limitation, whether the property is jointly or separately owned. However, if husband and wife file separate tax returns, each is subject to a separate $100 limitation for the loss by theft, regardless of whether the property is jointly or separately owned.

In money or property losses due to theft and embezzlement, your deductible loss is the actual amount of money taken, or the value of the other property on the adjusted basis. From this you deduct the amount of insurance or other recovery (such as surety or fidelity bond proceeds) that you received or may expect to receive.

Deduct in the year of discovery of the theft and embezzlement losses. You don't have to prove the date that the property was stolen, just the date when you discovered the loss.

Clear proof of loss through theft or embezzlement is required. The losses may be for business or nonbusiness property; they are deductible only by the person who owns the property and sustained the loss.

Double-check your deduction with your accountant or local tax information office before setting down the sum, telling them the specific instance of loss and how you arrived at your figure. Details given here are necessarily simplified and condensed. They are a general guide, provided primarily to alert you to take a proper deduction on any loss due you.

THEFT TAX DEDUCTION CHECKLIST

☐   DO take all permitted tax deductions on losses from thefts or other crimes.

☐   DO deduct, within the regulations listed, for losses in stolen and embezzled property, and vandalism.

☐ DO figure deductions on business as well as personal losses due to crime.

☐ DON'T overlook the fact that deductions must be taken in the year of *discovery* of the loss, with clear proof of loss.

☐ DO check such deductions with your accountant or local tax information office.

50

HOW TO PROTECT GOVERNMENT CHECKS YOU RECEIVE

YOU MUST pay close attention to Treasury Department warnings if you regularly receive government checks. Here are the four main precautions recommended:

1. Many burglars habitually check mailboxes for government checks at times they are expected to arrive. Therefore try to have some member of the family at home when the checks are due to be delivered, and remove from the box as soon as possible after the postman's arrival.

2. If you cannot have someone home when government checks are due, make sure that your mailbox has a strong lock, not just a lid or latch.

3. Don't endorse the check when you receive it, but only in the presence of the person at the bank where you deposit the check, adding the words "for deposit" when you endorse the check. If you cash checks in a store or elsewhere, endorse only at the time of cashing.

4. Try to cash your checks at the same place each time— at the bank or a store or wherever—to make identification easier and the procedure quicker.

Follow these four points urged by the Treasury Department if you *cash* government checks for others:

1. Make absolutely certain that the person presenting a government check properly identifies himself as being entitled to cash it.

2. Don't cash the check unless you are certain that you

can locate the person for whom you cashed the check, if you should learn that the check is forged.

3. Again, know your endorser—and demand that the check be signed by the endorser in your presence.

4. After you cash the check, initial it and make a note of the kind of identification offered if you don't know the endorser well.

Penalties are high. Persons convicted of forging and altering U. S. Government checks may face heavy fines and imprisonment for many years. Those convicted of making, passing, or possessing counterfeit bills may receive lengthy sentences and large fines. Heavy penalties are assessed also for counterfeiting coins. Individuals having knowledge of counterfeiting activities can be fined and imprisoned if they don't make such knowledge known to the authorities. It has been said that "nothing counterfeit can be lasting"—except the punishment for the crime.

CHECKLIST ON PROTECTING GOVERNMENT CHECKS

- [ ] DO try to have someone home when checks are delivered lest they be stolen from the mailbox.
- [ ] DON'T fail to have a strong lock on your mailbox.
- [ ] DON'T endorse the check except in the presence of the person who will cash or deposit it.
- [ ] DO follow strict precautions in cashing checks for others— be sure that you identify the individual positively, that you have his address, and that the check is endorsed in your presence.

51

HOW TO KEEP FROM BECOMING
A CRIME STATISTIC

ACCORDING to a government bureau, in the past nine years, the chances of the individual in the United States becoming a crime statistic have about *doubled*. At this writing, serious crimes in just one representative state are up almost 25 per cent over the last statistical year. Robberies increased 51 per cent, murders 30 per cent, the total value of property stolen rose 18 per cent. It becomes increasingly imperative for you to take every possible protection step.

About 400 years ago, a nobleman wrote: "The house of everyone is to him as his castle and fortress, as well as for his defense against injury and violence as for his repose." Today, as then, you seek peace in your home, whether house or apartment, in city, suburb, or country, for your family and yourself. If you use the precautions recommended, your home and family will be much safer against injury and losses from burglaries. Inform every member of your family of the steps to safety and keep them on their toes on protection measures. Police records prove that greater safety comes from taking precautions. . . . "He is safer from danger who is on guard even when safe."

Keep aware at all times of new developments which you can use to help protect your family, your home, yourself. As people become increasingly aware of the need, new products and services will be offered, in addition to the many excellent aids recommended in this book. New and improved alarm systems are being perfected, as one example. However, don't put off taking available protective measures right now. It's worth it not

294

only to reduce the chances of loss, damage, and personal injury, but also to gain greater peace of mind—immediately.

Always cooperate with the authorities in every way you possibly can—this cannot be emphasized too much. It has been proved time after time that public cooperation can be enormously effective in fighting and conquering those outside the law. For example, West German television has telecast some information and clues from actual unsolved crimes one night each week. The West German Federal Criminal Police, convinced of the value of cooperation by the public, give viewers pertinent facts on open cases and show pictures of wanted subjects. Asked to be "armchair detectives," many individuals have pitched in to help.

As a result of clues and information reported by private citizens, a fugitive discussed on the first telecast was identified and arrested while the program was in progress. An extortionist who had threatened to dynamite express trains if his demands were not met was tracked down. Other cases have been solved with clues received from viewers, and good leads gathered which point to further solutions. All the cases publicized on the television programs were those in which little material and few leads were available to the police. Help from the public was and is essential to speed up effective enforcement, and to stop many criminals before they commit more crimes.

Of course you will use your common sense in putting protective recommendations into effect yourself. This book tells you what you can do, and gives you clear warning of the need for proper protective precautions. There is no guarantee that these measures will result in 100 per cent protection, or 100 per cent prevention. But your chances are far better against trouble if you take the precautions and follow the proved recommendations here. Remember that two primary elements are involved in most criminal activity: (1) the desire to commit a burglary or other crime; (2) the opportunity to do so. You help safeguard your family, your home, and yourself to the maximum when you reduce opportunity on your premises and person to the minimum.

Emphasize the Need for Protection

Speak out about the need for protection in your neighborhood and community if conditions demand improvement. Get together with neighbors and others to raise your voice and exert your power as a tax-paying, law-abiding citizen. It works. Control of criminal activities is possible.

Even the worst conditions can be overcome successfully if everyone cooperates. In a busy business area, hijacking of trucks and general pilfering mounted so sharply that losses climbed to over $50 million a year. Some protests were made, but the crimes continued. Finally, the area's trucking industry heads got together with the police to plan protection measures that would result in some immediate improvement. Conferences were held and decisions made.

Authorities ordered police to "saturate" the area with increased forces. The locality was cleared of many known thieves, loiterers, pimps, prostitutes, and other criminal elements. Did this cooperative action do any good? Within one week, hijackings and pilferage were reduced by a dramatic 70 per cent. The chairman of the drive said, "For the first time in many months, it is safe to walk in the area at night."

This is further proof that if all the law-abiding forces of society cooperate and proper protective measures are put into effect, then "the situation," as one leader put it, "can be contained." The citizen has the enormous combined strength of hundreds of millions of allies like himself, but that force must be exerted to be effective in combating crime.

Band together with others in your immediate neighborhood or apartment house to get added protection in a hurry until authorities can improve the situation. In some public housing projects, crime has been reduced by having tenant volunteers act as observers who keep criminals away just by their living presence. Each volunteer observer gives an hour or two a week, or every couple of weeks, however it works out according to the numbers available. In some middle-class apartment houses, tenants have gained greater safety by contributing to the cost of hiring lobby guards. In various concerned neighborhoods, block associations have been formed to hire a watchman to patrol the streets at night. Although these measures haven't wiped out all crimes in those places, the number of episodes has been brought down sharply.

Never give in to the pessimistic view of some listless people who say, "What's the use? We can't win against the criminal element." Public action and knowledge of how to protect one's property helps prevent crime; the criminal feeds and counts on public apathy, ignorance, and inaction. To prove this point, a TV station in Miami cooperated with the police to stage and film a number of the most common crimes—faked in these cases by actors. They acted out shopliftings, attacks on an officer of the law, child kidnappings, store robberies, and other simulated incidents. All these were viewed by bystanders, members of the onlooking public, unaware that the crimes were faked—yet onlookers intervened in only four cases out of more than fifteen staged. Most people watching didn't even go for a phone in a shopping center when they saw what seemed to be a real kidnapping.

When these individuals were accused of listlessness and of shirking responsibility, their usual comment was, "I thought somebody else would do something about it." Yet quick phone reports of crimes have often resulted in catching criminals who were then no longer free to endanger the life and property of you and your family. The personal cooperation of each citizen is a primary aid both in self-protection and in prevention of more crimes. There is a pertinent saying that "he who does not prevent a crime when he can, encourages it."

One police chief puts it to you this way, "People have to be the eyes and ears of the police department. If they see anything suspicious, they should call us. They see a lot more than we do." There can be no question that in spotting crimes, hundreds of eyes are better than two.

Don't be concerned if you can't take all the precautions

detailed. No one can. Do take the simplest steps, or use what recommendations you find most practicable in your case. The aim is not to impel you to regard everything with fear and suspicion, but rather to help you live with greater self-assurance and enjoy a comforting sense of safety along with conscious responsibility.

Knowledge adds to your ability to live more fully, hopefully, and happily, rather than fearfully. You know that ignorance is not bliss. Ignorance is a burden and a delusion which can lead to danger. Socrates said: "There is only one good, that is knowledge; there is only one evil, that is ignorance." Another philosopher affirmed: "True knowledge is modest and wary; 'tis ignorance that is bold and presuming."

It is up to you to use the knowledge you gain from these pages in your own most effective ways. The goal is utmost safety and lifelong benefits for yourself and your loved ones.

CRIME-AVOIDANCE CHECKLIST

☐ DO take every practicable precaution starting *today;* your chances of becoming a crime statistic have about *doubled* in the past decade.

☐ DO keep apace of all new protection developments.

☐ DON'T fail to cooperate with the authorities in every possible way.

☐ DO speak out about the need for protection locally and nationally, adding your voice and cooperation to neighbors and others.

☐ DON'T be pessimistic; crime control *is* possible if everyone law-abiding cooperates fully.

☐ DON'T despair if you can't take all the precautions detailed in this book (no one can); you'll profit by being alert and putting into effect all the protection measures you reasonably can.

☐ DO remember that two basic elements involved in criminal activity are (1) the desire to commit a burglary or other crime and (2) the opportunity; it is up to you to follow the precautions and protective steps given here in order to reduce to a minimum the *opportunity* to commit a crime on your premises or person.

Appendix:
A 7-POINT PROGRAM
TO COMBAT CRIME

IT IS vital that you recognize your responsibility as a law-abiding citizen not only to do everything legally and practically possible to protect yourself, your family, and your home (as advised throughout this book)—but also to join with local authorities and other forces to help combat and reduce crime at every level. Toward that end, for your thoughtful consideration and cooperation in the future, here in very brief, condensed form are the general basic objectives recommended by the President's Commission on Law Enforcement and Administration of Justice in the report, "Challenge of Crime in a Free Society":

1. Prevention of crime beforehand must be reinforced by providing all Americans with an equitable share in the benefits and responsibilities of American life, aided by strengthening law enforcement and by cutting down considerably the opportunities for crime.

2. Improvement of the system of criminal justice must be forwarded energetically and with all possible speed to develop a much broader range of techniques for dealing effectively with individual offenders.

3. Existing inadequacies and faults in criminal justice must be rectified in order to gain the cooperation and fullest regard for our judicial processes from all segments of American society.

4. More people and better people must be enlisted in the whole system and all processes of criminal justice, including judges, defense and prosecuting attorneys, police, and parole, probations, and corrections officers and officials—more people of knowledge, thorough integrity, vigor, and dedication.

5. More study, research, and planning in depth must be instituted and conducted promptly and assiduously, to help solve the multitude and magnitude of problems involved in providing effective criminal justice and control—both inside and outside the basic systems and procedures.

6. Realistically, more money must be provided—in considerably greater amounts, not just meaningless token increases—in order to help the courts, the police, and other correctional and control agencies deal with and curb crime more effectively.

7. All levels of government and citizenry, including citizens as individuals, civic and business organizations, and religious associations, must cooperate and coordinate their energies and actions. This combined effort can be exerted toward forwarding and putting into effect the preceding points in this recommended program. The result would be to reduce crime by a very sizable degree.